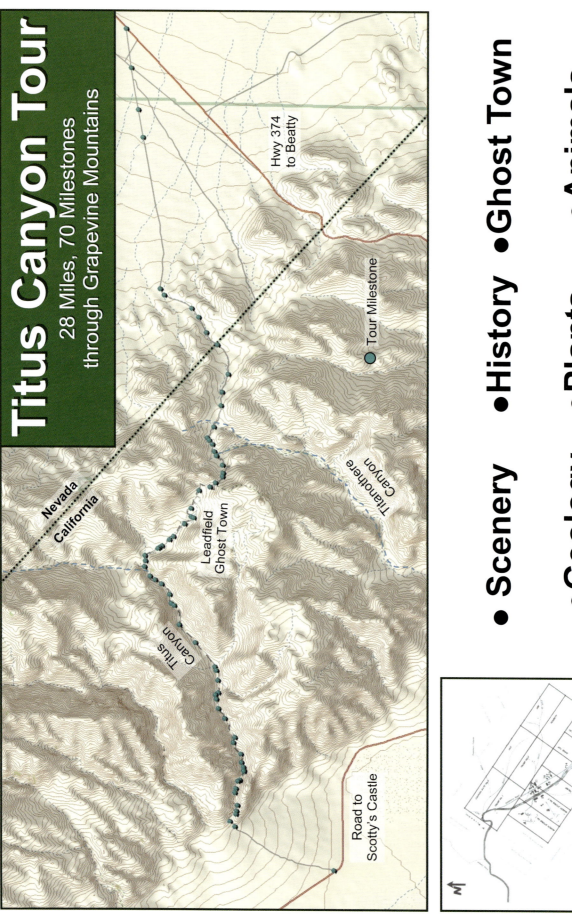

Death Valley's
Titus Canyon & Leadfield Ghost Town
Ken Lengner and Bennie Troxel

Second Edition

This volume is the second edition and reflects improvements on the first edition printed in 2002. This edition is in full color. There is additional photographic and historical material on the ghost town of Leadfield in its heyday and the present, additional material on prehistoric animals that lived in the ancient Titus Canyon area, corrections, improved graphics, tour locations by GPS and odometer, and a more user friendly appearance. A companion volume to this work deals with the detailed history of the Leadfield ghost town.

Ken Lengner 2008

™ DEEP ENOUGH PRESS

ISBN: 978-0-9820883-0-2

Copyright© 2002, 2008 Kenneth E. Lengner
First Printing 2002
Second Printing 2008
Library of Congress
Cataloging-in-Publication Data
Lengner, Kenneth, Death Valley's
Titus Canyon/Kenneth E. Lengner
Includes bibliographical references
Second Edition Design by Danny Ray Thomas
™Deep Enough Press

A 26-mile excursion, encompassing elevations from sea level to over 5,000 feet, through the southern Grapevine Mountains and the Death Valley region's most remarkable and enjoyable canyon. An integrated geology, plant, animal, and history work unfolds.

The text, with over 375 photographs and illustrations, can be used as a simple road log (over 70 milestones), a tool for more dedicated amateur geologists and naturalists, or a source of reference material for the Death Valley enthusiast.

Spectacular Titus Canyon, and the colorful rocks seen enroute to the canyon, provides fascinating glimpses into many of the geologic events and processes that have shaped this remarkable portion of the Death Valley region. The geologic story begins 600 to 525 million years ago when the Titus Canyon area was on a shallow continental margin intermittently beneath an ocean filled with simple life forms. Rocks in adjacent mountains display continuing deposition in the intermittent marine environment as late as 290-million years ago. No rocks, which were deposited for the next 263-million years, are alongside the tour route; however, previously deposited rocks display folded rock beds, occurring during the era of dinosaurs, when the western part of the continent suffered major deformation and volcanoes. The Titus Canyon Formation deposited late Eocene to early Miocene (~37 - 16 My) records a time of successive savannahs with long extinct giant mammals and massive volcanic eruptions that covered the region with tuff. Spectacular folds and faults viewed along the tour showcase the tectonic forces, which are still down dropping basins and uplifting rugged mountains. View the scenery and learn the exciting geologic story as you progress from milestone to milestone on the tour.

The Titus Canyon area supports plant communities from sea level to higher than 5,000 feet elevation. Become acquainted with more than seventy plants that have been photographed and are discussed. Color photographs of 48 flowers and shrubs have been provided. Read about Desert bighorn sheep, coyotes, Gamble's quail, chukar, chuckwalla lizards and other animals.

Native American artifacts and petroglyphs have been found in the Titus Canyon area. The history of boomtowns like Rhyolite and Bullfrog are summarized while Leadfield is discussed in detail. Learn about explorers, prospectors, financiers, and scientists who visited the area.

i

The Lower Narrows of Titus Canyon are cut into overturned sea floor rocks that are more than 520-million years old.

Mitchell W. Reynolds conducting geologic mapping west of the Little Belt Mountains, Montana, July 2001.

Dedicated to:

Mitchell W. Reynolds whose doctoral thesis (University of California, Berkeley) on the "Stratigraphy and Structural Geology of the Titus and Titanothere Canyon Area, Death Valley, California" and subsequent papers remain the definitive geologic works on this region. His maps, stratigraphic columns, and erudite descriptive prose provided much information as well as many hours of reading pleasure. He enthusiastically, patiently, and with great diligence contributed his technical and editorial skills to improving the content of this manuscript.

Mitchell W. Reynolds began his professional career with the United States Geological Survey (USGS) studying the geology of part of south-central Wyoming and the area bordering the west side of the Nevada Test Site. Six years later he joined the faculty in Geology and Geophysics at the University of California, Berkeley, where he was an Assistant Professor of Geology, teaching field geology, tectonics, and stratigraphy. Mitchell returned to the USGS, which he has served during the past thirty years. He has conducted field investigations to understand the geology of areas in the western United States, principally Montana, Wyoming, southeastern California, and southern Nevada. His responsibilities involved development and funding of national geologic programs in the USGS. For seven years, he was Chief of the Office of Regional Geology responsible for the National Geologic Mapping Program and programs in astrogeology and geology of the disposal of radioactive waste. Reynolds was one of the principal authors of the National Cooperative Geologic Mapping Act passed by Congress in 1992.

About the authors

Ken Lengner, originally from Wanaque, New Jersey, was an Aerospace Engineer for 34-years. He started his career as a Systems Engineer on the Apollo Moon Landing Program and retired from Boeing as Chief Project Engineer of Space Shuttle-Orbiter Subsystem Managers. For approximately 30-years, a parallel "career" entailed frequent visits to Death Valley National Park. He is an avid photographer and student of the Death Valley region's history and natural sciences. He has been a full time resident of the area for the past ten years. He has published three books on the Death Valley region and has more in progress.

Bennie Troxel, a native of Osawatomie, Kansas, moved to California in 1939 where he subsequently became a builder of World War II airplanes at what was, at the time, Douglas Aircraft. He later moved to Northrop Aircraft. During the war, he also was in the United States Army and served in India and China. Later he earned a college degree at UCLA and worked as a geologist for the California Division of Mines and Geology. At the suggestion of Lauren Wright, he developed a career in Death Valley geology that he has followed since 1952. He has written numerous papers on Death Valley geology.

Acknowledgments

The authors express particular appreciation to the following:

Danny Ray Thomas applied skills and historical knowledge to facilitate the second edition, greatly improved the appearance of the text and cover, provided GPS locations, created new maps, and climbed requisite mountains.

Blair Davenport (Death Valley National Park Curator, (DEVA)) helped with research.

Alan Van Valkenberg (DEVA Interpretation) and **Dana York** (DEVA Botanist) helped with plant identification.

Terry Baldino (Chief of Interpretation) reviewed the manuscript and recommended improvements.

Dr. Allan A. Schoenherr provided correction and clarification of plant and animal names, zones, and survival strategies.

James W. Hagadorn provided photographs of Late Proterozoic and Early Cambrian trace fossils.

Nancy Lengner improved the manuscript's appearance and provided her editorial skills.

John Stark (DEVA Engineering) and **John Patton** (BLM) provided U.S. Mineral Survey 5883 maps and field notes. **California State Archives Staff** and **Inyo County Recorder's Office** provided Leadfield research material.

Bighorn sheep and petroglyphs near Titus Canyon's Klare Spring.

Table of Contents

1.0 Introduction vi
   Applying This Book vi
   Where Is Titus Canyon? 1
   Trip Planning, Preparation and Facilities 1

2.0 The Story 2
   How Titus and Titanothere Canyons
   Got Their Names 2
   Death Valley Region's Geology 3
   Titus Canyon Area's Natural History............... 4
   Plants Overview 18
   Animals Overview 25
   Humans and Titus Canyon 27

3.0 Tour Overview 31

4.0 Up the Fan 38

5.0 Land of Titanotheres 68

6.0 Through Titus Canyon 106

Appendices 145

References 164

Glossary 166

Index 173

Prince's plume.

Leadfield buildings and mine waste.

1.0 Introduction

Many Death Valley enthusiasts consider the one-way, 26-mile tour through the Titus Canyon area as the best single-day experience in the Death Valley region (Death Valley National Park and immediate surroundings).

Section 2 provides background information on the area's geology, plants, animals, and history.

The tour, Section 3, starts in the high Amargosa Desert at ~3,600 ft. elevation, climbs an alluvial fan to ~5,000 ft. at White Pass, descends and crosses a steep drainage tributary to Titanothere Canyon, and switchbacks its way up to ~5,250 ft. at Red Pass. The tour then progresses downhill along a drainage channel flowing into Titus Canyon and arrives at the ghost town of Leadfield, the scene of a boomtown that made a lot of noise but did not produce lead. Leadfield is covered in some detail herein and is the subject of a companion book to this book. Next, the tour winds its way through the spectacular scenery in the Titus Canyon and finally emerges at the canyon mouth with a view across Death Valley's floor to the Panamint and Cottonwood Mountains. Along the way, visitors encounter fascinating and complex geologic phenomenon, diverse plant communities, hopefully some wildlife such as Desert bighorn sheep, and evidence of past human activities in the area.

At milestones (designated both by GPS and odometer readings) along the trip route, this guide provides information on geological history and structures, plants and animals, and human history. Strongly believing that "A picture is worth a thousand words", we have included many photos and illustrations. In order to make this book user friendly, it is constructed such that it can be used simply as a road log or as a source of more detailed information. If you just want to read the headlines and look at the pictures, do so. If you just want to read only about geology, plants, animals, or history, do so.

How do I apply this book to meet my personal needs?

Decide what your goal is.

We don't intend for you to read through the entire text as if it were a novel. You might get mired down in a level of depth with material that may not interest you a great deal. The most important thing to do is to decide what is your goal(s) relative to Titus Canyon. Here are some possible goals:

Level 1:
I want to take the best 1-day tour in Death Valley region and am curious about what I see.

Level 2:
I am very interested in geology, plants, animals or history.

Level 3:
I am more of a multi-disciplined naturalist (geology, plants, animals, and history), and as such, am very interested in what the Titus Canyon area provides.

How do I achieve my goal?

Level 1:
Read, "Where is it?" and "Preparation and planning" in the Introduction. In The Tour section, read the milestone's location and headline for each stop and scan photos and illustrations as they interest you.

Level 2:
In both "The Story" and "The Tour" sections, read those paragraphs highlighted for the discipline you are interested in. Program your GPS.

Level 3:
In both "The Story" and "The Tour" sections, to the level of depth you desire, review the geology, plants, animals, and history sections.
Program your GPS.

Where is Titus Canyon?

East-central Death Valley National Park along California and Nevada border (Figure 1.2)

North of Furnace Creek, California and southwest of Beatty, Nevada

Start one-way tour at turnoff from Nevada Highway 374

Ends in Death Valley National Park, north of Stovepipe Wells on the road to Scotty's Castle.

Trip planning, preparation, and facilities

- Plan 1-hour from Furnace Creek to the start of the tour and 1-hour to return to Furnace Creek from end of the tour.
- Plan 4-6 hours on the tour.
- Spring is best for flowers. Call the DEVA to find out when what is blooming for that year. (760) 786-3200.
- Call DEVA to find out if the road conditions allow access. (760) 786-3200.
- Drive high clearance or four-wheel drive vehicle, if possible.
- Check to ensure that you have a good spare tire and an operating car jack.
- Fill your gas tank.
- Bring warm clothing in the fall through early spring.
- Bring a lunch and plenty of water.
- Bring your camera with ample film.
- When stopping, do not block the narrow one-way road.
- Toilet facilities are at the canyon exit.

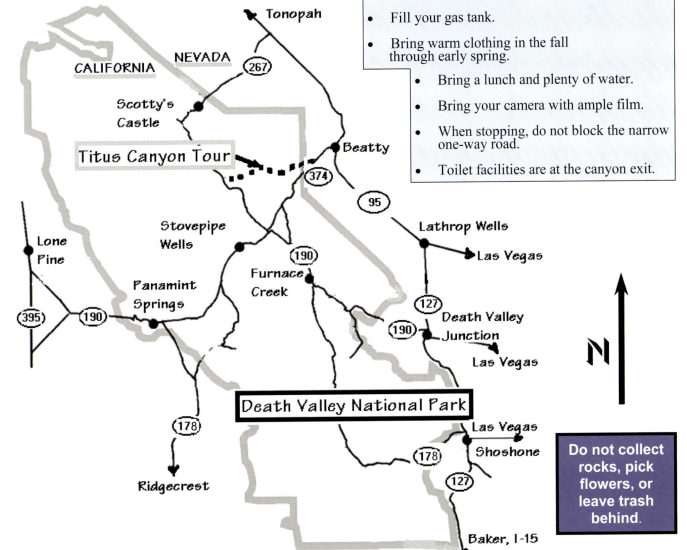

Figure 1.2 Titus Canyon is located in Death Valley National Park

Do not collect rocks, pick flowers, or leave trash behind.

2.0 The Story

This section provides an overview of the Death Valley region and Titus Canyon area. The following section entitled "The Tour" provides more detailed geology, plant, animal, and historical information associated with the milestones along the tour route.

2.1 How Titus and Titanothere Canyons got their names

Titus Canyon

On June 20, 1905, three inexperienced prospectors left Bullfrog, Nevada, for the Panamint Range. The three were John Mullan and the brothers-in-law Edgar Morris Titus and Earle C. Weller. They had 19 burros and 2 saddle horses with them. On the first day, they covered 20 miles to Wood Canyon and found the promised spring dry. They then doubled back to Mud Springs in Death Valley. The next day they left Mud Springs with 20 gallons of water for themselves and their stock. On June 26, they turned down a wrong canyon and found a spring that produced only a cup of water every 4 hours. Finding it to be insufficient for themselves and their stock, Titus continued down the canyon in search of a better spring. He never returned. The next morning, Weller left with the burros to search for Titus and water. He also never returned. The next day, Mullan searched for his missing companions. He got sunstroke and disoriented but managed to find his way back to camp. He was too weak to get out of the canyon. He remained there for two weeks until found by a Hispanic who helped him back to Bullfrog.

There is some evidence that an experienced prospector, Judge Lawrence Bethune of Tonopah, Nevada, might have met Titus and Weller. It is assumed that Bethune was unable to save both them and himself. Two dead men and one man who survived for an hour and a half were found in northern Death Valley. They had discarded some of their clothing in their delirium and hence had no identification. However, a burro belonging to Bethune and some of Titus's burros later showed up at Grapevine Ranch. Another version of the Titus and Weller disappearance has it that union miners with whom they might have had earlier difficulties while operating a Weller family gold mine in Telluride, Colorado, murdered them.

Weller's father came to Death Valley three years in a row to search for the bodies of his son, Earle, and son-in-law, Edgar Titus. He failed to find their remains but found a sign in the canyon that now bears his son-in-law's name.

The sign read:
Hurry on! I am going down to investigate the spring.   Titus

Titanothere Canyon

Although we only cross the tributary drainage to this canyon and do not explore the canyon itself, its rather unconventional name merits an explanation. The titanothere (also known as brontothere) was an herbivorous, hoofed mammal that evolved and became extinct during the Eocene Epoch (58-37 My). Initially, it was approximately fourteen inches tall at the shoulder. It continued evolving into the late Eocene at which time some species resembled a rhinoceros with a forked horn on the end of its nose. One species of titanothere, *Brontotherium platyceras* **(Figure 2.1)** evolved to a prodigious size (over 8 feet, 4 inches tall at the shoulder with an 18 inch span of its forked horn).

Titanothere Canyon is named for fossils Donald Curry, early park service naturalist, found in the upper portion of this canyon in 1934. Under the auspices of the California Institute of Technology, D. Curry, along with Chester Stock, Francis D. Bode, D. Scharf, L. Bolles, and J. Beck, excavated **(Figure 2.2)** the fossilized remains of two species of titanotheres.

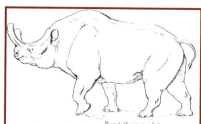

Figure 2.1 Huge *Brontotherium platyceras*.   Charles Knight

Figure 2.2 In 1934, Don Curry, Dr. Chester Stock, and others excavated fossil remains of titanotheres and other Late Eocene (37 My) mammals.
Courtesy of Los Angeles. Museum of Natural History

In honor of its discoverer, one species was named *Protitanops curryi*. The actual fossil resides in the Los Angeles County Museum of Natural History. A replica of the skull found at the excavation site is on display at the DEVA Visitor Center **(Figure 2.3)**. A poorly preserved facial portion of another species of titanothere was found in the same rock sequence as the other titanothere, making them approximately contemporary. Stock believed this titanothere was smaller than *P. curyyi* and had horns trihedral in cross section.

Figure 2.3 *Protitanops curryi's* mold can be seen in the DEVA Visitor Center. *Courtesy DEVA*

2.2 The Death Valley Region's Geology

So that you may better appreciate and understand Titus Canyon area, we briefly discuss the major geologic events that created Death Valley region and then concentrate on the Titanothere and Titus Canyon area. For your reference, a list of geologic terms and their definitions are provided in the Glossary.

The geologic history of the Death Valley region is long and varied. With some interruptions it stretches from 1.7 to 2.5 billion years ago (By) to the present. The region has been torn asunder by continental rifting, compressed by converging tectonic plates, sheared by tectonic plates sliding alongside one another, and, once again, torn asunder. It has drifted around the globe and endured climates ranging from a freezing environment to hot, humid, equatorial conditions. It has been submerged beneath oceans, freshwater lakes, lava flows, ash falls, and sediments from surrounding mountains. Summer and autumn deluges eroded the region and created world-class alluvial fans and wineglass canyons. Humans arrived and they blew-up, dug-up, and hauled off the region's minerals. Now, the Death Valley region is undergoing extension and shearing. It is a region that has had a very complex geologic history leading to its current dynamic state. The area we are visiting is part of that story.

For a summary of Death Valley region rocks types and the sequence in which they were deposited, please see **Appendix A**. Some of the sources for the region's sedimentary rocks are from an ancient continent called Rodinia, transgressing and regressing seas during the early Paleozoic Era (~543-245 My), continually eroding mountains, and a series of lakes during the Pleistocene Epoch ~2,000-10Ky). The igneous rocks were derived from Mesozoic Era (245-66 My) and Cenozoic Era (~66-0 My) volcanoes ejecting rhyolitic, andesitic, and basaltic rocks or rising magma domes that cooled beneath the earth's crust and yielded granitic structures. Throughout the Proterozoic (~2,500 – 543 My) to the present, metamorphic rocks were formed beneath the earth's surface by intense pressure and/or temperature changing pre-existing rock. One excellent location to view many of the rock types found in the Death Valley region is Dante's View **(Figure 2.4)**

Figure 2.4 Dante's View, provides a view of youthful valley floor and ~ billion year-old rock in foreground.

2.3 Titus Canyon's Natural History

This natural history section discusses the Titus Canyon area's geology and prehistoric animal life.

As part of the Death Valley region, the Titus Canyon area shares part of the Death Valley region's geologic history. However, the Titus Canyon area does not display all of the rocks found in the Death Valley region. **Figure 2.5** is a sketch of a geologic map of the Titus Canyon area and its immediate surroundings. When we look at this map, we see that along the tour route is an area that is comprised mostly of Cambrian (and some very late Precambrian) marine sedimentary rocks, Eocene-Miocene Epochs nonmarine sedimentary rocks, Tertiary volcanic rocks, and Quaternary sediments. Other rocks may be visible in the distance but are not readily accessible. Let's restrict our definition of the Titus Canyon area to the tour route and readily accessible to the motorist. In the varied geologic settings, both marine and terrestrial animals were present.

Late Precambrian and Cambrian Geology… beneath the ocean

The oldest rocks you will see on this tour are late Precambrian and Cambrian Period **marine** sedimentary rocks deposited approximately 580-500 million years ago (My). Starting from oldest to youngest, geologists have grouped these rocks into categories referred to as the Stirling Quartzite, Wood Canyon Formation, Zabriskie Quartzite, Carrara Formation, Bonanza King Formation, and Nopah Formation. A brief description of each is given in **Box 2.1** with more detailed descriptions in **Appendices C1. to C6.** (To find out the names of the rocks deposited in the overall Death Valley area prior to and after the aforementioned Titus Canyon tour rocks, refer to **Appendix A**.)

From the Late Precambrian and throughout the Cambrian Period, for a total of over 350 million years, what was to become western North America was beneath shallow seas. It was on a "**passive continental margin**". That is to say, it was in the area between the continent and the deep ocean in a region characterized by slow accumulation of sediments and, in general, a lack of earthquakes and volcanic activity. This area was created after an ancient continent called Rodinia spread apart (rifted) around 750 My. As that continent spread apart, the ocean gradually filled the gap. Spreading continued and a passive margin was established. The Death Valley region and its Titus Canyon area were on a shallow shelf as seen in **Figure 2.6**. During this time span, the sea levels rose (transgressed) and receded (regressed) as a result of increased or decreased global glaciations, continental margin sinking or rising, variations in sea floor spreading rates, and the variable rate of sediment deposition. Intermittently, the seas moved far inland as seen in **Figure 2.7**.

This transgression and regression resulted in (a) the formation of different types of sedimentary deposits (sandstone, quartzite, conglomerate, siltstone, mudstone, limestone, dolomite, and chert) in a range of depositional environments and (b) those deposits occurring in layers to a thickness that are a function of length of time beneath the sea, erosion, and other factors.

Generally speaking, **sandstone** results from dune, beach, coastal lowland stream, and intertidal depositional environments. This corresponds to when the seas had receded and the Death Valley region was near the shoreline. As time passed and more sediments were deposited upon the sandstone, it was deeply buried and converted to **quartzite**.

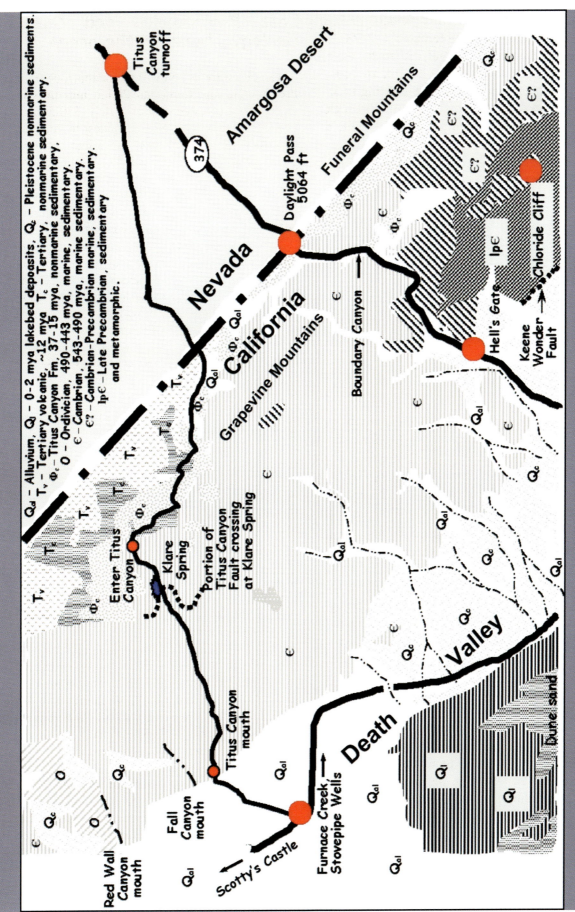

Figure 2.5 Sketch—Geologic map of the region surrounding the Titus Canyon area

Box 2.1 Generalized columnar section – rocks deposited in Titus and Titanothere Canyons over the past 585-million years

Time	Unit/Thickness	Lithology (Rock Description)
Quaternary Period (0-2My)	**Alluvium, Colluvium**-300'	Gravel, sand, angular rock fragments; stratified and unstratified, mostly unconsolidated. *No fossils.*
	Older Gravel-0 to 100'	Gravel, sand; well rounded clasts. *No fossils.*
Pliocene Epoch (2-5 My)	**Conglomerate**-80'	Gravel, sand; stratified, consolidated; angular and well-rounded clasts. *No fossils.*
Miocene Epoch (5-24 My) 15 My start of: a) Great Basin extension which drops basins and uplifts ranges, b) CA coast right lateral tectonic plate movements produce same motion in DV.	**Welded Tuff**-1200'+	Welded tuff (pale red, grayish red, blackish red near base). *No fossils.*
	Crystal Lithic Tuff-650' to 800'	Tuff (pale red and grayish pink). *No fossils.*
	Vitric Tuff and Associated Sedimentary Rocks	Tuff (pale greenish gray, greenish brown, to pale grayish orange); Sedimentary rocks (thin-bedded, cross-bedded; well rounded clasts); Lava flow (phenocrysts, brownish gray, weathers brownish black). *Fossil fish.*
Late Eocene-Oligocene Epochs (24-37 My) Savannah like plain with camels, horses, titanotheres, etc. and streams from nearby Sierras.	**Titus Canyon Fm** – 1850 to 2600' (total Fm) *Late Eocene to Miocene* Deposited from late Eocene into the Miocene. (~15-37 My)	Green Conglomerate Facies (greenish gray to light brown; well rounded pebbles and cobbles; sandstone and limestone interbeded; tuff near center; tuff beds). *Locally contains algal remains.*
		Siltstone, mudstone, marl, sandstone and conglomerate (pale red, reddish brown, yellow, orange, pale green; well rounded pebbles and cobbles, scattered algal limestone beds) *Titanothere and other mammal fossils. Fossil trackways (Miocene?).*
		Breccia (Angular carbonate rock fragments interbedded with siltstone). **Base**
	Megabreccia Deposits Oligocene-Pliocene	Breccia of Cambrian carbonate rock. *No Fossils.*

The Rocks between the Cambrian and Oligocene are not exposed along the Titus Canyon tour route. However, Ordovician, Silurian, and Devonian rocks can be seen far in the distance from Red Pass. (Some of these "missing" rocks are found in many other parts of Death Valley National Park. Essentially Mesozoic, Paleocene, and Eocene rocks are missing from Death Valley region.

Time	Unit/Thickness	Lithology (Rock Description)
Cambrian Period (490-543 My) Planet Earth sees an explosion of life (e.g. trilobites) following a massive Permian extinction. DV region is beneath ocean on a shallow "passive" coastal margin. Waters alternating move inland and recede (sea level changes due to glaciations) creating bedded marine deposits.	**Nopah Fm**-1300'	Dolomite (1210', medium dark to dark gray with light gray bands in lower half); Dolomite, Limestone, and Chert (320' medium gray to brownish gray); Claystone (110' pale yellowish brown). **Base**. *Abundant fossils in lower part.*
	Bonanza King Fm-3600'	Dolomite (600', medium to dark gray with light gray bands); Dolomite and Limestone (1100', alternating dark gray, light gray, medium gray); Dolomite (275', dark gray); Dolomite and Limestone (white); Dolomite (210', dark gray); Dolomite and Limestone (1300', dark and medium dark gray; mottled). **Base**. *Fossils fragments in many units.*
	Carrara Fm-1560'	Limestone (815' medium to dark gray); Limestone (160', medium to dark gray with white "cap"); Siltstone (290', variegated olive and red); Limestone (115', medium to dark gray); Siltstone, Thin Limestone, Quartzite at base (180', olive, gray, brown). *Fossils in all units.*
	Zabriskie Quartzite-950'	Quartzite (930', grayish purple to brownish gray, forms ledges). *No fossils.*
	Wood Canyon Fm-2600'	Siltstone and Quartzite (325', olive gray, brown gray); Dolomite Limestone (350', moderate and yellowish brown). *Fossils in dolstone and siltstone.* **Base**.
Proterozoic Eon (543- 2500 My) Continent of Rodinia Begin rift (1100) apart through DV region. Coast uplifts, down drops, yields passive margin (580).		Siltstone and quartzite (1080', olive, green, brownish gray); Conglomeratic Quartzite (380', light gray to purple); Quartzite and Sandstone (500', green gray to olive black); Dolomite, Siltstone, Quartzite (635', yellowish brown, olive gray, brownish gray). **Base**.
	Stirling Quartzite-800' (Late Proterozoic)	Quartzite (light to pinkish gray); Dolomite center of formation (yellow brown). **Base**. *No fossils. (Can be seen at great distance when passing Titianothere Canyon)*

1. Beds are listed in order of upper to lower with "Base" designating the lowest beds. 2. Rocks older than Stirling Quartzite are not exposed in the Titus Canyon area. 3. Rocks up to 1.7 By are exposed in other parts of Death Valley National Park) 4. **Red lines** *indicate an unconformity or "missing" rocks between deposits, possibly lost to erosion.*

Lengner derived from Reynolds

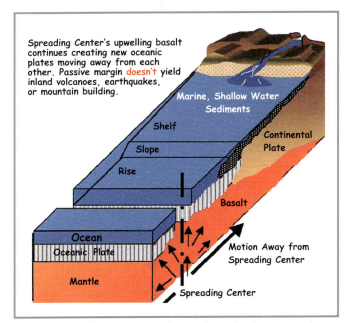

Figure 2.6 Sediments along the shallow passive margin include limestone and dolomite derived from a marine environment and sediments for sandstone, conglomerate, and siltstone that were derived from inland sources such as rivers or deltas.

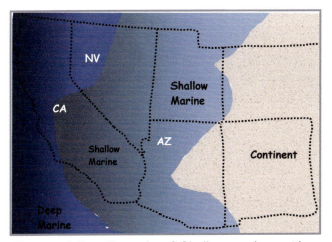

Figure 2.7 Example of Shallow marine setting. From Cambrian to early Triassic, seas intermittently extended far inland.

Siltstone or **mudstone** was deposited in coastal swamps, deltas, and near shore shallow marine environments such as tidal flats. Mudstone could also be deposited farther offshore in a deep, quiet environment.

When the sea level rose, **limestone** (calcium carbonate from seawater creatures) would be deposited in an off shore, shallow marine environment. In some cases and for reasons not completely understood, the calcium of the limestone would be replaced by magnesium and **dolomite** would be the result. **Chert** (silica oxide from seawater) would also be deposited in this environment.

Sea Level Changes Created Different Colored Layers Exposed on the Irregular Mountain Slopes

At times the depositional environments were: inland, delta, shoreline, near shore marine, and offshore marine. Consider the following example to understand how different sedimentary rocks accumulated and weathered differently. The following discussion pertains to the Titus Canyon area and the Death Valley region.

During a time when the ocean waters had receded and the ancient Titus Canyon area was on the beach as in **Figure 2.8**, sediments deposited along this shoreline would eventually become sandstone or quartzite. Sandstone colors vary with the impurities in the sand and it can weather into slopes. Quartzite is more weather resistant and can form cliffs. Farther offshore, in the waters of the shallow passive margin, sediments that would eventually form siltstone and limestone were being deposited.

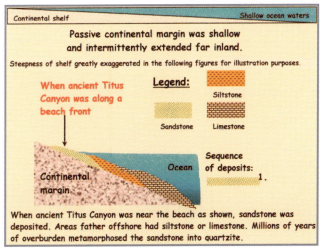

Figure 2.8 Example, when ancient Titus Canyon was beachfront property sandstone was deposited in the area. It would eventually metamorphose into quartzite like the purple Zabriskie Quartzite seen on the tour.

Assume that global sea levels rose either due to increased sea floor spreading rates or a warming climate that melted glaciers. The ancient Titus Canyon area was then in deeper water as shown in **Figure 2.9**. The shoreline that was once at Titus canyon has now moved far inland. The previously deposited sandstone is now overlain by limestone from marine sea shells or from precipitation. Limestone is weather resistant and forms ledges in an arid climate.

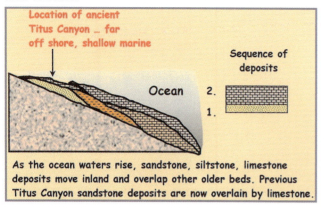

Figure 2.9 Example, when next the sea level rose and ocean waters covered ancient Titus Canyon, limestone (later changing to dolomite) was deposited.

Now, assume there has been yet another change in Earth's climate. Once again it becomes colder and more water is captured in glaciers or sea floor spreading rates decrease. The sea level recedes and ancient Titus Canyon is once again near a shoreline as shown below. The previously deposited sandstone and limestone is now overlain with another layer of sandstone **Figure 2.10**. Perhaps there are different impurities in the two different layers of sandstone. Millions of years pass and these two layers have a slightly different color and composition.

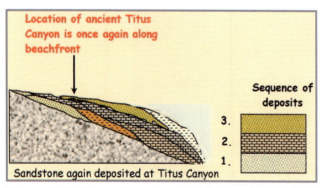

Figure 2.10 Example…when next the sea level fell and ancient Titus Canyon was again beachfront…3.

Now a sequence of three different rock layers exists. Millions of years pass, more layers are added and the sandstone converts to quartzite. Many more millions of years pass as more and more layers are added, plate tectonics changes a number of times, mountains are created as uplift occurs, groundwater flows through permeable rocks, and erosion wages its constant contest with those forces that uplift mountains. Once again our example sequence sees the light of day and winds and rain erode it. As we mentioned, the layers weather differently both in shape and color. in **Figure 2.11**. Sandstones may vary in color due to impurities and slope due to how well it is cemented.

Figure 2.11 Weathering has affected the various rock deposits. Depending on the rock type and content, different slope steepness, shape, and color have resulted in our hypothetical example.

Marine Life in the Late Precambrian and Cambrian Titus Canyon Area

Before we discuss marine life in the Titus Canyon area, be reminded that everywhere on Plant Earth's continents, the mountains and valleys were devoid of plant and animal life during the late Precambrian and Cambrian.

However, the seas were a different story and were the scene of the appearance of the earliest animals (multicelled metazoans) after billions of years of single celled life. The currently defined (and debated) sequence of evolving life is as follows:

1) ~3.75 - 1.35 By: marine life was single celled prokaryotes (i.e. no nucleus), formed stromatolites.

2) ~1.35 –.700 By: marine life included single celled eukaryotes (i.e. with nucleus).

3) ~700 My: first metazoans (multicelled, animals), no skeleton, called Ediacaran.

5) 543 My: <u>current</u> USGS definition of beginning of Cambrian Period.

6) ~500 (?) My: Burgess Shale in Canadian Rockies deposited with animals having broad range in anatomical designs not seen before, or since, included skeletons.

The Wood Canyon Formation, which you will see after Leadfield and in the beginning of Titus Canyon, was witness to the remarkable Precambrian beginnings of multicelled life, the soft bodied Ediacaran, and the later Cambrian skeletal animals, such as trilobites **(Figure 2.12)**, along with crinoids (sea lilies), sponges, snails, corals, and brachiopods, **Figure 2.13**.

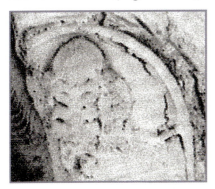

Figure 2.12 Trilobite fossil in Carrara Fm., Death Valley. *USGS*

Detailed description (**Boxes 6.1 to 6.3**) of this transition of life forms will be reserved for that portion of the tour (Segment 3) where the Wood Canyon is visible.

Figure 2.13 Trilobites on the seafloor with tall crinoids in the background. *Heinrich Harder 1903*

A 453-million year gap exists in the rocks visible in the Titus Canyon area.

Following the Cambrian Period (~490 My), there is approximately 453 million years worth of rock deposits not easily visible in the Titus Canyon area. Look at the middle of **Box 2.1**. However, from Red Pass, Ordovician, Silurian, and Devonian formations are visible far in the distance on the northwest flank of the Grapevine Mountains. There are no Mesozoic Era, Paleocene Epoch, or Early to Middle Eocene Epoch sedimentary rock found anywhere in the Death Valley region. The gap closes with the appearance of the Late Eocene-Miocene Titus Canyon Formation (~37-15My). Later deposits are found throughout Death Valley.

If you desire to know what rocks were deposited in the Death Valley region other than in the Titus Canyon area, see Appendix A.

Tectonic plate subduction started 250-million years ago and reshaped rocks of the Titus Canyon area.

Although there are no sedimentary rocks of the Mesozoic found in the Death Valley region, tectonic activity in that timeframe reshaped the rocks previously deposited.

Prior to the beginning of the Triassic Period (245 My) movement of the Earth's crustal plates changed. West of what is now California coastline an oceanic plate (Farrallon) and/or displaced terranes converged with the continental Plate (North American). The heavier oceanic plate rocks (comprised of the oceanic crust and the lithosphere) dived under the lighter continental plate rocks into the plastic or pliant asthenosphere. As it dived, it began to melt so that silica-rich magma rose to form granitic plutons or rhyolitic or andesitic volcanoes. This process is called subduction and is illustrated **Figure 2.14**.

The plate collision or subduction resulted in: (a) the Death Valley region rising above sea-level, (b) rising plutons that formed granitic masses (if they cooled within the earth) or violent volcanoes spewing forth rhyolite and andesite or more benign volcanoes flowing basalt, (c) earthquakes, and (d) compressive forces.

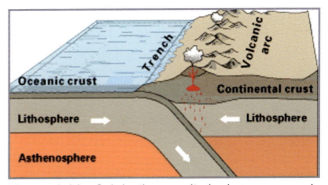

Figure 2.14 Subduction resulted when an oceanic plate dove underneath a continental plate. Compressive forces were transmitted inland. Volcanoes erupted, plutons rose, and earthquakes shook the Death Valley region. *USGS*

Very visible in the Titus Canyon region are the results of these compressive forces. During the Paleozoic and Mesozoic timeframe, the Wood Canyon Formation, Zabriskie Quartzite, Carrara Formation, and Bonanza King Formation were still covered by thick layers of rocks. These layers subjected the Titus Canyon rocks to great temperature and pressure. Possibly with the aid of rising gneiss domes, the temperature and pressure softened the rock. The compressive forces then produced folds (bends) in the previously horizontal deposits. You will see numerous examples of folded rock beds. Some will be the size of mountains and some too small to be noticed easily. A fine example is the folded layers of the Bonanza King Formation as seen at Leadfield. In **Figure 2.15**, notice the building in the right foreground that provides the scale for the size of the fold.

During the Late Eocene to Miocene (37-15 My), the Titus Canyon region was a savannah with trees, shrubs, streams, volcanoes, and eventually grasses.

Titus Canyon provides us with rocks (Titus Canyon Formation) that are late Eocene to early Miocene(~37-15 My) in age and some mammal fossils that are Late Eocene (~37 My). They are a view into the past.

Geology-Floodplain and Volcanic Deposits

By the late Eocene (~37 My), the environment in the Death Valley region had cooled resulting in a flat, open woodland-savanna with some trees, shrubs, streams and lakes. The ancient Sierra Nevada was closer to Death Valley than today. The Sierra Nevada had not reached the height of today's mountains nor did they display granite outcrops seen today. Large stream channels flowed through the savannah. Their sources came from the north. The streams deposited rounded rock debris, sand, and mud that was later to become the Titus Canyon Formation. Occasionally, violent rhyolitic and andesitic volcanoes erupted with explosive force as they spewed forth lava, tan to pink ash, and gases. Eruptions continued into the subsequent Miocene Epoch.

The rocks of the Titus Canyon Formation were deposited from approximately 37 to 15 My. **Appendix C-5** provides a stratigraphic column defining the formation's composition and sequence of the deposits, how you can identify the formation, and where it is located. **Figure 2.16** shows the rounded clasts indicative of parts of the Titus Canyon Fm.

Figure 2.15 Behind Leadfield, there are beds of the Bonanza King Formation, which were folded due to compressive forces.

Figure 2.16 The rounded, often fractured or bruised, clasts suspended in a finer grained matrix are indicative of the conglomerates of the lower Titus Canyon Formation and can be seen between White and Red Passes.

Animals from the Late Eocene (37 My): Titus Canyon Area Fossils and Contemporaries

Dinosaurs had been extinct for some 29-million years and the Age of Mammals was in full swing when some animals left behind their fossilized remains to be found in 1934-5 by Monument naturalist H. Donald Curry and famed paleontologist, Chester Stock and his California Institute of Technology colleagues. **Appendix C-7** identifies and describes these animals along with contemporary animals which lived at the same time in nearby, compatible environments and may have frequented the Titus Canyon-Death Valley area.

One of the many fossilized species found in the vicinity of Titanothere Canyon, *Mesohippus* was an ancestor of today's horses, **Figure 2.17**. The three-toed, perissodactyl (odd toed), *Mesohippus* was only 20 inches high and 40 inches long and browsed on leaves and pulpy fruits. It was a widespread species in North America with fossils also being found in the Dakotas, Montana, Nebraska, and Saskatchewan. Its descendants would evolve their teeth to become grazers and survive on the future grasslands of North America until climatic changes would result in their migration to Asia.

Fossils of two families of rodents, *Ischyromyidae* and *Aplodontidae*, were found by Stock and colleagues. The latter family would have one species evolve into the mountain beavers found in today's Rocky Mountains. Twenty inch long Eocene beaver, *Agnocastor*, may have dammed savannah streams.

On the opposite end of the spectrum were the fossils of two species of titanotheres. They are also known as brontotheres which translates to "Thunder Beast," an animal in Sioux mythology which ran across clouds and created thunderstorms. There were various species of large brontotheres roaming North America's west during the middle and late Eocene. Some characteristics included: distinct frontonasal prominence or horn, elephant sized, bulky, short neck, stocky body, relatively short limbs.

Very large brontotheres (titanotheres) had a shoulder height greater than 8 feet, were 12 to 14 feet in length, and weighed 4 to 5 tons. Some male's horns were up to 45-inches from the base of the skull to the tip of the horn. Classified as perissodactyls, their forefeet had four digits and their hind feet had three digits. They lived in herds and were sexually dimorphic… males were larger. They were browsers and possibly had lips and a long tongue to grab the leaves and twigs they fed on. Their cheek teeth were low crowned resulting in rapid wear if they fed on high silica vegetation such as grass. Failure of teeth to become high crowned and adapt to grazing may have led to their extinction. There were long-horned and short-horned species and variations in overall size. Size and shape of horns may have been used by the brontotheres to distinguish their species from another species.

The males are believed to have been contentious beasts trying to use there large, blunt horns to attack the flanks of their opponents as seen in **Figure 2.18**.

Having started out as small beasts such as *Lambdocerium* and *Eotitanops* (**Figure 2.19**) in the Early

Figure 2.17 Early horse herd, *Mesohippus*, gallops across a savannah interspersed with trees and shrubs.
Fossils found in MT; ND; SD; NE; Saskatchewan and **Titus**.
Heinrich Harder

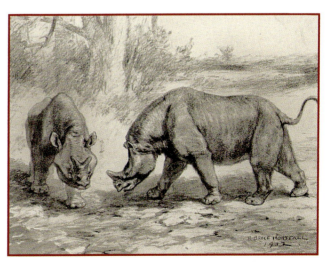

Figure 2.18 Two male titanotheres begin to spar. Note the open background with occasional trees and shrubs.
Robert Bruce Horsfall

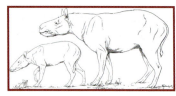

Figure 2.19 Early Eocene brontotheres: *Lambdocerium* (~28" long x 16" high) and *Eotitanops* (~50" long x 25" high).

E. S. Christman

Eocene (~55-50 My) they grew into the Thunder Beasts (**Figures 2.20-2.24**) by their demise in the Late Eocene (~37 MY).

The fossils of two titanothere species were found in the vicinity of Titanothere Canyon. *Protitanops curryi* was a large titanothere that may have resembled contemporary *Duchesneodus* or *Megacerops,* **Figure 2.20**. There were insufficient fossil remains of the second species to attempt to establish its identity. Which, if any, of the **Figure 2.20** to **2.24** brontotheres definitely frequented the Death Valley region beside *Protitantops cureyi* is unknown.

Figure 2.20 *Megacerops:* **Large to very large-sized. Long** horns that are directed laterally or forward, and roughly elliptical in cross section. Resembles *Protitanops curryi*. Fossils found in SD, NE, CO, MT, and Saskatchewan. *Charles Knight*

Figure 2.21 *Protitanotherium:* **Large-sized. Short** but prominent **horns** that are laterally directed and elliptical in cross section. Fossils found TX, UT, WY. *Charles Knight*

Figure 2.22 *Brontops robustus:* **Very large-sized**, approaching the size of *Brontotherium platyceras*. **Short** horns. Fossils found in SD, WY, UT, NE, Saskatchewan. *Charles Knight*

Figure 2.23 *Menodus (Menops)* **Very large-sized** brontothere. **Horns relatively large**, laterally directed, and strongly trihedral in cross section. Fossils found in SD, NE, CO, Saskatchewan. *Charles Knight*

Figure 2.24 *Brontotherium platyceras*: **Very large-sized**. **Long horns** are forked. Perhaps the largest of all brontotheres. *Charles Knight*

Stock and colleagues found fossils of two other perissodactyl families… the tapirs and rhinoceroses. During the Early Eocene Epoch (~50 My), the two families had diverged. They were originally immigrants from Europe. The tapir fossil find belonged to medium sized to large, *Colodon*. A contemporary and in the same family was *Protapirus* seen in **Figure 2.25**. Stock's group found fossils of the rhinoceros *Telataceras mortivallis* and another unidentified family member. In 1987, Kelly and a group from the University of California, Berkeley, found additional unidentifiable rhinoceros fossils. *Telataceras* was a small, browsing rhinoceros that also left its fossils at another site in the Mojave Desert. A contemporary and possible another Titus Canyon area rhinoceros was the very widespread *Hyracodon* or "Running rhino" illustrated in **Figure 2.26**. It was 4' at shoulder and 8' nose to tail. It had a 14" skull and long, slim legs which aided it in running from predators.

Figure 2.25 The browser *Protapirus was a* medium-large sized member of the tapir family known exclusively from river channel deposits. Fossils found in Saskatchewan, SD, WY, MT, NE, CO, and NV (Mineral County and Smith Valley). *Robert Bruce Horsfall*

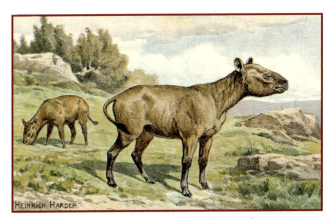

Figure 2.26 Running rhinoceros, *Hyracodon*. Fossils found in SD;NE; WY; UT; MT; CO; TX; Saskatchewan; Mexico. *Heinrich Harder*

Several individuals of *Agriochoerus* (**Figure 2.27**) *transmontanus* were found in the Titus Canyon area. These artiodactyls (even toed) were members of the Oreodont family which have been described as appearing like a cross between a pig and a sheep. They had enlarged canines, a long body, short legs, short neck, large head, long tail, 4 toes and walked digitigrade. *Protoreodon transmontanus* was a contemporary oreodont found at multiple sights in Ventura and San Diego Counties, CA.

Figure 2.27 The oreodont *Agriochoerus* stops to drink at a stream running through the late Eocene Titus Canyon area savannah. Fossils found in WY; CO; UT;TX; Saskatchewan. and **Titus**. *Robert Bruce Horsfall*

Members of the camel family, also artiodactyls, first appeared in Mid Eocene when drying conditions were producing open woodlands and savannas. Although relatively rare in Eocene with no fossils found in the Titus Canyon area, it is still possible that the Late Eocene *Poebrotherium* (**Figure 2.28**) frequented Titus Canyon and Death Valley.

The artiodactyls family Leptomerycidae migrated

Figure 2.28 Early camel *Poebrotherium*. Variable in size. 3-4 feet long. Longer neck than *Poebrodon*. Fossils found in TX, SD, WY, MT, NE. *Robert Bruce Horsfall*

from Asia to North America in the Middle to Late Eocene (40 MY). A portion of the jaw and molars of a family member were found. *Leptomeryx blacki* (**Figure 2.29**) was small, lightly built, deer-like, a ruminant, and hornless. It lived in wooded environs feeding on fruits, tender shoots, and possibly insects.

Figure 2.29 Small and deer-like *Leptomeryx* browsed in wooded environments. Fossils found in MT, WY, SD, ND, NE, CO, northern Mexico, Saskatchewan, **Titus**.
Robert Bruce Horsfall

Another hornless ruminant family that migrated from Asia to North America in the Middle to Late Eocene (40 MY) and possible inhabitant of the Death Valley region was the Hypertragulidae. One genera was *Hypertragulus* which was notable for its small size and short forelimbs. Fossil sites include NE, SD, CO, MT, and CA (Ventura and Kern Counties).

The family Protoceratidae originated in North America in middle Eocene. It started out as a family of small and hornless browsers. The Late Eocene saw some members moving to hypsodont (high crowned teeth) and thereby adapting to the grassland environment which would eventually predominate. The left jaw and teeth of a family member, *Poambromylus robustus,* was found in the Titus Canyon area. Its fossils have also been found in SD, WY, UT, NM, and TX. *Leptotragulus* was another genera in this widespread family. It left its remains in UT, WY, SD, MT, TX, NE, British Columbia, Saskatchewan, and CA (San Diego). Speculating that *Leptotragulus* also frequented the Death Valley region is not unreasonable.

The remains of only one member of the Order Carnivora was found in the Titus Canyon area. It was a fragment of the left mandible of a slender jawed canid, Family Canidae. Today's dogs, wolves, fox, etc. are part of that family. Stock commented on the similarities and differences of the Titus mandible to that of the canid *Pseudocynodictis* (*Hesperocyon*). *Hesperocyon* or "Western dog." (subfamily Hesperocyoninae) was fox-sized but mongoose like because of its long slender body (2'-6", short limbs, 4" skull, and long tail). Its forefeet were subdigitigrade and claws probably retractile allowing it to climb trees. It may have hunted small mammals in riparian forests and adjacent grasslands. Possibly it is the ancestor to all current canines. This genus was active from the Late Eocene to Late Oligocene (~39-27 My) and very common leaving its remains in Canada, MT, WY, SD, ND, CO, and NE.

Many other carnivores were probably preying on the adult and young herbivores found in the Late Eocene Titus Canyon area. They may have included the contemporary carnivores like hyena-like *Hyaenodon* (**Figure 2.30**), the pig-like *Archaeotherium* (**Figure 2.31**) and lynx-sized and cat-like *Dinictis* (**Figure 2.32**). The list goes on with names like *Hoplophoneus* (cat-like but not true cat, leopard sized), *Miacis* and *Protictis* (from an extinct family of weasel-sized predators) and *Daphoenus* (from an extinct family of "Beardogs").

Contingents of snakes, lizards, land tortoise, aquatic turtles were also present.

Figure 2.30 *Hyaenodon* "Hyaena-toothed" *horridus* Migrant from Europe 40 My. Scavenger-predator. This genus would leave remains in CA (Simi Valley and San Diego) and numerous sites in Central Great Plains from the Late Eocene to Late Oligocene. Sizes would vary greatly. Robert Bruce Horsfall

Figure 2.31 *Archaeotherium* (39.5-24 My). Omnivorous, scavenger eating carrion and plants (roots, tubers). Bone crushing jaws. Species were 3-6' tall at shoulder. Common in floodplain environments of northern Great Plains. Robert Bruce Horsfall

As time progressed the terrain would remain essentially flat and the volcanic activity continue. However, the climate became cooler and more arid resulting in the demise of open woodlands and their replacement by grasslands. Those herbivores that could not evolve hypsodont teeth to withstand wear by the high silica content grass became extinct as did the predators who couldn't deal with the new herbivores. Next, beginning by the Late Miocene Epoch (~15 My), even the terrain had changed.

Figure 2.32 *Dinictis* was saber-toothed with serrations; had a sleek body, short legs, powerful jaws, retractable claws, long tail; and walked plantigrade. Fossils found in SD, ND, CO, NE and WY   Robert Bruce *Horsfall*

Fifteen million years ago the shape of the land began to change as mountains rose, valleys dropped, and volcanoes erupted

As a result of another period of change, Death Valley would be torn lengthwise and mountains surrounding Death Valley would rise and the valleys sink. Along a fault, the Grapevine Mountains and Titus Canyon moved to the south while Death Valley would move to the north. The Grapevine Mountains rose and erosion cut into them (creating Titus, Titanothere, and other canyons) as draining waters sought the sinking Death Valley. Faults appeared where rising mountains and sinking valleys met.

Long before the late Miocene time, plate tectonics activity west of the California coast changed. Roughly 30 My the Farrallon oceanic plate had nearly been consumed in its headlong dive beneath the continental North America plate as seen in **Figure 2.33**.

By approximately 20 My, subduction had ceased west of the Death Valley region and the remnants of the Farrallon Plate were split into two plates, the Cocos Plate and the Juan De Fuca plate. A "transform" boundary with lateral motion between the plates had formed. By 10 My, the transform had expanded farther north and south. Then the North American Plate moved southeast and the Pacific Plate moved essentially northwest. Today, in most of California, they still grind along beside each other while in northern California the oceanic Juan De Fuca plate continues to dive underneath the North American plate and create the volcanoes of the Cascade Range.

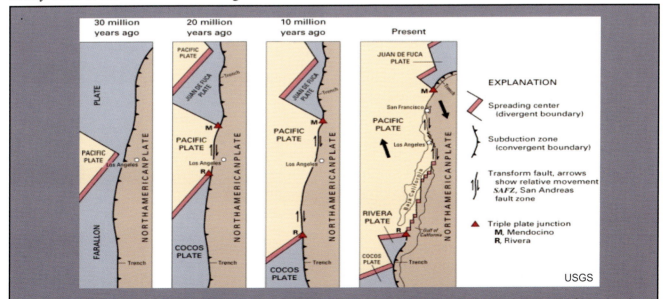

Figure 2.33 West of the Death Valley region, the plate tectonics along the coast changed from having the oceanic Pacific Plate diving underneath the continental North American Plate to today's tectonics where the plates move laterally with respect to one and another in southern California. The change is still felt far inland, including the Death Valley region. Lateral motion along the northern Death Valley fault zone is seen at the end of the Titus Canyon tour.

The current San Andreas fault zone only takes up part of the North American and Pacific plates' boundary's right lateral slipping motion requirement. Other right lateral faults like the San Jacinto, Furnace Creek and Death Valley fault zones (northern Death Valley fault zone is seen at the end of the Titus Canyon tour), account for some additional right lateral slip on the continent. Estimates vary on how much displacement has occurred from one side of the Death Valley faults to the other. The high estimate seems to be about 80 miles while the low is 30 miles. Just imagine one side of the region now being 30 to 80 miles farther north than the other side.

Besides the change to the grinding, transform boundary, another change greatly impacted the region from the Sierra Nevada east through Nevada to Utah. This area is known as the Great Basin and includes the entire state of Nevada and parts of California, Utah, Oregon, and Idaho. This vast region has been stretched (extended) since about approximately 17 My. Geologists call this process, "extension." Noted Death Valley geologists Lauren A. Wright and Bennie W. Troxel were among the first to recognize that this process existed in the past and is ongoing. The cause is not completely understood. The Great Basin is being stretched approximately from east to west. Ranges are being uplifted and the basins are being down dropped. The most simplistic view is provided in **Figure 2.34**. Basically, extension is causing the tensional forces that create the **Figure 2.34** normal faults and associated basin and ranges.

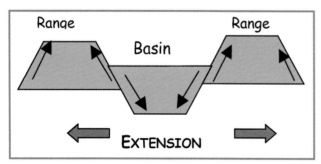

Figure 2.34 A very simplified illustration of normal faulting. Ranges uplift and basins down drip.

In real life, the ranges and basins across the Great Basin are different elevations as are the basins. For example, Death Valley is approximately sea level while Pahrump Valley, to the east, is approximately 2400 feet elevation. **Figure 2.35** is a more detailed sketch of what can occur in the presence of normal faulting. Note that smaller faults, some parallel to the main faults and some not, can result in fault blocks dropping different distances.

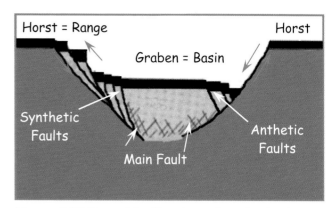

Figure 2.35 Normal faulting down dropping basins and uplifting ranges. *From Twiss and Moores*

When we look at the mountains, we can see that their layers (beds) are sometimes tilted. The tilting of the mountains (fault blocks) is explained by something called listric normal faults and detachment faults which are illustrated in **Figure 2.36**. Listric faults shallow with depth while detachment faults are low angle faults that mark a major boundary between unfaulted rocks below and deformed and faulted rocks above.

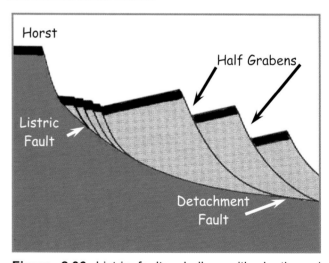

Figure 2.36 Listric faults shallow with depth and result in rotation (tilting) of fault blocks. Hanging wall fault blocks are parallel (imbricate) and synthetic. *From Twiss and Moores*

In summary, **Figure 2.34** identifies the basic fault processes which cause the Great Basins basin and ranges to form while **Figures 2.35 and 2.36** provide a little additional insight regarding how the terrain is formed.

Extension thinned the Great Basin's crust resulting in volcanoes and fissures spewing forth whitish-pinkish rhyolitic and andesitic flows and airborne debris and dark basaltic lava flows The Timber Mountain caldera complex, 35-miles east of Titus Canyon, erupted rhyolitic debris from 16-11 My and coated the flat landscape that was to become the eastern slopes of the Grapevine and Funeral Mountains. The caldera had basaltic eruptions during two subsequent periods. The latest was only 10 thousand years ago (Ky).

Volcanic activity far from the Death Valley region generated airborne ash that also coated the Death Valley region. During the Pleistocene Epoch, Huckleberry Ridge (Yellowstone, 2.1 My), Long Valley Caldera (near Bishop, California, 758 Ky), and Lava Creek (Yellowstone, 665 Ky), spread tephra (volcanic ejecta) deposits across the Death Valley region. Mount St. Helens, Figure 2.37, is an example of a modern day, violent, rhyolitic volcano that deposited ash in western states.

Various types of volcanic tuff beds are found in the Upper Titus Canyon Formation (Early Miocene), as shown in **Appendix C-5**. Various Middle Miocene tuffs are found in the area as described in **Appendix C-6**. While driving on the tour from prior to White Pass to the Leadfield area, these volcanic rocks will be to the right and much earlier (older) marine rocks to the left.

While plate tectonic driven extension caused the ranges to rise, the basins to drop, and the volcanoes to erupt, the forces of weathering and erosion caused by wind and water, broke down, carved, and carried off what had been built by tectonic forces. Canyons (Titus and Titanothere) were cut through the mountains. Debris, eroded from the uplifted mountains, began to fill the adjacent down dropping basins. The land was scarred. Today's topography was created. The processes continue today.

Remember that before this extension started, the entire region was a flat plain. The thousands of feet of mountain uplift and valley subsidence have created the Grapevine Mountains that you will be driving through on this trip as well as the nearby Panamint, Cottonwood, Funeral, and Black, Mountains. As a result of vertical displacement, tilting, and resulting erosion, you will be able to view the Cambrian rocks that were once deeply buried.

Figure 2.37 May 18, 8:32 am, 1980 Mount St. Helens erupted causing a gigantic rockslide and debris avalanche and triggering a major pumice and ash eruption. Within 9 hours the plume was 15 miles above sea level. Ash reached Idaho by noon. Five more eruptions occurred in 1980. *USGS, Austin Post*

2.4 Rocks observed on the tour

Box 2.1 provides a summary reference of the sequence and description of rocks deposited in the tour area. Use it for future reference.

You will see, colorful volcanic rocks produced by the Timber Mountain Caldera region 16 to 11 million years ago and rocks that were deposited as long as 600 million years ago (My) in an ocean environment. There are the remnants of stream channels that flowed from the direction of the Sierra Nevada and/or from the north and produced the Titus Canyon Formation. Rock walls display many folds and faults. Lower Titus Canyon has high, steep walls, fascinating examples of erosion, and the mosaic like displays of calcite and breccia.

2.5 Plants...an overview

A plant is a living organism that utilizes photosynthesis, a process whereby sunlight is utilized to create chemical energy. They are at the base of the food chain and produce their own food. Plants vary greatly in their appearance and the environments they live in. Plants are the kingdom Plantae that has eleven subdivisions and a vast number of species. A list compiled of Death Valley National Park plants has over six hundred entries. Flowering plants, angiosperms, are the most prolific and receive the most attention from Park visitors.

Knowing the name of a plant is not the same as knowing the plant. Becoming somewhat familiar with some of the basic flowering plant structure and functions will help to both understand the plant and aid us in determining plant identities.

Flowering plant structure and functions

The structure of a flowering plant (angiosperm) consists of roots, stem, leaves, and flowers. The roots absorb water and minerals from the soil and store food. The stem contains two systems of tubes, which transport water and minerals towards the leaves and plant food from the leaves to the stem and roots. Leaves are responsible for creating plant food by the process of photosynthesis. Leaf shapes margins, and arrangements vary greatly and are aids to identifying specific plants. Flowers are the reproductive organs of the plant. Flowers are the first thing most of us look at when we see a plant and the primary tool many of us use for identifying a plant.

What are flowers?

Flowers are flowering plants' sexual organs. Flowers provide a sexual display that improves the plant's reproductive success. Flowers attract (color, odor, food source) animals to unwittingly transfer pollen from one plant to another. The stationary plant uses mobile animals, including bees, beetles, moths, butterflies, flies, and hummingbirds, as part of its courtship and consummation ritual. Flowering plants first appeared 150 My and rose to being the dominant land plant because of the capability to attract pollinators. The earliest flowering plants were woody. Herbaceous (lacking wood) types evolved later. Annuals evolved from the long-lived or perennial herbaceous types.

Flowers are leaves that evolution has modified into sepals, petals, stamens, and carpels as illustrated in **Figure 2.38**. Sepals are at the base of the flower and protect the other three "leaves" as the bud develops. All the sepals are collectively known as the calyx. Just above the sepals are the petals, which are often colorful and fragrant, thereby attracting animals. When a flower's color is identified, the petal color is what is generally

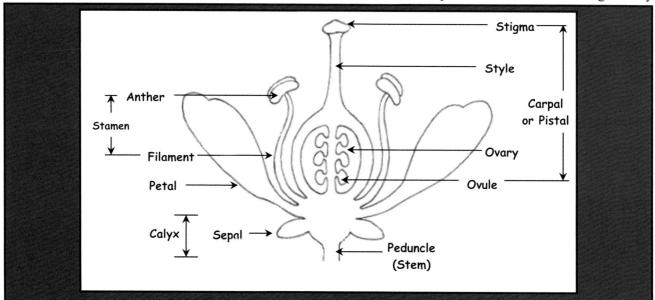

Figure 2.38 Flowers consist of four evolved leaves called sepals, petals, stamens and carpels. Complete flowers have all four leaves. Male flowers lack the carpels while female flowers lack the stamen.

referred to. Stamens are the male reproductive structures and are attached just above the petals. Most stamens are comprised of a long, slender filament with an anther on the tip. The anther produces pollen. The female reproductive structures, carpels, are at the highest position on the flower. Carpels consist of a stigma (catches pollen), style (tube that connects the stigma to the ovary), and the ovary, (contains one or more ovules). When mature, each ovule becomes a seed while the ovary becomes the protective, edible, and/or adhesive container called the fruit. Some flowers lack one or more of the four "leaves". This results in male (lack carpels) and female (lack stamens) flowers on the same or different plants.

An angiosperm's flower display can vary greatly from plant to plant. Arrangement on a stem, shapes, symmetry, size, color, and sexuality can differ. Members of the sunflower family have many tiny flowers making up what appears to be one flower head but is a composite of many tiny flowers. The sunflower family's composite head can contain many ray flowers, disk flowers, or both. Refer to the "Jepson Manual, Higher Plants of California" for more detail.

Table 2.1 and 2.2. have frequently used terms that require a clear understanding.

Table 2.1 Frequently used terms

annual	Completing life cycle (germination through death) in one year (or growing season), essentially non-woody. Herb.
biennial	Completing life cycle (germination through death) in two years or growing seasons (generally flowering only in the second) and non-woody (at least above ground), often with a radiating cluster of leaves near ground level during the first season. Herb.
herb	A plant that has little or no wood above ground. Above ground parts are of less than one year (or growing season) in age. (All plants called annual, biennial, or perennial, according to Jepson, are herbs.)
herbaceous	Lacking wood. Having the characteristics of an herb.
perennial	Living more than two years (or growing seasons). Herb.
shrub	A woody plant of short maximum height and much branched from the base.
subshrub	A plant with lower stems woody, the upper stems and twigs are not woody (or less so) and dying back seasonally.
tree	A woody plant of medium to tall maximum height, with generally one relatively massive trunk at the base.

Table 2.2 Flowering plant structure and functions

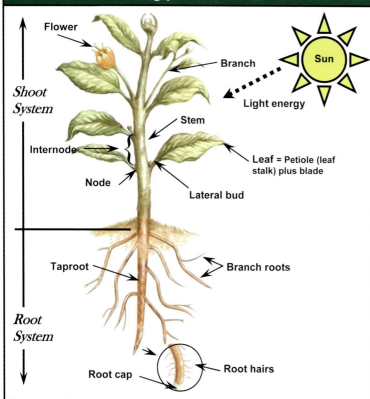

Figure derived from Audesirk

Photosynthesis

$$CO_2 + H_2O \xrightarrow[\text{chlorophyll}]{\text{light}} CH_2O + O_2$$

Carbon dioxide (from the air) plus water (originally absorbed by the roots) have their molecules rearranged by the light energy (absorbed from the sun by chlorophyll) into energy rich carbohydrates and oxygen.

Flowering plants are divided into two groups: monocots and eudicots.

Monocots have one cotyledon (seed leaf), usually parallel veins in leaves, parts (e.g. petals) usually in multiples of three, fibrous root system, and tubes scattered across stem diameter. Eudicots have two cotyledons, veins in leaves are usually netlike, parts (e.g. petals) are usually in fours or fives, taproot system, and tubes in the stem are arranged in a ring.

Structure	Definition/Function
Axil	The angle between the upper side of the stem and a leaf, branch, or petiole.
Branch	An offshoot of the stem.
Flower	Reproductive organs. See Figure 2.38.
Leaf	Contains chloroplasts and creates plant food via photosynthesis. Grows from node in stem. Arrangements include opposite and alternate along stem, whorled (multiple leaves per node), and basal. Various shapes include elliptical, linear, round, and needlelike. Margins include toothed, wavy, lobed, and cleft. Simple (one leaf per petiole) or compound (multiple leaflets per petiole (palmate)) leaves.
Node	Part of the stem from which a leaf, branch, or aerial root grows.
Petiole	A leaf stalk.
Root	Anchors and supports plant. Absorbs water and minerals and channels to stem. Stores plant food.
Stem	Bear leaves. Main support of plant. Contains plant's two-way transport system made up of two systems of tubes. One system carries water and minerals up from roots. After leaves produce food, the other tubes carry food to stem and back to roots for storage.
Tap root	Main root of some plants. Extends straight down under plant.
Terminal bud	Bud located at tip of stem.

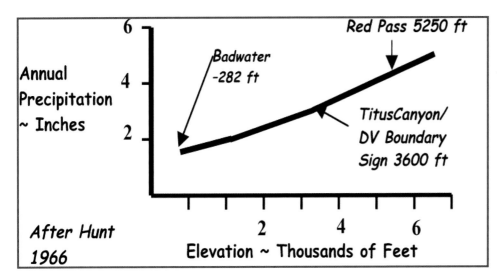

Figure 2.39 Death Valley region's low annual precipitation threatens plant and animal survival.

Plants must adapt to a harsh environment.

Plants must adopt strategies that allow them to survive the environments in which they are "rooted." They must deal with climatic factors (e.g. **moisture** and **temperature**) and available **soil environments**. In particular, desert plants must deal with drought, high temperatures, extreme variations in daily and yearly temperatures, coarse soils that do not retain water, clay that does not readily absorb water, and alkaline soils.

The Death Valley region is primarily part of the hot, "biological" Mojave Desert and yet has aspects of the high and cold Great Basin Desert. A desert is an area that receives less than an average of ten-inches of rain per year. Death Valley's floor receives less than two-inches of rain per year. More **moisture** is available at the higher elevation as shown in **Figure 2.39**. Note that there is a rather significant relative precipitation difference between Badwater and Red Pass. The majority of these rains usually occur in January through March and that is the coldest time of the year. Valley floor air **temperatures** soar to the high 120's in the summer. Peak temperatures occur in July. The highest recorded temperature was 134 degrees Fahrenheit on July 10, 1913. Due to the lack of moisture in the air, the day/night temperature extremes vary greatly (e.g. 30 to 40 degrees).

Plants are distributed over a range of **soil environments** as illustrated in **Figure 2.40**. Each of these environments poses challenges, which plants meet by various survival strategies. For example, moving down the desert slopes, soil particle size decreases and alkalinity increases. Also, the higher, coarser, soils absorb but do not retain water. In addition, the lower, clay-like soils tend to initially shed water but then retain it for long periods of time. Furthermore, the soils become "saltier" the closer you get to the valley floor. Note that these environments overlap and grade into one and another.

To survive in these diverse climatic and **soil environments**, plants have adopted various strategies which include storing water (e.g. cacti), going dormant during periods of drought (e.g. loss of leaves (sages)), having large and deep root systems (mesquite), having small leaves (sages), having small, coated leaves to reduce transpiration (e.g. Creosote bush), excreting salt from their leaves (e.g. Desert holly), thriving only in areas of constant water (e.g. Stream orchids), losing their above ground parts during drought (e.g. Coyote Melon), or living their entire life cycle in less than one season (e.g. annual wildflowers).

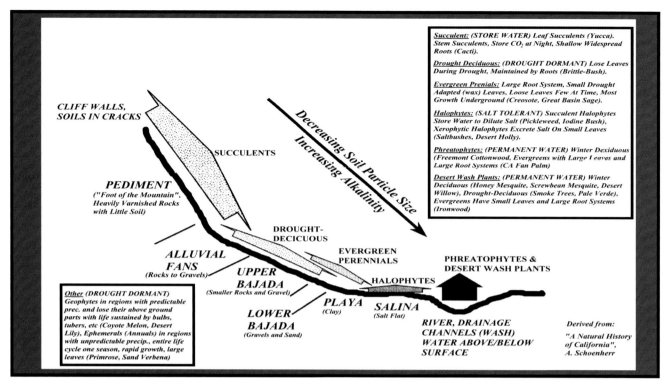

Figure 2.40 In addition to temperature extremes and lack of moisture, desert plants must meet the threats posed by various soil conditions. Plants develop different survival strategies to meet these threats.

Confusion in plant names... and the fix(s)

Most of us who are not botanists use a "common" name when we refer to or identify a plant. It is easy and comfortable for us because the common name is in English and refers to some obvious attribute (s) of that plant. Usually it works. Unfortunately, all too frequently, confusion arises because one plant has two or more common names. Cheesebush, burrobrush, and white burrobrush are the same shrub...we think. Sometimes a common name can be used to refer to a number of different plants. Burrobrush has been used to identify cheesebush and burrobrush (bur-sage). Sometimes burroweed is substituted for burrobrush. You should be confused by now.

To retain the comfort associated with common names, all plants in this book will have a photo along with the most common "common" name followed by other common names in parenthesis. For example: Cheesebush (burrobrush, white burrobrush).

The most rigorously correct approach is to utilize the "scientific" names that the botanists have derived. The plant kingdom has been broken down (top to bottom) into divisions having subdivisions that have orders having families that have... genera (singular, genus), species (singular, species), and subspecies (or varieties). As you progress from top to bottom, more specific and like attributes are identified until you get to species that can "interbreed" or are most closely related to one another than other plants in that genus. Unfortunately Latin and Greek, instead of English, are used. This tends to frighten off the non-professional. However, it is the only method to identify a specific plant properly. With some help from acknowledged people, we have included the scientific names along with the common names. The family, genus, species and, if required, subspecies will be identified.

We will see flowering plants in the sunflower, poppy, figwort, potato, legume, spurge, geranium, mint, buckwheat, cactus, lily, evening primrose, loasa, mustard, rose, phlox, waterleaf, orchid, cattail, goosefoot, gourd, and mallow families. Members of the sunflower family will be prevalent while members of the orchid and cattail families will be singular. We will discus a few interlopers, ephedras, from the pine family (not a flowering plant).

What clues can we use to anticipate where we might see specific plants?

Plants tend to group into communities based on the challenges they are presented with as seen in **Figure 2.40**. Areas with more moisture, coarse rocks, and low alkalinity (higher up on slopes) have different plants than areas that have fine clay-sized particles and are high in alkalinity (low on slopes). On coarse (small rocks and gravel), low alkaline slopes, you will see some succulents (cacti) and drought deciduous plants (Brittlebush) which lose their leaves in the dry season. As the particle size decreases from gravel to sand, as altitude decreases, and as alkalinity increases there are more evergreen perennials which rely on large root systems and have small leaves which are only lost a few at a time as drought conditions continue. Typical of this group are creosote bushes and various sages. Drought deciduous, evergreen perennials, and succulents dominate most of the Titus Canyon tour. On the alluvial fan at the end of the tour, you will see some halophytes (salt tolerant) such as desert holly. At Klare Spring, you will see phreatophytes (permanent water) such as cattails.

Let's simplify and tailor the **Figure 2.40** discussion on soil conditions, survival strategies and plant types to give us clues to where we might see specific plants. We will define five environments in which plants tend to group into communities and use them to identify which plants we may anticipate seeing therein.

1) **Alluvial fans** (e.g. beginning of tour to Mile 6.0, exit Titus Canyon to valley floor)…including: creosote bush, ephedras, sages, lupines, cacti, cheesebush, pincushion, thornbush, tackstem, eriogonums, gravel ghost, and desert five-spot.

2) **Upper slopes** (e.g. both sides of Red and White Pass)…including sages, spiny mendora, Mojave desert rue, snakeweed, lupines, and saucer plant.

3) **Cliffs** (e.g. at Red Pass, Titus Canyon walls)…including Indian paintbrush, Stans-bury cliff-rose, desert rock goldenbush, desert tobacco, Death Valley sage, and desert rocknettle.

4) **Wash** (e.g. stream channels in alluvial fans, Titus and Titanothere Canyon main and tributary drainage channels)…including spectacle pod, Stansbury cliff-rose, rabbitbrush, groundsel, coyote melon, pygmy cedar, and desert rocknettle.

5) **Riparian** (e.g. the constant water source at Klare Spring)…including stream orchids and cattails

See **Table 3.1** for a list of plants and typical locations and **Table 3.2** for color plates.

Wildflowers add many colors... particularly during spring.

If you make this trip during the early spring, you may be treated to a wide-ranging display of wildflowers. Their blooming seasons vary. You can visit the region one-week and return the next week to a new suite of flowers. Red, orange, yellow, green, blue, indigo and violet flowers (all colors of the spectrum) can be seen along with a multitude of variations on white. Annuals include white tackstem, golden evening primrose, pebble pincushion, desert five-spot, desert dandelion, Indian paintbrush, fiddleneck, white margin euphorbia, various phacelias, Layne milkvetch, and many others. Perennials include desert sage, Stansbury cliff-rose, Death Valley sage, and various cacti.

Cottontop cactus blooms in the summer while others, like rabbitbrush or desert rock goldenbush, bloom in the fall.

Rare plants grow in the Grapevine Mountains.

There are a number of rare plants growing in the Grapevine Mountains. These rare plants include rocklady maurandya, prickle-leaf, bear poppy, and napkin ring buckwheat. We do not identify a location for them because we prefer that they be completely left alone. However, we would like you to enjoy them. Therefore, we will discuss some of these rare plants in the following paragraphs.

Rocklady maurandya (*Maurandya petrophilia*), Figwort family, **Figure 2.41**, LL is the scarcest wildflower growing in the park. This **perennial herb** has pale yellow petals approaching yellow near the stem. The leaves are dark green, about one inch long and wide, and are edged with bristly teeth (*Maurandya*, Dr. Maurandy, teacher of botany at Carthagena; L., *petrophilia*, pale yellow.)

Figure 2.41 White Rocklady maurandya is extremely rare.

Prickle-leaf (*Hecastoclais shockleyi*), (Shockley's prickle-leaf), Sunflower family, **Figure 2.42** is a rare, rounded, and many-branched **shrub** that grows from 1-1/2 to 3 feet tall. The leaves are narrow, yellow green, and spine-tipped. Oval bracts, that are straw colored and have spines on the margins, are on the end of the branches. A single flower is partly enclosed in a bract. (*Hecastoclais*, Gr., "each shut up", referring to each flower being enclosed in its own involucres; Shockley, W. H. mining engineer and plant collector in western Nevada and eastern California, 1855-1925.)

Desert bearpoppy, (*Arctomecon merriamii*), (Desert poppy, White bear poppy), Poppy family, **Figure 2.43** grows only in the Death Valley region and southern Nevada. This **perennial herb's** flowers have six white petals and yellow stamen and carpels. Each flower appears on the end of a stem. Leaves are spread out around the base. The leaves are as intriguing as the flowers because the leaves are covered with numerous silver "hairs" from which this poppy derives its name. (Arctomecon, Gr., "bear poppy", referring to the hairy leaves and stems; Merriamii, D. C. Merriam, Chief of U. S. Biological Survey from 1885 to 1910.)

Napkin ring buckwheat, (*Eriogonum infractum*), (Jointed buckwheat), Buckwheat family, **Figure 2.44** is a **perennial herb** that has erect, leafless stems that are solitary, and unbranched except where the flowers grow. When old, the stems look like napkin rings. (*Eriogonum*, Gr., wooly joint or angle; *infractum*; L., broken within.)

Figure 2.42 Prickle-leaf has spine tapped leaves.

Figure 2.43 Bearpoppy has white flowers and leaves with long silver hairs.

Figure 2.44 Dried stems of napkin ring buckwheat look like rings stacked upon one and another.

> Titus Canyon is a particularly sensitive area due to the rare and unusual plants growing there.
> # PLEASE DO NOT PICK ANY FLOWERS

2.6 Animals...overview

Animals are the Kingdom Animalia. They are metazoan. Animals do not produce their own food like plants do. Animals must eat other organisms to obtain energy. They eat plants, animals, or both. They are more complex than plants because they have muscles and nerves that allow them to move around their environment in a controlled manner.

Like plants, animals have common names which most of us use. There is also a formal, hierarchical system identifying/defining a specific animal. Top to bottom is Kingdom, phylum, subphylum, class, subclass…and finally families, genera, species and subspecies. We will deal with the last four.

Animals include sponges, jellyfish, anemones, insects, spiders, worms, snails, clams, squids, starfish, urchins, and, of course, vertebrates. Vertebrates include jawed vertebrates such as fish, sharks, rays and terrestrial vertebrates. Terrestrial vertebrates include mammals, reptiles, amphibians, and birds. Focusing on the Death Valley region, **Appendix B** provides a summary list of the region's native mammals, birds, reptiles, fish, and insects as compiled by the National Park Service.

Although the Titus Canyon tour does not pass through all of the Death Valley National Park's environments, the visitor may still encounter many different animals. **Table 2.3** identifies some of the animals that live in the area. **Figure 2.45** provides pictures of some of these animals. If you are particularly lucky, Bighorn sheep may be seen peering down from the canyon's walls.

Sightings of the larger mammals will be rare. To a large extent, we can blame that on the area's arid climate and resulting plant life. The plants are on the bottom of the food chain. Plants produce their own food and are the source of food for herbivores. Generally, it takes 1,000 pounds of plant life to support 100 pounds of herbivore. The herbivores are the food supply for the carnivores. That 100 pounds of herbivore will only support 10 pounds of carnivore. Extrapolating this, 12,000 pounds of edible plant life, in this desert environment, would be required to support a 120-pound mountain lion. Other factors, such as time of day and time of the year will impact your ability to see larger mammals. Lions hunt and herbivores generally feed and move at night. Sheep may feed during the day on cool days, but they (including that mountain lion) will be at higher altitudes during the hot summer months.

Animals must adapt to their harsh, desert environment.

As is the case for plants, animals must adapt to the challenges posed by harsh environment (s) such as temperature extremes, drought, and a sparse food supply. They do this by having "strategies" to survive each of the aforementioned threats. We will briefly touch on those threats and strategies herein. We recommend Dr. Allan Schoenherr's "A Natural History of California" for a thorough discussion.

The desert environment has both daily and seasonal temperature extremes. Over-heating can be dealt with by panting or by avoidance. Avoidance is

Table 2.3 Some of mammals, birds, reptiles, and insects living in the Grapevine Mountains			
Desert cottontail	Coyote	Raven	Alligator lizard
Kangaroo rat	Desert woodrat	Roadrunner	Speckled rattlesnake
Various Mice	Gray fox	Red-tailed hawk	Sidewinder rattlesnake
Kit fox	Badger	Desert tortoise	Kingsnake
Ringtail	Bobcat	Desert iguana	Harvester ants
Mountain lion	Bighorn sheep	Chuckwalla	Tarantulas
Mule deer	Gamble's quail	Zebra-tailed lizard	Scorpions
Black-tailed jack rabbit	Chucker	Collared lizard	Blister beetles

preferable to panting because it doesn't use the meager water supply. Cold temperatures can be accommodated by fur, feathers, or seeking a heat source. Rattlesnakes and other reptiles can be found along warm, dark, asphalt roadways at night or den in deep rock crevasses when cold, winter temperatures occur.

Strategies for dealing with drought like conditions include water storage, flexible water sources, heat avoidance, dormancy, and tolerance to bodily water loss. Desert tortoises store a quart of water in their urinary bladder. Besides drinking water at a spring or seep, animals such as coyotes and kit fox derive water from the animals they devour. Tortoises and others obtain water from the vegetation they eat. Animals avoid the direct rays of the sun on hot days by getting in the shade of a rock or tree, climbing into trees to avoid the hot sands, or burrowing underground. Some animals can still function with loss of body water content. Examples are humans (10%), bighorn sheep (20%), burros (30%), spadefoot toads (40%) and Gamble's quail (50%).

Seasonal changes in food supplies are survived by storing fat, changes in diet items, and reduced reproduction. Chuckwalla store fat in their tails and Gamble's quail change what vegetation they will consume. Some of the many animals found in the Titus Canyon area are depicted in **Figure 2.45**.

Figure 2.45 Many different animals are found in the Titus Canyon area.

2.7 Humans in the Titus Canyon area

Native Americans

Archaeological studies indicate that Native Americans did not arrive in the Death Valley region until 9-10,000-years ago. The "Nevares Spring Culture" (Death Valley I) consisted of hunters who periodically visited, hunted big game, and left behind tools (**Figure 2.46**) that were predominately scrapers suitable for shaping wood atlatls and removing meat from skins. An arid climate followed and humans did not return until increased precipitation returned. The "Mesquite Flats Culture" (Death Valley II) maintained a hunter-gatherer existence 5,000-2,000 years ago, left behind the first petroglyphs, and saw the beginning of the replacement of the atlatl with the bow. The climate became arid again 2,000-years ago. The Saratoga Springs Culture (Death Valley III) was comprised of hunter-gatherers who adapted to the arid climate and left behind rock alignments, more numerous petroglyphs, and gravesites. The Saratoga Springs Culture reflects the time period from the adoption of the bow to the introduction of pottery. The "Panamint (Shoshone) Culture" (Death Valley IV) prospered since 1,000-years ago, created the first bighorn sheep petroglyphs, painted the first pictographs and made pottery. Some of their petroglyphs are preserved at Klare Springs. Some of their utensils found in Titus Canyon are seen in **Figures 2.47** and **2.48**. Their descendants, the Timbisha Shoshone, still live in Furnace Creek and surrounding regions. The Timbisha (Panamint, Coso) legend has them originating in Ubehebe Crater.

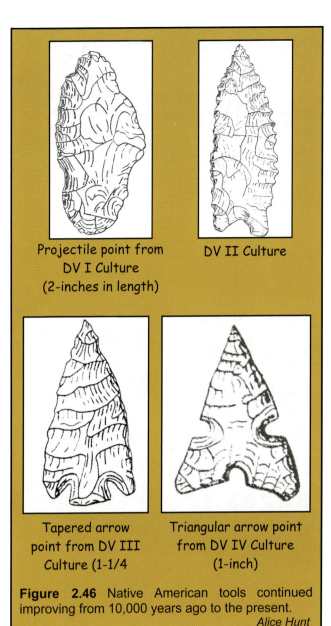

Projectile point from DV I Culture (2-inches in length)

DV II Culture

Tapered arrow point from DV III Culture (1-1/4

Triangular arrow point from DV IV Culture (1-inch)

Figure 2.46 Native American tools continued improving from 10,000 years ago to the present.
Alice Hunt

Figure 2.47 Panamint Shoshone crafted this water jug found in Titus Canyon.
Death Valley National Park

Figure 2.48 Shoshone split willow branches and wove it into a winnow basket that was later found in Titus Canyon.
Death Valley National Park

Explorers, Prospectors, Miners...

Explorers (possibly as early as 1834) and immigrants (e.g. Bennett-Arcane party of 1849) passed through the Death Valley area in the 1800's but left no specific reference to Titus Canyon.

Early prospectors included Mormons and Hispanics. Later prospectors sought legendary mines like the Gunsight and Lost Breyfogle. However, serious mining didn't start in the Death Valley region until 1871 with the discovery of silver and the founding of the town site of Chloride Cliff. Prospectors probably covered the Titus Canyon area before and after the Chloride strike. In 1891, Clinton Hart Merriam organized the biological expedition led by botanist Frederick Vernon Corville. Edward William Nelson, or a number of members of that party, collected specimen in the Grapevine Mountains in "Bighorn Canyon" that is currently believed to be Titus Canyon.

The year 1905 saw prospecting and limited mining in the area. Leadfield, **Figure 2.49 and 2.50**, saw a burst of prospecting and mining activity in 1924-26 but past into oblivion soon thereafter. Leadfield and its main promoter, Charles Courtney Julian, make an interesting tale that will be covered in detail in Segment 2 of the tour. Consider one of his advertising lines...

"Possibly it's too close to your back door for you to realize that such an immense treasure could exist, but let me tell you I am not the biggest "DUMB-BELL" at large..."

–C. C. Julian

Now, all that remains at Leadfield are dilapidated buildings, abandoned mine prospects, debris, history and the wind. "Leadfield... Death Valley Ghost Town" tells the interesting story of this boomtown.

With the creation of Death Valley National Monument in 1933, visitors and Park Naturalist Don Curry frequented Titus Canyon. After Curry's initial discovery of part of a fossil titanothere, scientists Chester Stock, Francis Bode, and others discovered additional Late Eocene fossils in the Titus Canyon region and documented their initial finding in 1935.

During the Great Depression, members of the Civilian Conservation Corps resided in Death Valley. They built new roads and maintained old ones. According to C. B. Glasscock, they helped to maintain the Titus Canyon road originally built by Julian.

Some of the early geologists (**Figure 2.51** to **2.57**) who worked in Titus Canyon and or the Grapevine Mountains region include Grove Karl Gilbert (1871), J. Edward Spurr (1903), Frederick L. Ransome (1905-10), S. H. Ball (1905, 07, 10), H. Donald Curry (1935-6), the aforementioned Stock and Bode (1935), Levi Fatzinger Noble who was

Figure 2.49 Miners and investors survey Leadfield, 1926.

Figure 2.50 Hidden by an encroaching creosote bush, one of Leadfield's remaining buildings is a shadow of its 1926 self.

responsible for publishing a generalized map of the Death Valley area including the southern Grapevine Mountains in 1954, Henry J. Cornwall and Frank J. Kleinhampl (1960, 61, 64), and Charles Butler Hunt and D. R. Mabey (1966). From 1961 to 1963, Mitchell W. Reynolds performed detailed geological mapping of the 110 square miles of the Titus and Titanothere Canyons region. His manuscript and maps represent the most comprehensive geological study of this region to date. Many other scientists, and an occasional engineer, continue to study the region's features.

Figure 2.51 Grove Carl Gilbert - 1898

Figure 2.52 J. Edward Spurr - 1866

Figure 2.53 Levi Fatzinger Noble

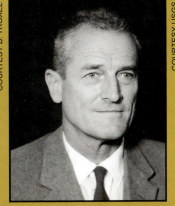

Figure 2.54 Charles Butler Hunt

Figure 2.55 H. Donald Curry

Figure 2.56 Mitchell W. Reynolds. Leadfield, Dec. 12, 1961 (while mapping Titus Canyon region)

Figure 2.57 Portion of "Preliminary Geologic Map of the Bullfrog District" by Frederick L. Ransome, 1907. Original Bullfrog mine is middle of left side, and Montgomery Shoshone mine (not on this Figure) is above and to the right of Rhyolite. Tiny + symbols denote Tertiary volcanic rock while shaded areas are alluvium.

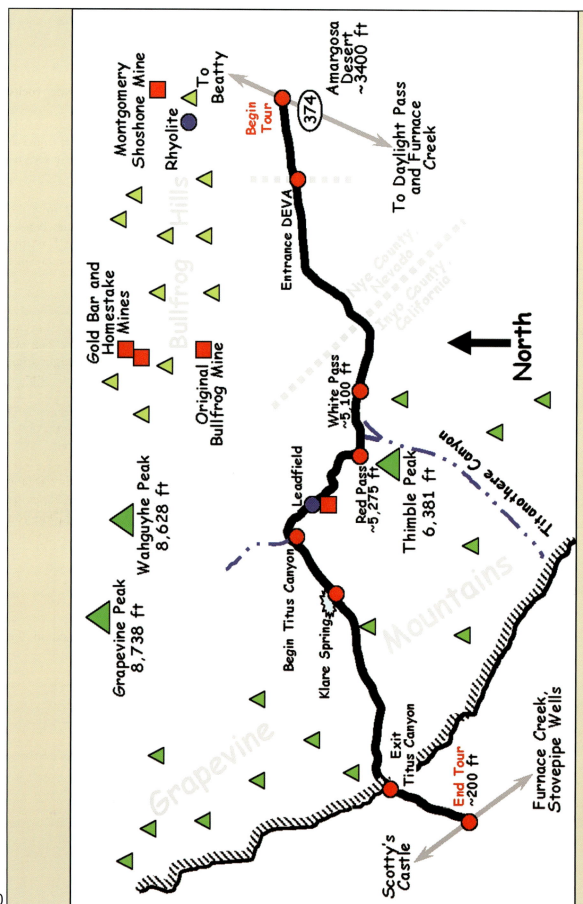

Figure 3.0 Overview of Titus Canyon tour (Total length: 28-miles. Maximum altitude: 5250 ft., Minimum altitude: 200 ft.)

3.0 Tour overview

On the tour, we will stop at specific locations and discuss its geology, identify representative plants and animals, and discuss relevant history. Read the route milestones, look at the pictures, and select the items you care to read about in depth.

3.1 The Route

The tour, **Figure 3.0**, is approximately 28 miles on a one-way, unpaved road. It stretches from the Titus Canyon turnoff on Nevada Highway 374 to the Scotty's Castle Road in Death Valley. The route and altitudes at key points are provided in following maps. There are no intersections to confuse you. Maximizing your vehicle's speed is guaranteed to minimize what you will see. We suggest that you occasionally park your vehicle, safely off to the side of the road, and walk around. You will see many more interesting things than while driving.

The tour guide is divided into 3-segments because these segments roughly correspond to geological and biological groupings.

The segments are:
1. **Segment 1:** Up the (eastern alluvial) fan to White Pass
2. **Segment 2:** Into the land of the titanothere and the ghost town
3. **Segment 3:** Down the drain and through Titus Canyon (and down the western alluvial fan)

3.2 Geology overview

The geology sections identify and describe what rock types are exposed, the environment when the rocks were deposited, and some geologic structures and how they formed.

The rock types you will see are:

1. **Cambrian** (543-490 My) **marine rocks** (Wood Canyon Formation, Zabriskie Quartzite, Carrara Formation and Bonanza King Formation) will be **to your left** from the beginning of the tour until you reach the townsite of Leadfield.

2. Tertiary **volcanic rocks** (erupted from the Timber Mountain Caldera and elsewhere ~ 16-11 My) will be **to your right** from the beginning of the tour to the entrance to Titus Canyon proper.

3. Late Eocene-Oligocene (37-24 My) **sedimentary rocks** (Titus Canyon Formation) will also generally be beneath you or on lower slopes **to your right** from White Pass to the entrance of Titus Canyon proper.

4. In **Titus Canyon**, different types of Cambrian marine rocks surround you.

You will start and finish the tour on alluvial fans created by debris eroded from the Grapevine Mountains. We provided maps that will inform you specifically what types of rocks you will see beside the tour route.

Geologic conventions

You will see the following symbols used in the following segments.

Fault — — — — — Fold - - - - - - - - -
Contact —·—·—·— Drainage —··—··—··
Road ——————

Q = Quaternary period (2-0 MY)
T = Tertiary period (65-2My)
Є = Cambrian period (543-490 My)
N = True north   **MN** = Magnetic north

31

3.3 Plant overview & roadmap

What plants

We have tried to select the most conspicuous and representative flowering plants (angiosperms) that you might see in the Titus Canyon area. We haven't covered them all; however, we did present pictures and discussion on eighty plants. We certainly did not cover all the plants seen in the Park. *Contact a National Park Service (NPS) Ranger at the Furnace Creek Visitor Center in order to get a complete list of DEVA plants.*

When seen

When and if you can see specific flowers is a function of when the fall and winter rains occurred as well as climatic conditions for that particular time of the year. It is impossible to say, in this book, specifically when you will see what flowers. Most plants bloom in the spring. One suite of plants will bloom one week and be replaced by another suite a week later. Some plants, such as rabbitbrush, bloom in the fall while cottontop cactus bloom in the full heat of the summer. **The NPS prints lists of what flowers are currently blooming for that particular time of year and approximately where they can be seen.**

Locating and identifying

It is difficult to say exactly where you will find a specific plant. To aid locating and identifying specific plants as you progress along the tour route, we created the plant roadmap in **Table 3.1**. We list the plants in the order they are discussed in the text, which is also close to the order in which you may encounter them. The segment in which a plant is encountered, the letter designation of the plant on the color plate, the text's page number where the plant is discussed in detail, and the typical type of location where the plant can be found are provided for the reader. **The photos presented herein were taken at the tour milestones in which the plants are discussed**. You have a good chance of seeing a perennial where we photographed it; however, annuals are also a function of the wind but should be in the tour segment where photographed or type of location identified in **Table 3.1**. Check **Recommended Reading** after the **Appendices** for a list of books that will help you identify plants.

Plant description...convention

A **"Plants"** heading alerts the reader that a description of plants, specifically seen and photographed <u>at that tour milestone</u>, occurs in following paragraphs. The convention used to describe plants is:

Desert globemallow (*Sphaeralcea ambigua*), (Apricot mallow), Mallow family, Figure 6.30, **CP-QQ**
<u>where:</u>
Desert globemallow = common name
Sphaeralcea ambigua = scientific name for plant genus and species
(Apricot mallow) = another common name for the same plant
Mallow family = the plant family in which the plant genus and species belongs
Figure 6.30 = the plants Figure number in the text
CP-QQ = if included, identifies the color plate of the plant in **Figure 3.1**. which provides close-ups and comparisons to other Titus Canyon area plants.

The text includes identification of annual, perennial herb, subshrub, shrub, or tree.

At the end of each plants description are parenthesis that enclose the translations of the *Greek* (Gr.) and *Latin* (L.) scientific names.

Where and when to see specific animals is even harder to specify than locating blooming plants. **Animal photos included herein were taken at or near the trip milestone being discussed.** Look for quail and chukar scurrying across the road.

3.4 Animal overview

The slower you drive, the more you will see. Get out of your vehicle and walk. The more you walk, the more you will see, Examine large rocks for lizards or snakes sunning themselves. Inspect flowers for insects pollinating them. In the canyon, watch for Bighorn sheep watching you. Be alert for coyotes walking along the road or Chukar crossing the road.

Table 3.1 Plant Roadmap for Titus Canyon Tour... approximate plant locations, descriptions, and color plates.

1) Shaded box indicates that plant is found in that numbered tour segment and, assuming reasonable blooming season, usually visible from roadside. A plant might be present, but not readily visible, in a tour segment for which the box is unshaded.
2) The * bold letters alongside the plant name identify the plant's color photograph in **Figure 3.1**.
3) The number in the shaded box is the page number in the text where plant is discussed
4) Plants bloom in spring except where noted by parentheses. (Fall)

Tour segment / Plant	1	2	3	Typical Location	Tour segment / Plant	1	2	3	Typical Location
Creosote bush	40			Alluvial fan	Green ephedra *Y	58			Upper fan
Bursage *A	40			Alluvial fan	Chia *Z	59			Upper fan
Cheese bush	40			Alluvial fan	Stansbury phlox *AA	59			Upper fan
Thornbush	41			Alluvial fan	Big sagebrush *BB	60			Upper fan
Desert purple sage *B	41			Upper fan					
Cooper golden bush	42			Alluvial fan	Prince's rock cress	61			Upper fan
Layne milkvetch	42			Alluvial fan	Brittlebush *CC	61			Fan-wash
Pebble pincushion *C	42			Alluvial fan	Royal desert lupine DD*	63			Upper fan
Fiddleneck *D	43			Alluvial fan	Prince's plume *EE	63			Alluvial fan
Whitemargin euphorbia	43			Fan, wash	Saucer plant *FF		71		Upper fan
Tackstem	43			Alluvial fan	Fremont phacelia *GG		71		Fan, slopes
Red stem filare *E	43			Alluvial fan	Honey mesquite		73		Fan, water
Death Valley ephedra	49			Alluvial fan	Desert milkweed *HH		74		Fan-wash
Nevada ephedra	49			Alluvial fan	Threadleaf snakeweed		78		Uppr slopes
Hop-sage *F	49			Alluvial fan	Desert pricklepoppy *II		78		Uppr wash
Spiny mendora	50			Upper fan					
Desert alyssum *G	50			Fan-wash	Desert rock goldenbush (Fall)		88		Cliff
					Grape soda lupine *KK		88		Alluvial fan
Indigo bush *H	50			Alluvial fan	Skeleton, Birdnest, &		89		Alluvial fan
Bladder sage *I	50			Upper fan	Pagoda eriogonums		90		
Calif. buckwheat *J	51			Alluvial fan	Mojave desert-rue *LL		90		Uppr slopes
Winter fat *K	51			Alluvial fan	Hedgehog cactus *MM		90		Fan-cliff
Mojave aster *L	51			Fan-cliff	Rabbitbrush (Fall)			112	Wash
Silver cholla *M	52			Alluvial fan	Desert tobacco *NN			114	Cliff
Beavertail pricklypear *N	52			Fan-slopes	Death Vly. phacelia *OO			114	Wash
Fishhook cactus *O	52			Alluvial fan	Cottontop cactus *PP (Summer)			117	Fan-slopes
Weakstem mariposa *P	52			Alluvial fan	Desert globemallow *QQ			119	Fan, wash
Indian paintbrush *	53			Fan-cliff	Groundsel *RR			119	Wash
Desert hyacinth *R	53			Alluvial fan	Pigmy cedar			119	Wash
Desert trumpet	53			Alluvial fan	Stream orchids *SS			120	Klare Sprg.
Desert dandelion *Q	53			Alluvial fan	Cattails			120	Klare Sprg.
Gold. eve. primrose *S	53			Fan-wash	Woody forget-me-not			130	Cliff
Shred eve. primrose *T	54			Alluvial fan	Death Valley sage *TT			138	Cliff
Parish larkspur *V	54			Alluvial fan	Desert holly			138	Lwr. Al. Fan
	54				Coyote melon			139	Wash
Wooly sunflower				Alluvial fan	Arrow-leaf			140	Cliff
Yellow eyed lupine	55			Upper fan	Desert rocknettle			141	Cliff, wash
Blazing star *W	55			Alluvial fan	Desert five-spot *UU			143	Lwr. Al. Fan
Spectacle pod	55			Fan-wash	Gravel ghost *VV			143	Lwr Al. Fan
Stansbury cliff-rose *X	58			Wash-cliff					

Figure 3.1 Color plates of selected plants on the Titus Canyon Tour

Letter designates color plate identified in text. Key for detailed plant description is on page 33.

Y. Green ephedra

Z. Chia

AA. Stansbury phlox

BB. Big sagebrush

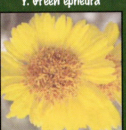
CC. Brittlebush

DD. Royal dsrt lupine

EE. Prince's plume

FF. Saucer plant

GG. Fremont phacelia

HH. Desert milkweed

II. Pricklepoppy

JJ. Rckldy maurandya

KK. Grape soda lupine

LL. Mojave dsrt-rue

MM. Hedgehog cactus

NN. Desert tobacco

OO. Dth Vly phacelia

PP. Cottontop cactus

QQ. Desert globemallow

RR. Groundsel

SS. Strm orchid

TT. Dth Vly sage

UU. Desert 5-Spot

VV. Gravel ghost

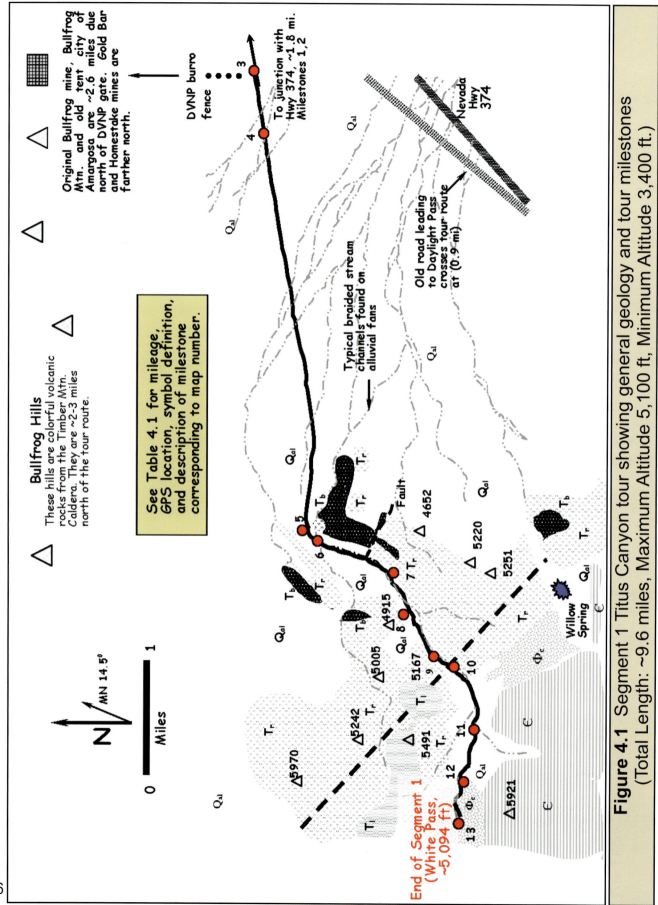

Figure 4.1 Segment 1 Titus Canyon tour showing general geology and tour milestones (Total Length: ~9.6 miles, Maximum Altitude 5,100 ft, Minimum Altitude 3,400 ft.)

Segment 1 Milestones (MS) of Titus Canyon Tour - Odometer Mileage and GPS Locations

MS	Miles	GPS	Description	MS	Miles	GPS	Description
1	0.00	N36° 51' 32.9" W116° 50' 45.9"	Highway 374 and Titus Canyon Rd., 3,400 ft, Bullfrog Hills, sages, Rhyolite ghost town. Start up the alluvial fan, sages, cacti, and flowers.	8	7.20	N36° 50' 04.0" W116° 57' 51.6"	Solitary remnant of volcanic ash flow
2	0.90	N36° 51' 26.8" W116° 51' 43.3"	Rhyolite to Dayligt Pass road	9	7.60	N36° 49' 54.5" W116° 58' 14.0"	Dip in road. Rhyolitic ash beds
3	1.85	N36° 51' 18.3" W116° 52' 44.1"	DEVA boundary and gate, Bullfrog mine	10	8.00	N36° 49' 40.9" W116° 58' 32.4"	Volcanic rock forms craggy hillside
4	2.50	N36° 51' 12.5" W116° 53' 26.0"	Large drainage channel	11	8.77	N36° 49' 27.9" W116° 59' 15.6"	Small valley
5	6.00	N36° 50' 51.2" W116° 57' 09.7"	Miocene volcanic rocks	12	9.21	N36° 49' 35.2" W116° 59' 41.8"	Volcanic rocks right Marine rocks left
6	6.20	N36° 50' 46.3" W116° 57' 19.5"	Drive into and along stream channel, stream deposits, plants change, Stansbury cliff-rose	13	9.56	N36° 49' 36.4" W117° 00' 02.4"	White Pass Elevation 5,094 ft. View Amargosa Desert and Titanothere Canyon
7	6.90	N36° 50' 12.3" W116° 57' 38.4"	Rhyolitic rocks and colorful lichen			Mileages are based on GPS readings with accuracy within 25 ft.	

Map Legend

Q_{al} – Alluvial fan debris (boulders, cobbles, gravel, sand) eroded from Grapevine Mountains

T_b – Miocene and younger volcanic – basalt (dark gray to black)

T_l – Miocene latite flow (brown-gray to red-brown)

T_r – Miocene and younger volcanic – rhyolite (gray to red-brown)

Φ_c – Oligocene (24-37) and younger Titus Canyon Fm, (green conglomerate, multi-colored and composition, breccias)

ϵ – Early Cambrian marine sedimentary (e.g. Wood Canyon Fm (slopes), Zabriskie Quartzite (purple cliffs))

Δ – Peak with elevation in feet

4.0 Segment 1... Up the fan to White Pass

Mile 0.0 - Starting point: Park at junction of Nevada Highway 374 and the Titus Canyon road
N36° 51' 32.9" W116° 50' 45.9"
Altitude 3,417 feet

Segment 1 takes us from the start of the tour to a scenic viewpoint, called White Pass, that overlooks the drainage into Titanothere Canyon. In Segment 1, the road progresses westward up an alluvial fan that slopes gently eastward and downward from the Grapevine Mountains. The fan helps to create the environment for a creosote bush and sage dominated plant community. Proceeding up the fan and still on the east side of the Grapevine Mountains, we enter an area that has Tertiary volcanic rocks on our right (northward) and predominately Cambrian marine sedimentary rocks on our left (southward). In this area, we observe a transition into a different plant community. Finally, we reach White Pass.

Segment 1 map and milestones are presented in **Figure 4.1**. Stop frequently and get out of your vehicle to look around. Remember to park your vehicle on the side of the road so that fellow explorers and Death Valley National Park rangers can get past your vehicle.

Start the tour by parking here and looking around. We are at an altitude of approximately 3,400 ft and on a large alluvial fan composed of rock debris eroded from the Grapevine Mountains (**Figure 4.2**) that are ahead of us (southwest and west). The mountains were named by the Lt. George Montague Wheeler survey expedition of 1871. The name refers to grapevines found in some canyons (e.g. Scotty's Castle's "Grapevine Canyon"). North are the colorful, tilted, volcanic Bullfrog Hills, **Figure 4.3**.

Geology

Directly north from the starting point, the Bullfrog Hills consist of east tilted, volcanic rocks that are underlain by normal faults at a shallow depth (**Figure 2.36**). In places, the volcanic rocks are enriched by quartz bearing gold and have been intensely explored by prospectors. The volcanic rocks were erupted from the Timber Mountain Caldera (located in the Nevada Test Site) during middle Miocene time (16-11 My).

The highest peak off to the northwest is Wahguyhe Peak (8,628 ft). Farther north and slightly west is Grapevine Peak (8,738 ft).

Figure 4.2 View looking southwest to the snow-capped Grapevine Mountains. Out of view and farther left, the extreme north end of Funeral Mountains meets the south end of the Grapevine Mountains along Boundary Canyon.

What does a geologist see when he studies the volcanic rocks of the Bullfrog Hills? **Figure 4.4** answers that question. He sees tuff (volcanic rock) beds that provide him with a record of the last 16 My in this region. These deposits, starting with Tertiary quartz and latite lava flows (Tql) and ending with Tiva Canyon member of the Paintbrush tuff (Tpc), were originally erupted from a volcanic source 12.9 to 16(?) My and laid down sequentially in approximately horizontal beds. Potassium-argon analyses of the ages of the tuffs and chemical analyses of the tuff beds correlates them to volcanic sources in the Timber Mountain caldera in the Nevada Test Site to the northeast of the Titus Canyon area. Volcanic activity and extension (spreading apart due to tensional forces) of the Great Basin might be attributable to North American continental plate overriding a midoceanic ridge that extended north from the Gulf of California. This extension has produced the north-south trending mountain ranges and valleys (basins) across the Great Basin. The specific cause of this extension is still being debated. Analyses of the types and geometry of the faults indicates that rocks of the Bullfrog Hills extended west along the **Figure 4.4** detachment fault 8-10 My. The tuff beds broke along normal (tensional) faults and tilted downward to the east as movement progressed along the detachment fault.

Figure 4.3 Looking to the north, the colorful, volcanic Bullfrog Hills are seen. They were the location for gold mining towns such as Rhyolite, Bullfrog, and Homestake.

Figure 4.4 Close-up of Bullfrog Hills and Bullfrog Mountain showing Miocene volcanic rocks dipping into the upper detachment fault. QTac (Quaternary and Tertiary) alluvium and colluvium, Tql (Tertiary) quartz and latite lava flows, Tlr (Tertiary) Lithic Ridge Tuff, Tcb (Tertiary) Bullfrog member of Crater Flat Tuff, Tpc (Tertiary) Tiva Canyon Member of Paintbrush Tuff.

Plants

The large shrubs that are about 4 to 6 feet tall and have multiple grayish stems with small shiny, waxy leaves are called **creosote bush** (*Larrea tridentata*), (Greasewood, Chaparral), Caltrop family, **Figure 4.5**. This shrub's common name refers to its characteristic odor that is evident after a rain. During the spring, numerous tiny yellow flowers, **Figure 4.5**, appear. Small, fuzzy, white fruit follows the yellow flowers. Creosote bush is the most common plant below snow-level throughout the California desert. Estimated to be more than 11,000 years old, a creosote bush in the Mojave Desert may be the oldest living plant in the world. Creosote is an extremely hardy plant. It has a large root system that can draw moisture out of the soil better than any other desert plant. Its leaves are coated with a substance that minimizes loss of water due to transpiration (evaporation of water through a plant's leaves). The creosote **gall midge**, *Asphondylia auripilia*, causes the one-inch diameter, leafy balls often seen in creosote bush. A moth larva, **creosote bagworm**, *Thyridopteryx meadi*, creates a 1-1/4 inch long, cigar shaped silk cocoon. Native Americans boiled the shrubs for

Figure 4.5 Creosote bush has yellow flowers and fuzzy, white fruit, and occasionally a gall midge.

Figure 4.6 Bursage (yellow-green) appears tortoise shaped and has stems that appear to be "wooly".

Figure 4.7 Cheesebush is rounded and waist high, has threadlike leaves and 5-petaled fruits, and exudes a rank smell when its leaves are crushed.

Medicinal tea, used the sap for glue and burned it as firewood. It also has been used externally as an antiseptic and poultice for rheumatism and internally for gastric problems. It is an antioxidant that has medicinal applications for treatment of herpes, breast cancer, asthma, liver disorders, and others. (*Larrea* refers to John Anthony de Larrea, Spanish promoter of science; *tridentate*, L., "3-toothed".)

A smaller (approximately up to 2-feet high), tortoise-shaped, plant is called **bursage** (*Ambrosia dumosa*), (Burro bush, Burro-weed), Sunflower family, **Figure 4.6, CP-A**. The stems are whitish and the leaves are small, gray-green and lobed. The leaves somewhat resemble tiny oak leaves. The spring growth looks like yellow-green wooly stems. It is common on the fans and extends down to lower elevations in Titus Canyon. Burros and sheep are said to enjoy this **shrub**. In 1844, Captain Fremont gathered specimens along the Mojave River. (*Ambrosia*, Gr., "food of the gods"; *dumosa*, L., "bushy".)

Another **shrub** you will see is **cheesebush** (*Hymenoclea salsola*), (Burrobrush, White burrobrush), Sunflower family, **Figure 4.7**. Its crushed leaves do not smell like any cheese you would want to eat. This shrub grows to approximately waist high and has long, slender, threadlike leaves. Cheese bush looks like a soft, yellow-green bush. In the spring, it has fruit that looks like tiny, dirty white rosebuds. The buds later open to flat, 5-petaled, cream-colored flowers. It grows in washes and drainage courses throughout the region. (*Hymenoclea*, Gr., Membrane (i.e. wing) enclosed; *salsola*, the Russian thistle that it was thought to resemble.)

This area also has a pleasantly aromatic shrub commonly called **desert purple sage** (*Salvia dorrii*), (Great Basin blue sage, Purple sage, Desert sage), Mint family, **Figure 4.8, CP-B**. It has purple bracts and dark blue flowers. It grows at elevations of 4,000-6,000 feet. You will continue to see this plant for quite some distance up the alluvial fan. Native Americans dried the leaves and smoked them as medicine. (*Salvia*, L., an herb used for healing; dorrii, Dorr.)

Thornbush (*Lycium andersonii*), (Box thorn, Desert thorn, Anderson thornbush), Potato family, **Figure 4.9**, has light purple or blue, 5-petaled,

Figure 4.8 Desert purple sage (blue)

Figure 4.9 Thornbush has light-blue, five-petaled flowers.

Figure 4.10 Cooper golden bush.

Figure 4.11 Layne milkvetch

Figure 4.12 Pincushion (white) resembles its namesake. White moths pollinate this flower.

Figure 4.13 Fiddleneck (orange-yellow) has curly "fiddle" stems.

Figure 4.14 Whitemargin euphorbia (white) is mat-like.

flowers. The leaves are green and single lobed. The stems are gray. There are short, needle-like spines. This **shrub** grows approximately waist high. (*Lycium*, refers to Lycia in ancient Greek geography it was a region in southwest Asia Minor; *andersonii*, Dr. C. L. Anderson, 1827-1910, physician and naturalist, resident of western Nevada and central California.)

Cooper golden bush (*Ericameria cooperi*), Sunflower family, **Figure 4.10**, is a rounded **shrub** that grows to three-feet high. When the yellow flowers bloom in the spring, the shrub looks like a "golden bush." Evergreen leaves are short, narrow, and flat.

Layne milkvetch (*Astragalus layneae*), (Layne locoweed, Widow's milkvetch), Pea family, **Figure 4.11**, has leaves that resemble a fern and lie flat, close to the ground. One or more vertical, six-inch stems contain white and purple tipped flowers that are well spaced on the stem of this **perennial herb**. The close-up of a stem shows the shape and color of a single flower and flower spacing. (*Astragalus*, Gr., dry fruit was thought to resemble bones in human foot; *laynae*, Dr. Mary K. Layne (aka Brandgee), 1844-1920.)

You might see what appears to be orange-yellow layers of spaghetti or thread that someone has spread on some of the creosote, hopsage, or other bushes. This annual is the parasite called "**dodder**" (*Cuscuta denticulate*), (Witches hair, Toothed dodder), Morning-glory family. Dodder has pale yellow stems and small, urn-shaped white flowers. It will eventually kill the host plant. (Arabic, *Kush-kut; denticulate*, L., small-toothed.)

Pebble pincushion (*Chaenactis carphoclinia*), Sunflower family, **Figure 4.12, CP-C**, grows to about twelve inches high and can be many branched in wet years. This **annual** derives its name from the half-inch, diameter white flowers that look like pincushions due to its stamens standing up like many little pins.

(*Chaenactis*, Gr., "gaping ray," an enlarging orifice and limb of the marginal corollas found in most species simulating a ray; carphoclinia, Gr., "a small dry object" + "bed".)

Fiddleneck (*Amsinckia tessellata*), (Devil's lettuce, Checker fiddleneck, Bristly fiddleneck), Borage family, **Figure 4.13, CP-D**, stems curl at the top where the flowers are blooming and somewhat resembles a fiddle's neck. The "necks" straighten and flowers migrate upwards as this annual plant grows. Native Americans are said to have used this **annual's** small seeds and fresh green stems as food. The Jepson Desert Manual indicates that the seeds and herbage are toxic to livestock, especially cattle, due to alkaloids and high nitrate concentrations. The sharp plant hairs irritate human skin. (*Amsinckia*, Wilhelm Amsinck, Burgermeister and botanic patron of Hamburg, Germany; *tessellata*, L, "checkered," referring to arrangements of warts on the backs of the nutlets.)

Whitemargin euphorbia (*Chamaesye albomarginata*), (Rattlesnake weed), Spurge family, **Figure 4.14**, is a mat-like plant with white flowers and green, heart-shaped leaves. This **perennial herb** is very common and you will continue seeing it on up to Red Pass and into Titus Canyon. Native Americans used the milky sap from the stems and leaves in treating eye inflammation and infections. (*Euphorbia*, Gr. ancient name for a kind of prostate plant)

Tackstem (*Calycoseris wrightii*), Sunflower family, **Figure 4.15**, grows to twelve inches high. The flower heads are 1-1/4 inches in diameter, white with a tinge of pink, and have many flat petals that are saw-toothed on the ends. Leaves are much divided along the stems. This **annual** plant derives its name from tiny glands along the upper stems. These glands appear to be tiny tacks. (*Calycoseris*; Gr., cup + "Seris," a cichoriaceous genus; *Wrightii*, surveyor and teacher Charles Wright, 1811-1885, collected new plant species in Texas and California.)

Red Stem Filare (*Erodium cicutanium*), Geranium family, **Figure 4.16, CP-E**, magenta/pink/white flowers have five-petals and are one-half inch in diameter. Leaves appear fernlike. This **annual** plant was introduced from the Mediterranean area and has spread over most of California at elevations below 4,000 feet.

Animals

You might see a few lizards sunning themselves early in the morning or later in the day when it's overcast. Remember, unlike members of the mammal kingdom, reptiles use the sun or the shade to help regulate their body temperature. You might see others scampering through the brush after you have frightened them.

The carnivorous **Long-nosed Leopard lizard** (*Gambelia wislizerii*), **Figure 4.17**, is 8-15 inches long, slender, and has dark spots on its body, limbs, and tail. It shelters under clumps of vegetation as it hunts for insects, spiders, small lizards, and members of its own species. It hisses and will bite.

Figure 4.17 The spotted, carnivorous Leopard lizard hunting for its next meal.

Figure 4.15 Tackstem has white, saw-toothed petals.

Figure 4.16 Red Stem Filare

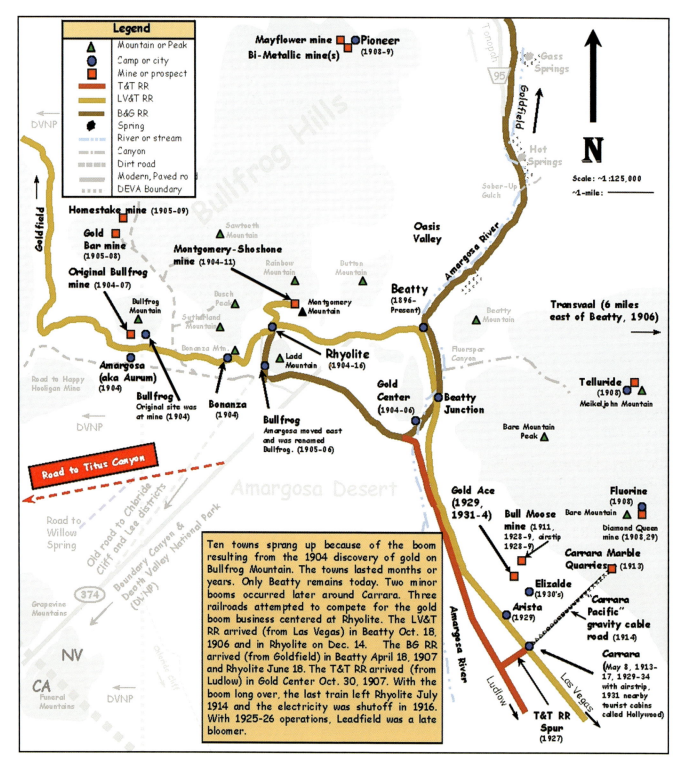

Figure 4.18 Nye County, Nevada's Bullfrog Hills was the scene of various mining operations long before the Leadfield boom (responsible for the construction of the road to and through Titus Canyon). Prospectors drawn to this area fanned out in search of strikes in other areas. Their efforts lead to multiple discoveries of lead deposits near the beginning of Titus Canyon.

History

With the discovery of gold in Tonopah (1900) by Jim Butler, and in Goldfield (1903) by Al Myers and Tom Murphy, miners and prospectors flocked to the surrounding regions of Nevada to try and strike it rich. Northeast from the starting point of this tour, are the remnants of the old gold mining town of Rhyolite which sprang up after two prospectors, Shorty Harris and Ed Cross, discovered the "green bullfrog" gold ore in 1904. As shown on **Figure 4.18**, Rhyolite was one of three mining towns that started up in the Bullfrog Hills. Rhyolite grew to approximately 10,000 people by its peak in 1907. The largest mine was the Montgomery-Shoshone (**Figure 4.19**). Characters like mine-owner Bob Montgomery, Nevada Senator William M. Stewart, steel-magnate Charlie Schwab, entrepreneur and later Nevada governor Tasker L. Odie, and Death Valley Scotty (**Figure 4.20**) frequented its streets. The Las Vegas and Tonopah, Bullfrog and Goldfield, and Tonopah and Tidewater railroads hauled freight and passengers to and from Rhyolite. Changes in the national economic environment and falling production saw the population fall to less than 1,000 people by 1910. By 1916, the electricity was shut off and the lights went out. Some of Rhyolite's buildings were moved to the Nevada, marble-quarry town of Carrara, located a few miles south of Beatty. The town of Carrara also became a ghost town.

Rhyolite is well worth a future side trip. Still visible are the remains of the J.S. Cook Bank (**Figure 4.21**), Porter Bros. Mercantile, jail, ornate train station (**Figure 4.22**), schoolhouse (**Figure 4.23**), the famous Bottle House (made from 50,000 beer and liquor bottles and mud cement by miner Tom Kelley), and many more buildings.

North of us, and west of Highway 374, is the modern day Bullfrog mine that was in production until 1999. It employed over 300 people and produced both gold and silver.

The region south of Rhyolite and the Bullfrog Hills and the region to the southeast is the Amargosa Desert through which the Amargosa River flows (above and below ground). The John Charles Fremont Expedition of 1845 so named the river because it means "river of bitterness" in Spanish.

To our left and behind us (southwest) are Daylight Pass (5064 ft) and the northern extremity of the Funeral Mountains and the beginning of the southern Grapevine Mountains. The boundary between the Funeral and Grapevine Mountains is the northeast-southwest trending Boundary Canyon. The Governor H. G. Blasdel Expedition (1866) named the Funeral Mountains. It is thought that the Funeral Mountains were so named because they bounded a portion of <u>Death</u> Valley.

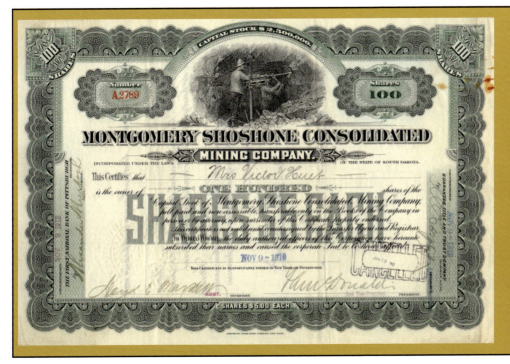

Figure 4.19
This Montgomery Shoshone Consolidated stock was issued in 1910. (The mine was located next to Rhyolite.) Note the two miners using pneumatic drilling equipment. The days of single and double jacking with drills and sledgehammers had passed. Now diesel air compressors (exterior to mine) and air hoses. Diesel pumps and water lines and water liners were needed to provide water for cooling the drills.

Figure 4.20 Death Valley Scotty in Rhyolite creating his usual turmoil.

COURTESY NEVADA HISTORIC SOCIETY, *Death Valley National Park, A. E. Holt*

Mile 0.0 - 6.0
Driving west up the alluvial fan

Continue the tour by driving up a six-mile long alluvial fan. There will be a number of milestones in the next six-miles. This is the first major alluvial fan we will drive on as part of this tour and is on the east side of the Grapevine Mountains.

We will finish our tour by driving two-miles down the final major alluvial fan. That fan is on the west side of the Grapevine Mountains, begins at the Titus Canyon mouth (exit), and extends into Death Valley.

Figure 4.21 J.S. Cook Bank is Rhyolite photographer's favorite.

Figure 4.22 The Rhyolite Las Vegas & Tonopah Railroad station was completed in June 1909 for $130,000. It is still an impressive building.

Figure 4.23 The Rhyolite schoolhouse is a concrete structure that was built to last generations of students.

Geology

Alluvial fans, **Figure 4.24**, are formed from rock fragments (boulders, cobbles, gravel, sand, silt, and clay) that are eroded from the mountains by occasional floods. In this region, the floods primarily occur in the summer. The waterborne sediment exits the canyons mouth at a high velocity. The velocity (energy) decreases as the debris moves downhill and also spreads out as shown in **Figure 4.25**. The sediment size decreases laterally and downhill. From an airplane, the debris pile has a fan shape with the hinge of the fan at the mouth of the canyon and the blades radiating outward and downward into the valley. As you drive up the fan, you will notice that the size of the rock fragments generally increases. This is illustrated in **Figure 4.25**.

After you complete this tour, take some time to look at the large, "world-class" alluvial fans in Death Valley. The largest fans are on the west side of the valley. They start at the canyon mouths of the Panamint Range. Smaller, steeper and very spectacular fans start at the canyon mouths on the east side of central Death Valley, between Furnace Creek Wash and Shoreline Butte. The west side of the Grapevine Mountains has some beautiful, steep fans. Along the Scotty's Castle Road and south of Titus Canyon, you can see the fan in **Figure 4.26**. You will see "braided" patterns and patches of

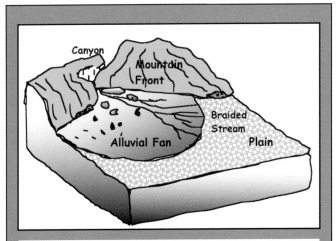

Figure 4.24 Alluvial Fan: A large fan or cone shaped pile of stream deposits that forms where a stream exits a mountain canyon with high velocity and spreads and slows as it emerges on a plain. Coarsest material accumulates where the stream exits the canyon with finer particles farther from the exit. Streams shift back and forth on the fan creating a braided pattern and a fan-like surface.

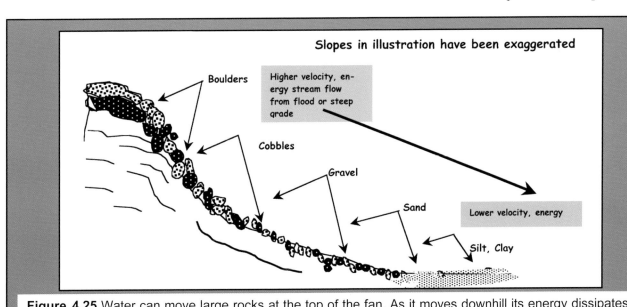

Figure 4.25 Water can move large rocks at the top of the fan. As it moves downhill its energy dissipates and only continually smaller rocks can be moved around. At the base where the water's energy has dissipated because its velocity is near zero, only clay-sized particles are moved.

Figure 4.26 This alluvial fan south of the mouth of Titus Canyon exit has braided drainage channels. Shades of sediments denote different ages of flooding events. You should be able to count at least four events here.

Figure 4.27 This gold "prospect" proved to be non-profitable and was abandoned prior to actual "mining".

Figure 4.28 "Desert pavement" is commonly covered with "desert varnish."

varying degrees of shading or darkness. The difference in shading indicates the relative ages of debris with darker being older.

When you first start driving, notice a white patch on the alluvium to north (right) and a road leading to it. The area of the patch was a potential low-grade gold mine but no mining was done due to profit projections. Farther east of that patch are notches (**Figure 4.27**) that look like stair steps cut into the side of the hill. These cuts were made in the early 1980's as part of early development for a "modern" gold mine that also never went into production.

As you continue driving west up the fan, you may notice small patches barren of vegetation that are covered with rock fragments. These patches contain tightly packed clasts and are known as desert pavement, **Figure 4.28**. They are formed by depletion of the fine-grained material such that the rocks concentrate on the surface. Another interpretation is that fine-grained material is added but migrates downward, beneath the protective cover of the rock fragments. Commonly the rock fragments have a dark coating on top (side exposed to the elements). The dark coating is called desert varnish. On this fan you see small patches that are, at most, a few hundred square feet in extent. If you turn rock fragments over, you will see pinkish to reddish iron stains on the underside of the desert varnished, opaque stones. Translucent fragments, such as quartz, usually have no varnish and the undersides have a thin coating of green algae. The algae require the sunlight that filters through the translucent stone to perform photosynthesis.

Plants

Driving up the fan, you will notice that the shrubbery is larger and lusher along the side of the road than farther from the road. The reason is water. The road is packed and not as absorbent as the surroundings. Therefore, the water is shed off the road surface and drains to the sides of the road. Those plants along the side of the roadway get their share from rain plus the water shed by the road.

You probably have noticed a shrub that appears to be a spiny, leafless plant that is about knee high. It is an ephedra and comes in different varieties in this region. **Death Valley ephedra** (*Ephedra funerea*), ephedra family, **Figure 4.29**, has gray-green stems spreading out from a node on the main stem at an angle of sixty degrees. This **shrub** has numerous main stems. In the spring, if you look closely, you should see small, scale-like leaves at the joints. (*Ephedra*, Anc. Gr., name use by Pliny for the horsetail which it resembles; *funereal*, L. "funeral.")

Nevada ephedra (*Ephedra nevadensis*), ephedra family, is quite similar except this **shrub's** stems spread out from a central node on a main stem at an angle of forty-five degrees. We shall see a third variety, **Green ephedra**, farther up the alluvial fan. Native Americans and settlers used ephedra to brew tea. (*Ephedra; nevadensis*. L., "of Nevada.")

Figure 4.29 Death Valley ephedra has many stems and small scale-like leaves.

Hop-sage (*Grayia spinosa*), (Spiny hop-sage) Goosefoot family, **Figure 4.30, CP-F**, is another shrub you probably have noticed from the onset of the tour. It is approximately one to four feet high, has widely spread gray branches that form a spiny point on their ends, and narrow, elliptical, green leaves approximately one-inch long. The densely packed, pink or white, papery, bracts crowded together on the branchlet tips are quite visible in the springtime. (*Grayia*, Asa Gray, 1810-1888, laid the foundations of botany in this country; *spinosa*, L., "thorny")

Figure 4.30 Hop-sage is 1-4 feet high and has sharp spines and very visible, papery, white or pink bracts.

Figure 4.31 Spiny mendora has sharp spines and 5-petaled white flowers.

Figure 4.32 Desert alysum has white, fragrant flowers.

Figure 4.33 Indigo bush has dark blue pea-shaped flowers.

Figure 4.34 Bladder sage has white to purple "paperbags."

Spiny menodora (*Menodora spinescens*), (Greenfire, Spiny desert olive), Olive family, **Figure 4.31**, grows at altitudes higher than approximately 3,500 ft. It is usually one to three feet high. Spiny menodora has widely spaced branches that form a stout, spiny point at their ends. This **shrub's** white flowers are tubular and have 5 petals. The leaves are small, oblong, and alternate. You will notice abundant spiny mendora at White Pass. Native Americans might have used the seeds for food.

Desert alyssum (*Lepidium fremontii*), (Desert pepper-grass, Desert pepperweed) Mustard family, **Figure 4.32, CP-G**, is a rounded, green-stemmed, perennial herb that grows one to two feet high and has small, white, fragrant flowers that eventually produce one-sixth of an inch long, flattened seedpods. The flowers densely cover this rounded, many branched bush. Leaves are basal. Desert alyssum is common in washes and where creosote bushes grow. Captain John C. Fremont collected a specimen 1844. (*Lepidium*, Gr., "small scale;" *fremontii*, Captain John C. Fremont.)

Indigo bush (*Psorothamnus fremonti*), (Fremont's indigo bush, Fremont's dalea), Legume family, **Figure 4.33, CP-H**, is a much branched shrub that grows one to three feet tall in this area. The leaves are grayish and can be wide or narrow. The stems and branches are white. Two to three-inch long spikes of dark blue, pea-shaped flowers bloom above the leaves. (*Psorothamnus; fremontii*, Captain John C. Fremont.)

Bladder sage (*Salazaria mexicana*), (Mexican bladdersage, Paper bag bush), Mint family, **Figure 4.34, CP-I**, is a two to three-foot high aromatic **shrub** with greenish-white branches that grow at right angles to the stem. The leaves are small, sparse, and opposite. When not blooming, it is very inconspicuous. When blooming in the later springtime, it has enlarged papery calyxes that enclose the fruit (four nutlets). The "paper bags" are white to light purple. When blooming in the late springtime, you can see these shrubs from here into Titus Canyon and might see Blister beetles mating in the branches. These love-starved, comical beetles are interesting to watch as they fall off branches during their somewhat backwards love making. However ludicrous they may appear, do not pick one up for they are aptly named and you might receive a blister. (*Salazaria*, Don Jose Salazar y Larreque, a Mexican astronomer; *mexicana*, Mexico.)

California buckwheat (*Eriogonum fasciculatum ssp. polifolium*), (Rosemary eriogonum, Eastern Mojave buckwheat), Buckwheat family, **Figure 4.35, CP-J**, is a two to three-foot high, many-stemmed shrub with small, narrow, gray leaves growing in bunches. When blooming in the late springtime, it has tiny, white flowers with pink stamens that are very conspicuous by their abundance. You will notice these shrubs from here into Titus Canyon. (*Eriogonum*, Gr., "wooly joint or angle" in reference to the hairy joints of some species).

Winter fat (*Krascheninnikovia lanata*), (White sage), Pigweed family, **Figure 4.36, CP-K**, is a one to three foot high **shrub** with long, narrow leaves growing alternately up the stem. The tiny, white flowers are so numerous that they look like tufts of white hair or wool. Perhaps, a fat and hairy pipe cleaner would be a good description. Blooming is in the late spring. A deep taproot enables it to withstand drought. It is a valuable winter grazing plant in the Great Basin. Native Americans chewed the fresh root and used it for burns. (Russian botanist, Stephan P. Krascheninnikov (1713-1755); *lanata*, L., "wooly.")

Mojave aster (*Xylorhiza tortifolia*), (Desert aster, Mojave woodyaster), Sunflower family, **Figure 4.37, CP-L**, is a one to two foot high **perennial herb** with gray foliage and spiny-toothed leaves. In mid springtime, it has large, 1 to 2 inch lavender flowers with yellow centers. You can see this plant from the beginning to the end of the tour.

During this tour, we shall see various types of cactus including cholla, pricklypear, fishhook, cottontop, and hedgehog cacti. Cacti and other succulents utilize a variation of the photosynthesis process discussed in **Box 2.2**. Cacti reduce water loss by opening stomates (minute pores) at night, instead of daytime, to collect and store carbon dioxide. The carbon dioxide is stored by combining it with an organic acid. The photosynthesis process then proceeds during the daytime using solar energy and the stored water and carbon dioxide. This physiological ability is known as crassulacean acid metabolism (CAM).

Figure 4.35 California buckwheat has a multitude of tiny white flowers tinged with pink.

Figure 4.36 Winter fat has a multitude of tiny white flowers that make this shrub appear "wooly".

Figure 4.37 Mojave aster has lavender petals and yellow stamen.

Figure 4.38 Silver cholla glows in the sunlight. When in bloom it has flowers with yellow-green petals tinged in red.

Figure 4.39 Beavertail prickly pear flowers have pink to magenta petals and yellow stamen.

Some of the cacti have flashy, red or magenta blossoms which make them easy to see among the other vegetation. When they are not blooming, they tend to fade into obscurity among their neighbors. Even when not in bloom, with yellow-greenish flowers tinged in red, **silver cholla** (*Opuntia echinocarpa*), (Strawtop cholla, Golden cholla, Staghorn cholla, Thorny-fruited cactus), Cactus family, **Figure 4.38, CP M**, can easily be spotted due to their long spines that seem to glow when hit by sunlight. This cactus has a distinct tree-like trunk with many short branching joints, all of which are rounded. This **shrub (stem succulent)** is found on the upper portions of fans and is less than two-feet high on this fan. Approach it with some caution. When lightly brushed against, its spines become painfully lodged in your flesh. If they cling to your clothing, dislodge them with a hair comb. (*Opuntia* Gr. thorny plant, Latin name derived by Pliny from city of Opus; *echinocarpa*, Gr., "hedgehog-fruited.")

Not so easily spotted when not in bloom, the **beavertail prickly pear cactus** (*Opuntia basilaris*), (Beavertail, Pricklypear), Cactus family, **Figure 4.39, CP-N**, grows in clumps. This **shrub (stem succulent)** has flat, somewhat elongated "pancake" pads (joints) that contain no vicious spines but have short, fine hairs that can be a real irritant if you touch them. The beautiful, magenta flowers grow on the periphery of the pads. Native Americans ate the beavertail's fruits. Joints were boiled and then dried. (*Opuntia*, Gr., thorny plant; *basilaris*, Gr. "regal.")

Fishhook cactus (*Sclerocactus polyancistrus*), (Mojave fish-hook, Pineapple cactus, Hermit cactus, Redspined fishhook cactus), **Figure 4.40, CP-O**, has more of a solitary nature than pricklypear or cottontop cactus for it does not grow in clumps. This **shrub (stem succulent)** resembles a fat cucumber standing on end. In this area, it is less than ten-inches long. Fishhook cactus has many long spines with a distinct, eighth-inch fishhook on the tip. When in bloom, it has numerous flowers with rose purple to magenta petals and throats that appear to be yellow and rimmed by pale green. This uncommon cactus grows above an elevation of 2,000 feet in a creosote bush environment. Native Americans ate their fruits. (*Sclerocactus; polyancistrus*, Gr., many fishhooks.)

Weakstem mariposa's (*Calochortus flexuosus*), (Straggling mariposa, Winding mariposa, Winding mariposa lily), Lily family, **Figure 4.41, CP-P**, stems twine on and through nearby shrubs or lie on rocky ground. This **perennial herb** has a pretty flower that has one to two-inch wide petals that are white and tinged with a light purple or lilac. Near the stem, the flower has a yellow band and central purple spot. Plants reach a length of approximately eighteen inches. It grows throughout the Great Basin at elevations where creosote bush and big sagebrush grow. Leaves are basal and alternate. During the dry times of the year, it loses above ground parts and sustains life by a bulb. Native Americans ate the bulbs. (*Calochortus*, Gr., beautiful grass referring to its grass-like leaves; *flexuosus*, L., full of turns.)

You will be able to see an **Indian paintbrush** (*Castelleja angustifolia*), (Desert Indian paintbrush, Desert paintbrush), Figwort family, **Figure 4.42, CP-Q**, because the bracts surrounding the greenish flowers are a bright fire engine red. This **perennial herb** grows in rocky desert areas from two to seven thousand feet in elevation. Native Americans used these for ornamentation, making soap, and may have eaten the seeds. (*Castilleja*, D. Castelleja, Spanish botanist; augustifolia, L., narrow-leaved.)

Desert hyacinth (*Dichelostemma capitatum*), (Wild hyacinth, Blue dicks), Lily family, **Figure 4.43, CP-R**, has pink to light purple, six-petaled flowers clustered at the end of a two-foot tall, leafless stem. This **perennial herb** grows in upper desert slopes from upper creosote scrub to Pinyon Pine woodlands during early springtime. Native Americans and early settlers, who called them "grass-nuts", used them for food.

Desert-trumpet (*Eriogonum inflatum*), Buckwheat family, **Figure 4.44**, is a very common and distinctive one to two-foot **perennial herb** with flat, one to two-inch, oblong, basal leaves, which have a silver sheen. The distinctive blue-green stem is slender at the base and expands to a 1/2 to 1-inch bulge or "trumpet" at the top where it branches and spreads to form new trumpets. Branchlets bear small clusters of tiny, yellow flowers. During the summer and fall, the reddish skeletons of the numerous desert-trumpets are very noticeable.

Figure 4.40 Solitary fishhook cactus flowers have pink to magenta petals and spines that have a hook on the end.

Figure 4.41 Weakstem mariposa creeps through brush and has white flowers changing to lavender with age.

Figure 4.42 Bright red Indian paintbrush.

Native Americans ate the stems raw. Large doses of seeds are thought to be unpleasantly hallucinogenic. This is another plant found by John C. Fremont, 1844 expedition. (*Eriogonum*, Gr., wooly joint or angle; *inflatum*, L., inflated.)

Desert dandelion (*Malacothrix glabrata*), Sunflower family, **Figure 4.45, CP-S**, has a white and canary yellow flower roughly one-inch in diameter. Often the flower has a bright-red button in the center. Leaves are basal. This **annual** plant grows in sandy areas of the Great Basin and resembles the dandelions (aka weeds) growing in your neighbors' front yards. (*Malacothrix*, Gr., soft hair; *glabrata*)

Golden evening primrose (*Camissonia brevipes*), (Yellow cup), Evening primrose family, **Figure 4.46, CP-T**, grows to more than a foot high and has rich yellow, four-petaled, cupped flowers. Flowers open at dawn. This **annual's** stems are reddish. Leaves are basal, serrated at the margins, and have reddish veins.

Figure 4.43 Desert hyacinth has purple petals and yellow stamen.

Figure 4.44 Desert trumpet has tiny, yellow flowers and a distinct bulge along the stem.

Figure 4.45 Desert dandelion.

Figure 4.47 Shredding evening primrose.

Figure 4.49 Wooly sunflower.

Figure 4.46 Golden evening primrose.

The plant can be found from sea level to four thousand feet elevation. During the early spring, you will see it in sandy or rocky slopes and in washes throughout this tour. (*Camissonia*; brevipes, L., short footed.)

Shredding evening primrose (*Camissonia boothii ssp condensata*), (Booth primrose, Booth's sun cup), Evening primrose family, Figure **4.47, CP -U**, has the same four-petaled configuration as the golden evening primrose and also appears in the early spring. This **annual's** flowers have four white petals, ball shaped stigma, and open at dusk. (*Camassonia; boothii*. Named by Scotch botanist David Douglas for M. B. Booth (unknown); *condensata*)

Parish larkspur (*Delphinium parshii*), (Desert larkspur), Crowfoot family, **Figure 4.48, CP-V** is a **perennial herb** with light, sky-blue flowers along the top of the stem. Compound, palmate, leaves are arranged along the stem, beneath the flowers, in a whorling pattern. Plants are one to two feet high. (*Delphinium*, Gr., dolphin, flowers somewhat resemble dolphins; *parishii*, S. B. Parish, pioneer botanical collector in southern California, died 1928.)

Wooly sunflower (*Eriophyllum wallacei*), (Wooly daisy, Wallace eriophyllum), Sunflower family, **Figure 4.49, CP-W**, is a small, branched plant with three lobed leaves at the tip. The wooly, five-petaled yellow flowers look like they would

Figure 4.48 Parish larkspur has sky-blue flowers.

like to lie down and form a doormat. This **annual** is found on gravely and sandy flats. (*Eriophyllum*, Gr. wooly leaf; *wallacei*, William A. Wallace who collected in the area of Los Angeles, circa 1854.)

Yellow-eyed lupine (*Lupinus rubens ssp. flavoculatus*), (Short-banner lupine), Legume family, **Figure 4.50**, is less than six-inches tall and has light green leaves. This **annual** has scented, pea-shaped, deep violet blue flowers with a yellow spot on the banner. The rich color of the flower is very noticeable. As in other lupine, the leaves look somewhat like palm fronds. (*Lupinus*, L., wolf; *rubens*, L., reddening; *flavoculatus*, L., yellow-eyed.)

Blazing star (*Mentzelia affinis*), (Yellow comet), Loasa family, **Figure 4.51, CP-W**, is one of many "Blazing stars". The **annual** has a flower that is deep yellow approaching bronze at the stem, one-inch in diameter, and five-petaled. (*Mentzelia*, Christian Mentzel, 1622-1701, German botanist; *affinis*, L., near.)

Spectacle-pod (*Dithyrea californica*), (Biscutella), Mustard family, **Figure 4.52**, is a spring **annual** with white to lavender, four-petaled flowers and small spectacle-shaped fruits. Leaves are basal, thick, and covered with hair. It is common in sandy places below four thousand feet altitude. (*Dithyrea*, Gr., two shields, referring to double, spectacle-like fruit; *californica*, of California.)

Figure 4.50
Yellow-eyed lupine have purple flowers each having a yellow "eye".

Animals

The **Blister beetle** (*Lytta magister*), **Figure 4.53**, can be seen consuming plant tissue of bladder sage and other desert shrubs. It is blue-black with a distinct orange head and upper thorax. Its upper legs are brownish-red with the outermost leg segments a blackish.

Mile 0.9 - Cross old road from Rhyolite to Willow Spring
N36° 51' 26.8" W116° 51' 43.3"

History

This road was originally built during the heyday of Rhyolite. Some maps also show this as an old railroad bed, refer to **Figure 4.18**. The road heads in the general direction of Daylight Pass (4317 ft) on the boundary between the Funeral Mountains to the southeast and the Grapevine Mountains to the northwest.

Figure 4.51
Blazing star has yellow petals that are red near the stem.

Figure 4.52
Spectacle pod has white flowers and spectacle shaped fruit.

Figure 4.53 Blister beetles feeding in Bladder sage.

Mile 1.85 - Death Valley National Park boundary
N36° 51' 18.3" W116° 52' 44.1"

History

The Death Valley National Park boundary is 1.85 miles west of the tour's starting point at the paved road. Originally established as a National Monument in 1933, the Monument was upgraded to a National Park in 1994 with acreage added. Now 3.3 million acres in extent, it is the largest national park in the lower 48 states.

Two and a half miles north of the road across the Amargosa Desert is the original Bullfrog mine, **Figure 4.54**. It is located on Bullfrog Mountain in the Bullfrog Hills. These "bullfrogs" are originate with Shorty Harris' description of the greenish gold ore he and Ed Cross found in 1904 as having the color of a bullfrog. Following the discovery, the first site of the town of Bullfrog and the tent town of Amargosa sprang up at the base of the mountain. The town of Bullfrog later moved to its second site southwest of Rhyolite. It only lasted from November 1904 until May 1905 because Rhyolite drained away people and businesses. All that remains of the town of Bullfrog, **Figure 4.55**, are some walls and a few gravesites, some of which have been pilfered. North of the Original Bullfrog mine are the sites of Gold Bar and Homestake.

Figure 4.54 The Original Bullfrog mine, source of the "bullfrog" gold, is located on Bullfrog Mountain in the Bullfrog Hills near the original town-site of Bullfrog.

Mile 2.5 Drive down into a large drainage channel
N36° 51' 12.5" W116° 53' 26.0"

This is one of a number of drainage channels that drain the alluvial fan and cross the road. Look at **Figure 4.1** for an overview of the channels. Ahead, other large channels cross the road.

Figure 4.55 The remnants of the second site of the town of Bullfrog are limited to the walls of an icehouse.

Mile 6.0 - Outcrops of Miocene (~11-16My) volcanic rocks
N36° 50' 51.2" W116° 57' 09.7"

Geology

The tan, beige, and pink rocks cropping out on the hillside to the northwest (right) are derived from volcanic eruptions. These rocks are called volcanic or extrusive igneous rocks because they originated when molten magma reached the surface of Earth where it fragmented and cooled. (Magma cooling below the surface is referred to as plutonic or intrusive igneous rock.) Some rocks formed from rhyolitic ash that was erupted from a volcano and carried by the winds until the ash settled. Rhyolite is a volcanic rock rich, from 60 to 80%, in quartz (silica) and has very little iron or magnesium. Most rhyolitic rocks are generally tan or pink in color. It is the surface equivalent (chemically) of granite, which crystallizes beneath Earth's surface. Volcanoes issuing forth rhyolite or andesite (less silica, more iron, and darker than rhyolite but still viscous) are violent or explosive. The eruption of Mount St. Helens is an example of a violent eruption.

Specifically, during middle Miocene time, volcanic eruptions in the Timber Mountain Caldera region (thirty five miles to the northeast in the Nevada Test Site) deposited layers of ash and debris, forming "tuff", across the current Grapevine Mountains and across part of the current Death Valley (tuff crops out southwest of Death Valley Buttes). During this time, the area from Timber Mountain to Death Valley was of low relief as evidenced by (a) the hundreds of feet thick succession of Timber Mountain tuffs found on Grapevine and Wahguyhe Peaks lacking evidence of ponding or impediments to flow and (b) the tuff units near Death Valley Buttes being tilted at moderate angles west and southwest into Death Valley. The Grapevine Mountains and Death Valley had yet to form. The different tuff beds are referred to as:

A) Bullfrog member of the Redrock Valley Tuff ~ <15 My,
B) Tiva Canyon member of the Paintbrush tuff ~12.5-13 My,
C) Rainer Mesa member of the Timber Mountain Tuff ~11.3 My, and
D) Ammonia Tanks member of the Timber Mountain Tuff ~11.1 My.

The darker outcrops in the background are also volcanic in origin: however, they are basaltic in composition. That is to say, they have a much lower content of quartz (45 to 50 %) but contain high quantities of iron and magnesium oxides (16 to 26%). The high iron and magnesium content makes basalt heavy and dark in color. Basaltic eruptions are not violent because they are nonviscous or low in silica content. The slow moving basalt flows from the Hawaiian volcanoes are examples. The basaltic outcrops you are viewing were produced " in place" (where you see them) presumably from fissures.

Mile 6.2 - Driving into and along a drainage channel
N36° 50' 46.3" W116° 57' 19.5"

Geology

The road leaves the fan surface and descends into a drainage channel that we will follow for the next few miles. At the point where we joined the channel, stop and look at the sides of the channel. You can see layers of sediments that make up the fan in the stream channel sides. Runoff from thunderstorms and heavy rains leaves distinct beds in the drainage channel, as illustrated in **Figure 4.56**. The energy of the flow (a clue to the rate and amount of rainfall) can be determined from the size of the rock fragments in the various beds.

Plants

Consider some of the changes you have seen in the shrubbery as you drove up the fan. Some of the shrubs became smaller and sparser as we gained altitude. The creosote bush is an example. Creosote bush does not do well in freezing temperatures above the snow line. We have climbed into the zone that gets snow on a more frequent basis than where the creosote predominates. Also we begin to see some distinctly new shrubs such as Stansbury cliff rose and green ephedra (Mormon tea). We are seeing a transition into a new plant community.

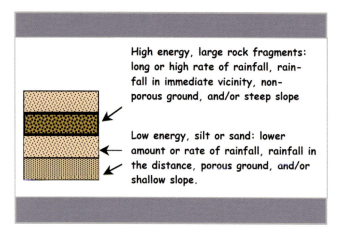

Figure 4.56 Sides of the drainage channel indicate amount of energy when the rocks were deposited. The amount of energy at any location is an indication of the proximity, amount, and/or rate of rainfall.

Figure 4.57 Distinctly green Stansbury cliff-rose grows along the roadside.

Bordering the road and in the surrounding area, we see **Cliff-rose** (*Purshia mexicana stansburyana*) (Quinine bush, Stansbury cliff-rose), Rose family, **Figure 4.57 and 58, CP-X** a fragrant plant when blooming in the spring. This **shrub** is wide-branched, gnarled, and shaggy barked, evergreen that grows eight to ten feet tall. Spring flowers are cream-colored and fragrant. Each fertilized flower will grow a long fuzzy tail that dispenses the seeds. The leaves are resinous and sticky. In the spring, you might notice caterpillars of the **Fotis hairstreak** (*Incisalia fotis*) in "tents" among the branches. Because the shrub is an evergreen, it will be apparent throughout the year. In other areas, deer browse on the plants in the winter. You will see cliff rose here, on Red Pass, and into Leadfield. Native Americans made cloth cords, mats, and sandals from the silky inner bark. (*Purshia*, Frederick T. Pursh, 1774-1820, botanical explorer; *mexicana*, Mexico; *stansburyana*, Captain Howard Stansbury who led government expedition into the Salt Lake region of Utah in 1850.)

In the same area, we also now see **Green ephedra** (*Ephedra viridis*) (Mormon tea, Desert tea, Squaw tea, Mountain joint fir, Mountain ephedra), Pine family, **Figure 4.59, CP-Y**, that is greener and significantly larger (3-4 feet high) than the Nevada and Death Valley ephedra we have seen previously. Also, the joints are thicker and

Figure 4.58 Cliff-rose has five-petaled, white flowers. Often "tents" of the Fotis hairstreak can be seen in the branches.

darker and the stems are more vertical. This **shrub** is a primitive conifer. Cones grow at the joints. It is found at elevations above 3,000 feet. You will see large areas covered with this plant along the roadside as you near Red Pass. Native Americans boiled the stems for use as both a medicinal tea and a beverage. The name would imply that settlers did the same. People who have tried the tea say that it has an unpleasant taste. (*Ephedra; virdis*, L., green.)

Chia (*Salvia columbariae*), (Chia sage), Mint family, **Figure 4.60, CP-Z**, has lavender to dark blue flowers arranged in globes. With basal leaves and four to twenty-inch leafless stems, the globes appear to float in the air. This **annual** is found in dry, disturbed, open areas in altitudes ranging from sea level to seven thousand feet. Native Americans cooked and ate the seeds. (*Salvia*, L., an herb used for healing; *columbariae*, L., like (Scabiosa) *Columbaria*)).

Stansbury phlox (*Phlox stansburyi*), (Cold-desert phlox), Phlox family, **Figure 4.61, CP-AA**, is four to eight inches tall with stout stems and narrow, hairy, gray-green leaves. This **woody based perennial** has pinkish-white, five-petaled flowers that peek up through other plants. It grows in stony areas at higher elevations. (*Phlox*, Gr., flame referring to brilliant flowers; Stansburyi, Captain H. Stansbury.)

Animals

In this area, **Gamble's quail** (*Callipepla gambelli*) occasionally scoot across the road or through the brush. They can be found in large coveys. Therefore, if you only see one or two, remain still and listen for their call. More might be hidden in surrounding brush. You might see a male, **Figure 4.62,** acting as a sentinel standing on a high rock or perched on a branch. The males and females have a teardrop-shaped plume feather. The males are more colorful than the females and have a distinctive reddish-brown or chestnut crest and black face outlined in white. They are quite similar to the California State bird, Valley quail, but the male Gamble quail's chest is a buffy white and unscaled while the Valley quail's chest is scaled with brown markings. They appear quite comical running along the ground. If you approach too closely, they will explosively take flight.

Figure 4.59 Green ephedra is distinctly "green". Settlers and Native Americans brewed it and drank it as a tea or medicinal.

Cones are found at the joints of this primitive conifer.

Figure 4.60 Chia resembles lavender or blue pincushions floating in the air.

Figure 4.61 Stansbury phlox has white, pink, or red flowers.

Mile 6.9-7.6 - Rhyolitic rocks with colorful lichens
N36° 50' 12.3" W116° 57' 38.4"

That colorful orange and gray-green crust you see on the rocks to your left is lichen, **Figure 4.63**. It is an example of a mutually beneficial arrangement of two separate species, alga and fungus. The fungus provides the means for attachment to the rocks while the alga provides food. The alga species uses a process called photosynthesis to create food. It utilizes energy from the sun and water (H_2O) and carbon dioxide (CO_2) from the air to create food in the form of carbohydrates (CH_2O) and to create oxygen (O_2) as a most useful byproduct. Native Americans ground lichen, mixed it with water, and used it as a poultice for mouth and other sores.

Mile 7.2 - "Tan Mountain," remnant of volcanic ash flow
N36° 50' 04.0" W116° 57' 51.6"

Geology

Stop at a wide spot in the road to look at this feature. A prominent point, **Figure 4.64**, which appears to be a solitary tan colored mountain, on the right is not a volcanic plug or neck. It is an erosional remnant of an ash flow that once covered the entire region. The rest has been eroded. This solitary remnant stands because it is more resistant to erosion than surrounding outcrops. From this point on to Leadfield, volcanic rocks are right (north) of the road and Cambrian sedimentary rocks are on the left (south).

Plants

Stop at the pullout to the right (north). Note the profusion of dark, green Stansbury cliff rose.

A short distance up the road from the lichen-covered rock, you can see a shrub called **big sagebrush** (*Artemisia tridentata*) (Great Basin sagebrush), Sunflower family, **Figure 4.65., CP-BB** This shrub is indicative of being in the biological Great Basin. It is the dominant plant in some 90-million acres in the western United States. Some characteristics include a clean and aromatic smell

Figure 4.62 Male Gamble's quail in foreground.

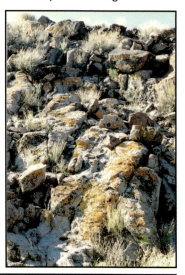

Figure 4.63 Colorful lichen covers rhyolitic rock.

Figure 4.64 This solitary sentinel is a remnant of a volcanic ash flow that once covered the area.

after a rain and three, rounded bulges on the end of each silvery leaf. It is probably the most abundant shrub in western North America. Unlike creosote, big sagebrush is a cold tolerant shrub. Native Americans chewed or boiled leaves as a medicinal tea to cure a variety of ailments or mixed leaves with water and used as a poultice for sores and infections. (*Artemisia,* Gr., Artemis the goddess of the hunt, *tridentate*, L., 3-toothed.)

Figure 4.65 Big sagebrush has flowering stems that rise above the foliage.

Look around in the area where the big sagebrush grows for a pink flower protruding from the sage's branches. This flower is a **perennial herb** named **Prince's rock cress** (*Arabis pulchra*), Mustard family, **Figure 4.66**. It is a single stemmed plant, grows to about eight to twenty four-inches high and has pale pink tubular flowers. (Arabis, L., from Arabia; *pulchna* L., beautiful).

Figure 4.66 Prince's rock cress has pink, tubular flowers.

Mile 7.6 - Dip in road, rhyolitic ash beds to right
N36° 49' 54.5" W116° 58' 14.0"

Airborne clouds of Miocene, rhyolitic ash settled here to form these beige ash beds. The source may have been northeast of the Timber Mountain

Mile 8.0 - Craggy, volcanic rock hillside
N36° 49' 40.9" W116° 58' 32.4"

caldera.

Geology

Wind and water have helped to erode these Miocene volcanic rocks into angular, rough appearing outcrops, **Figure 4.67**. Erosion affects different rocks with different results. As we progress on the tour we will see additional examples of erosion that will include steep cliffs, ledges, steep and shallow slopes, talus cones, and

Figure 4.67 Craggy volcanic outcrops are one example of the effects of erosion.

another large alluvial fan.

Plants

Brittlebush (*Encelia farinosa*), (White brittlebush, Incensio), Sunflower family, **Figure 4.68, CP-CC**, is a round, leafy shrub that grows two to three feet high. This **shrub** has bright yellow flower heads in loosely branched clusters on branched stalks that protrude well above the foliage. Leaves are a silver or gray. It is a striking plant, which often lines roadsides in the DEVA region, generally at elevations below 3,000 feet. Its fragrant resin was chewed by Native Americans and burned as incense by early California padres. (*Encelia*,

Figure 4.68 Brittlebush has yellow flower distinctly protruding above the leaves.

Animals

The **Side-blotched lizard** (*Uta stansburiara*), **Figure 4.69**, is a small (4-6 inches), long-tailed lizard that is brown with distinct blue on its sides. At night it feeds on insects.

The Titus Canyon region has two types of rattlesnakes, the Speckled and Mojave Desert sidewinder. Both are toxic and are to be avoided by looking where you are going, not stepping over objects when the other side is not visible, avoiding stepping near brush you cannot see into, and not putting your hands or feet into or on items you have not thoroughly looked over. Snakes would rather avoid you. They may slip off on their own and you will never be aware of their presence. Rattlesnakes may or may not rattle. If you see a rattlesnake, don't "play" with or "tease" it for your sense of humor is not compatible with that of the rattlesnake. Most victims of rattlesnake bites are eighteen-year-old boys who are showing their girl friends how brave and clever they are. Rattlesnakes are active from April to October. During other months, they are usually in a den. If you get bit, seek immediate medical attention.

Figure 4.69 Side-blotched lizard warms itself on rock ledge.

The **Speckled rattlesnake** (*Crotalus mitchelli*), (Panamint red), **Figure 4.70**, grows 23-52 inches long and has very potent venom. It is gray, brownish-orange, or sandy color with dark blotches on its back and dark rings on its tail. In DEVA, the orange color is dominant. It is usually a rock dweller and ranges up to 6,500 feet elevation. When cornered, it and may hold its ground. This is the snake that some call a Panamint red rattlesnake. The specimen pictured in **Figure 4.70** was seen beside the road beneath Stansbury cliff rose.

The **Mojave Desert Sidewinder** (*Crotalus cerastes*) grows 17-33 inches long and is moderately toxic. It has a light background and dark blotches. It prefers to be near rodent burrows in washes and sandy areas and ranges up to 3,500 feet elevation. It is nocturnal and may be in burrows during the day. The sidewinder has developed a method of locomotion that minimizes body contact with the hot sand. It appears to move "sideways", hence the name. It leaves tracks that look somewhat like elongated S's.

> ### Mile 8.77 - Small valley
> ### N36° 49' 27.9" W116° 59' 15.6"

Geology

At an obvious bend to the right, we turn into a small valley that trends northwest in the mountain range. The Titus Canyon Formation underlies this low terrain. The Formation is easily eroded and it underlies depressions in the mountain range.

On the skyline to our left (south), are the jagged outcrops of the Zabriskie Quartzite, **Figure 4.71**. Beneath the outcrops, the smooth mountain mass is made up of softer and more easily eroded rocks of the Wood Canyon Formation. You can read about the what, where to find, how to identify, and the origin of the Wood Canyon Formation and Zabriskie Quartzite in **Appendices C1** and **C2**, respectively.

On the right (north) side, all of the rocks at higher elevations are variously colored volcanic rocks. The source of the rocks was the Timber Mountain Caldera in the Nevada Test Site. Although other calderas (Long Valley and Yellowstone) deposited

Figure 4.70 After being disturbed, this three-foot orange-brown speckled rattlesnake rattled as it moved to a new location beneath a Stansbury cliff-rose.

Figure 4.71 Reddish brown to purple, craggy Zabriskie Quartzite overlies the gentler slopes of the brownish gray Wood Canyon Formation.

rocks in the Death Valley region, you will see volcanic debris only from the Timber Mountain caldera on this trip. The caldera is located approximately 35-miles to the east. It deposited volcanic debris along what was to be the Funeral and Grapevine Mountains and into what was to be part of Death Valley. It started erupting approximately 12 My and continued its violent, silica rich eruptions (rhyolite) until about 8.5 My.

Calderas are volcanic depressions much larger than the original crater. A caldera forms when a volcano's summit is blown off by exploding gases, such as Mt. St. Helens, or when the crater floor collapses down into a vacated magma chamber, such as Crater Lake, **Figure 4.72**.

> **Mile 9.21 - 9.56 - Volcanic rocks to the right and marine rocks to the left**
> **N36° 49' 35.2" W116° 59' 41.8"**

Geology

Miocene latite flows (dark brown) and rhyolitic ash-flow tuffs crop out to our right (north) and dark brown, craggy, Cambrian marine rocks crop out to the left (south).

Plants

Royal desert lupine (*Lupinus odoratus*), (Mojave lupine), Legume family, **Figure 4.73, CP-DD**, has brilliant, royal purple, fragrant flowers Young flowers have an ivory white spot at the base. Leaves are green and arranged in a palm-like pattern with seven leaves per stem. This **annual's** stems have sparsely placed, fine hairs. This plant is taller than the Yellow-eyed lupine. (*Lupinus*, L., wolf; *ordoratus*, L., fragrant.)

Desert prince's plume (*Stanleya pinnata*), (Desert plume, Paiute cabbage), Mustard family, **Figure 4.74, CP-EE**, is two to five feet tall and has many stems that have a long-yellow plume at top. Along the roadside, below White Pass, you will notice many of the bright yellow plumes, or their dried remnants. They can also be seen ahead on the way to Leadfield and into Titus Canyon. This perennial herb blooms in middle to late spring. Native Americans boiled the young leaves for greens. (*Stanleya*, Edward Stanley, Earl of Derby, 1773-1849, ornithologist; *pinnata*, L. feathered.)

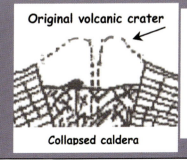

Figure 4.72 The Timber Mountain caldera is a volcanic depression similar to those illustrated on this figure.

Figure 4.73 Royal desert lupine is a striking display of royal purple flowers with an ivory white spot.

Figure 4.74 Golden yellow plumes of the Prince's plume protrude above the dome created by its leaves.

> **Mile 9.56 - White Pass, elevation 5,000 ft...**
> **End of Segment 1**
> **N36° 49' 36.4" W117° 00' 02.4"**

Geology

This is a good location to get out of the car and follow a path (right, north) up onto the small knob. Rocks of the sedimentary Titus Canyon Formation underlie the path. The well-rounded clasts (rock fragments) are composed of the hard, weather resistant rocks of the formations from which they were derived by weathering and erosion. These clasts include quartz, quartzite, and chert, (silica usually colored red, gray, or black) and rarely include limestone. Occasionally you can find a rock fragment of granite that resembles the type of granite that occurs in the Sierra Nevada or the north end of the Death Valley region. An occasional fragment of metamorphosed, Mesozoic, volcanic rock also is included in the conglomerate. Note the dark brown latite flow (**Figure 4.75**). The latite's source was a volcanic neck now exposed northeast of Red Pass.

The interpretation for the origin of the lower Titus Canyon Formation is that it was deposited in river channels and a floodplain. Besides rounded clasts transported in river channels, the formation includes mudstone units that were deposited in the flood plains in lower energy depositional environments. The upper Titus Canyon Formation is primarily volcanic. We will see outcrops of the Titus Canyon Formation, to our right (north) from here to just beyond Leadfield. You can read about the Titus Canyon Formation in greater depth in **Appendix C-5** and **C-6**. Farther along the path and rising before us are volcanic rocks that overlie the Titus Canyon Formation, **Figure 4.75**.

Transition to Segment 2 of the tour

Here, at this scenic viewpoint, we can look east, **Figure 4.76**, at the low relief and shallow channel and fan surfaces that we drove over to get here. The plant community behind us has changed. The steeper terrain that we are about to embark onto (west) seems to proclaim a change in the surface geological features. Here we begin segment two of our tour and enter "Into the land of the titanothere…" Look west, and begin segment two of the tour.

Begin Segment 2… Into the land of titanotheres and on to the ghost town

Figure 4.75 Sharply etched Miocene volcanic rocks contrast with the smoothly weathered slopes of the Titus Canyon Formation.

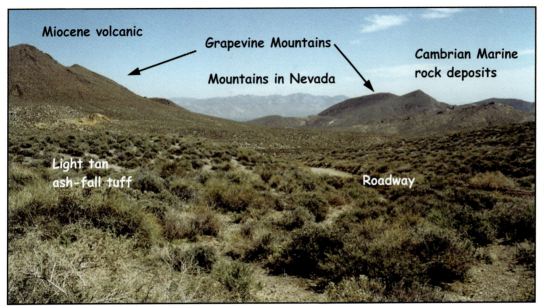

Figure 4.76 East of White Pass, shallow channels drain into the Amargosa Valley.

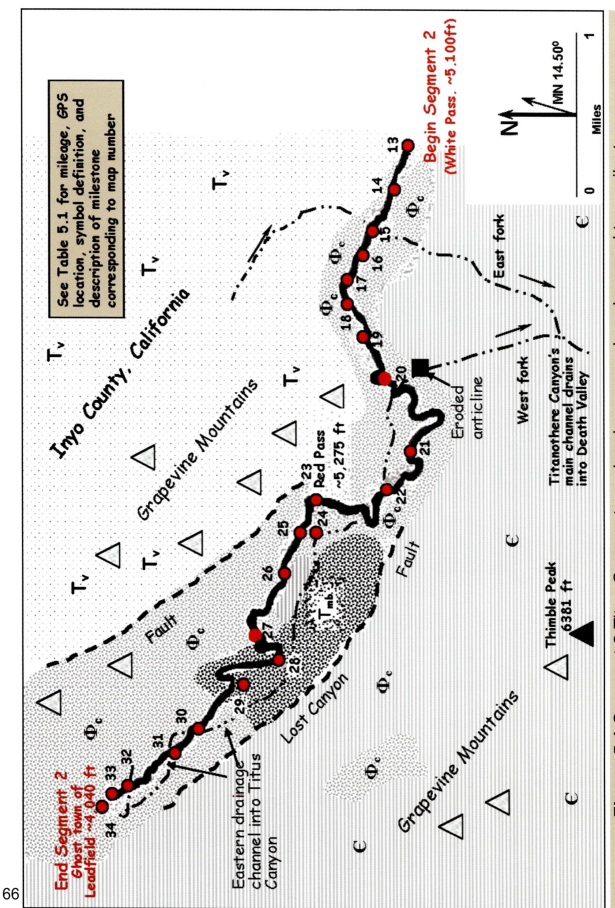

Figure 5.1 Segment 2 Titus Canyon tour showing general geology and tour milestones (Total length 5.8 miles, Maximum Altitude 5250 ft.)

Segment 2 Milestones (MS) of Titus Canyon Tour - Odometer Mileage and GPS Locations

MS	Miles	GPS	Description	MS	Miles	GPS	Description
13	9.56	N36° 49' 36.4" W117° 00' 02.4"	White Pass. GPS elevation: 5,094 ft. View Amargosa Desert and Titanothere Canyon drainage. Colorful volcanic hills.	24	13.02	N36° 49' 50.4" W117° 02' 02.3"	Very Dark Megabreccia.
14	10.13	N36° 49' 45.4" W117° 00' 33.8"	Looking down into Titanothere Cyn. Panamints and Sierras in distance.	25	13.52	N36° 50' 03.9" W117° 02' 08.1"	Eriogonums.
15	10.47	N36° 49' 53.3" W117° 00' 49.7"	Another drainage channel into Titanothere Cyn.	26	14.05	N36° 50' 13.8" W117° 02' 33.9"	Turnout.
16	10.56	N36° 49' 50.9" W117° 00' 53.9"	Honey Mesquite...unlikely place. Spring?	27	14.42	N36° 50' 13.5" W117° 02' 46.4"	Megabreccia.
17	10.68	N36° 49' 47.3" W117° 00' 59.6"	Parking area for break or hike.	28	14.55	N36° 50' 10.9" W117° 02' 48.5"	Hairpin curve.
18	10.89	N36° 49' 44.9" W117° 01' 10.1"	Megabreccia...Bonanza King Formation.	29	15.06	N36° 50' 22.0" W117° 02' 57.2"	Prospect and Hazard sign.
19	11.00	N36° 49' 42.1" W117° 01' 16.2"	Folded rock layers and fractured rocks	30	15.66	N36° 50' 35.6" W117° 03' 15.6"	Drainage channels into Titus Cyn.
20	11.44	N36° 49' 35.1" W117° 01' 30.1"	Colorful Red member of Titus Canyon Formation.	31	15.80	N36° 50' 40.2" W117° 03' 20.9"	Drainage channels into Titus Cyn.
21	11.90	N36° 49' 34.1" W117° 01' 41.6"	Looking back to White Pass. Spectacular view.	32	16.03	N36° 50' 49.4" W117° 03' 29.6"	Drainage channels into Titus Cyn.
22	12.00	N36° 49' 35.1" W117° 01' 47.4"	Look up to Titus Cyn. Fm at Red Pass. Colors, hoodoos, white marker bed.	33	16.10	N36° 50' 52.5" W117° 03' 32.1"	Drainage channels into Titus Cyn.
23	12.43	N36° 49' 43.4" W117° 01' 56.6"	Red Pass. GPS elevation: 5,276 ft. Great. views into Lost & Amargosa Vlys.	34	16.14	N36° 50' 54.3" W117° 03' 33.5"	Leadfield Ghost Town.

Mileages are based on GPS readings with accuracy within 25 ft.

Segment 2 - Map Legend

T_v - Miocene Volcanic rocks, Miocene (~12 My).	● - Tour milestone, stop and look around.
T_{mb} - Tertiary megabreccia.	N =north, MN = magnetic north
Φc - Titus Canyon Fm, conglomerate (24-37 My), red, brown, yellow, pale green.	△ Used to denote mountains in a region — — — — Fault
ε - Cambrian (505-570 My) marine sedimentary rocks.	╱ Road — · — · — · — · Drainage channel

5.0 Segment 2... Into the land of the titanothere and on to the ghost town

Mile 9.56 - White Pass, looking west into Titanothere Canyon
N36° 49' 36.4" W117° 00' 02.4"

Segment 2 proceeds downward and west from White Pass, into Titanothere Canyon tributary drainage, up to Red Pass, and finally down into the ghost town of Leadfield. Cambrian marine sedimentary rocks will be in the distance to your left. Eocene-Miocene sedimentary rocks of the Titus Canyon Formation will be along both sides of the road through Leadfield. Middle Miocene volcanic tuff will be to your right. See **Figure 5.1** for milestones and geologic formations.

Look across the valley to the north and try to imagine how it looked thirty-seven million years ago. It wasn't a valley and there were many strange animals roaming its environs. **Box 5.1** should help you visualize what this area once was like.

Geology

Today, looking north from White Pass we see a broad valley that drains into one of Titanothere Canyon's tributary drainage channels, **Figure 5.2**. Notice the steep-sided, deep drainage channel into Death Valley far below us. Turn around and look to the south at the area we passed through to get here. It has gentle slopes and shallow channels that drain eastward into the nearby, high elevation Amargosa Desert.

Why do these two topographies look so different? The answer lies in something called **potential energy** (**water density** multiplied by **gravitational acceleration** multiplied by **elevation drop**). Water that drains to the east drains into the Amargosa

Figure 5.2 View looking west into the headwaters of Titanothere Canyon. In the foreground, is a valley surrounded by Miocene volcanics, Eocene-Miocene Titus Canyon Formation, and Cambrian marine rocks.
In the distance, the drainage becomes steeper and a drainage channel is evident. There the water moves faster and continues cutting out steep and narrow Titanothere Canyon.

Box 5.1 Looking back: White Pass during the Late Eocene (~37 My)

Titanotheres on the Late Eocene savannah — Charles Knight

During the late Eocene, (~37 MY), near what was to become White Pass, the day is warm and a herd of titanotheres comes to drink along one of a number of streams flowing across the level savannah. Beside the stream, a few turtles bask in the sun. A bull titanothere, the size of today's elephant, surveys the savannah that was to become the red conglomerate of the lower Titus Canyon Formation. Other male, female, and young titanotheres browse in the background. Herds of the small, 3-toed early horse, Mesohippus, can be seen near the low hills further to the west. Small, two-foot high camels are beside the horses as is a large herd of herbivorous oreodonts, that resemble a cross between a sheep and a pig or dog. To the east, the remains of an ancient tapir are being consumed by a pack of canine like creodonts.

A small, fast, 5-foot long animal, resembling a horse but that is an ancient rhinoceros, runs past the carnivorous creodonts. Rodents are scattered throughout the savannah. Snakes, lizards, and tortoises are beneath the shrubbery. A small beardog is intent on catching one of the lizards. Predators and prey watch… and watch.

The Sierra Nevada is nearby and not as high as today. Streams flow from the north and creating and washing down rounded rock fragments. During periods of torrential rains or runoff from snowmelt, the streams become torrents and the size of the rocks and quantity of sediment deposits increase, as areas of the savannah are flooded. In the distance, a volcano smolders quietly.

Desert and reaches a relatively high base level of 3,000 feet elevation. Water that drains down Titanothere Canyon to Death Valley has a relatively shorter distance to travel to a much lower base level (sea level). A drop of water draining down Titanothere Canyon has much higher potential energy than its counterpart draining into the Amargosa Valley. The Titanothere Canyon drop can fall 5,000 feet while the Amargosa Desert drop can only fall 2,000 feet. Traveling the same horizontal distance, the Titanothere Canyon' droplet has 2--1/2 times the potential energy of its counterpart. As a droplet moves downhill (steeper for Titanothere Canyon), it gains velocity, and its potential energy is converted to something called **kinetic energy** (1/2 multiplied by **droplet mass** multiplied by the **square of the droplet's velocity**). The Titanothere Canyon's droplet can utilize its greater energy supply to help other droplets move larger boulders and cut deeper, narrower canyons.

Within 100 yards of the road, beneath the Titus

Figure 5.3 Middle Cambrian, marine rocks are visible southwest from White Pass.

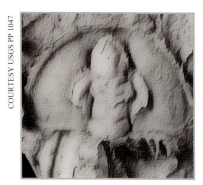

Figure 5.4 Trilobite fossil Olenllus gilberti, Carrara Fm., Titanothere Cyn.

Canyon Formation and left (south of the road) are prominent outcrops that are giant fragments of the Bonanza King Formation. These fragments fell from cliff walls of the drainage channel and were transported downstream by gravity and help from subsequent floods. The Bonanza King Formation was deposited during Cambrian (543-490 My) time. It is composed of dolomite, limestone, and shale that were deposited during the Cambrian Period when the Death Valley region was the site of a shallow sea. More detailed information on the Bonanza King Formation is provided in Appendix C-4.

Southwest from White Pass, is a prominent peak called Thimble Peak, **Figure 5.3**. The peak is moderately gray in color and has alternating horizontal layers of pale and darker gray. The Bonanza King Formation crowns the summit.

The closest ridge to the southwest is the Carrara Formation that is Early and Middle Cambrian in age. Fossilized trilobites, **Figure 5.4**, occur in the Carrara Formation. The ridge is crowned with the Bonanza King Formation.

The road from White Pass points to another prominent peak approximately two miles farther to the west. This peak is just east of Red Pass through which we will drive. The upper part of the peak is volcanic tuff. Below are greenish-gray to light brown beds that are upper layers of the Titus Canyon Formation. You may be able to see a thin white layer of crystal tuff within the upper part of the Titus Canyon Formation. We will drive towards that peak and will discuss it further as we get closer. Looking in the foreground, to the west-northwest, (**Figure 5.5**) we see colorful hills that are greens, pinks, grays, and browns. Rocks of these hills are various types of middle Miocene (11-16 My), differently colored volcanic rocks that were deposited upon the Titus Canyon Formation. The

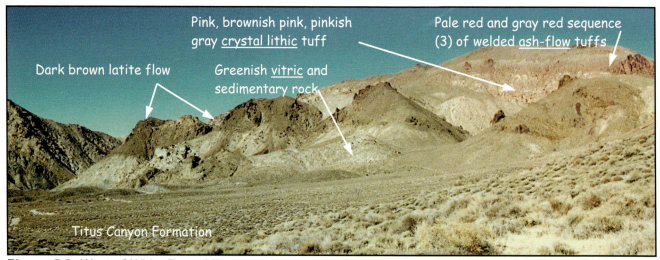

Figure 5.5 West of White Pass, Miocene volcanic rocks in the upper part of Titanothere Canyon drainage are colorful reds, greens, browns, and grays.

Timber Mountain Caldera, to the east, is the origin of many of these rocks. The youngest sequence is *welded ash-flow tuffs* that is pale red, grayish red, and black at the base and may have come from as far north as Nevada's Silver Peak area. The next is crystal lithic tuff that is pink, brownish pink, or pinkish gray. *Vitric tuff* is the oldest and is pale greenish gray, greenish brown, or pale grayish orange. It lies above the Titus Canyon Formation. An unconformity or gap in the rock record exists between the Titus Canyon Formation and the volcanic rocks. There is also an unconformity between the vitric tuff and the overlying crystal lithic tuff. Here, in upper Titanothere Canyon, is also a dark brown *latite flow* that filled an ancient valley and was surrounded by the preceding and subsequent vitric tuff. Interspersed within the crystal lithic and vitric tuffs are conglomerate and sandstone beds. The thickness of each tuff unit varies because the pre-tuff topography was irregular (i.e. comprised of hills and valleys). You will see these volcanic rocks again east and northwest of Leadfield. See **Appendix C-6** for additional information on these Miocene rocks.

From White Pass to a point beyond Leadfield, you will see Titus Canyon Formation along the road except for a short section north of Red Pass where megabreccia is exposed on both sides of the road.

Plants

The **Saucer plant** (*Oxytheca perfolita*), (Punctured bract, Roundleaf punctured bract), Buckwheat family, **Figure 5.6, CP-FF**, is a spreading **annual** plant with horizontal branches up to 1-foot. This spring annual derives its name from reddish-gray, fused bracts that make up a series of saucer-like discs that are 1/2 inch in diameter. With age, these bracts turn a reddish-gray. It grows in sandy or gravely soil from 2,400-6,000 feet elevation. (*Oxytheca*, Gr., "sharp cased" in reference to the spiny tips on the bract groups; *perfoliata*, L., leaf piercing.)

Fremont phacelia (*Phacelia fremonti*), Waterleaf family, **Figure 5.7**, is one of the many phacelias growing in the region. This **annual** grows from 4-10 inches high and has leaves that are longer than they are wide and are parted into leaflets. The flowers are blue to violet with a yellow throat. You might not like the flower's odor. (*Phacelia*, Gr., cluster, in reference to this plant's dense inflorescence; *fremonti*, explorer John Charles Fremont.)

USE LOW GEAR

Mile 9.56-10.2 - Crossing the upper drainage of Titanothere Canyon

N36° 49' 36.4" W117° 00' 02.4"

Geology

From White Pass to the base of the grade up to Red Pass, the middle portion of the Titus Canyon Formation is exposed beside both sides of the road. The middle portion is referred to as the variegated facies of the Titus Canyon Formation because of the wide diversity of rock types and colors that

Figure 5.6 Saucer plant's bracts are reddish-gray.

Figure 5.7 Fremont phacelia flowers have blue to violet petals and yellow throats.

Figure 5.8 Lower Titus Canyon Formation has conglomerate with rounded, polished, and fractured clasts of varying size, composition, and color in a fine matrix.

Figure 5.10 With a little imagination this becomes "Skull Rock."

Figure 5.9 Looking south (down) into the eastern drainage channel into Titanothere canyon. In the background, is the Panamint Mountain Range.

comprise it. **Figure 5.8** depicts some of the clasts found in the lower Titus Canyon Formation near this milestone. The formation is mostly sandstone and conglomerate. The conglomerate's clasts are resistant rocks such as quartzite, chert, casehardened carbonate rock, and vein quartz. Besides being comprised of clasts from the rock formations we see outcropping in today's Titus Canyon area (e.g. Wood Canyon, Zabriskie Quartzite, Carrara, and Bonanza King), the clasts are also comprised of the missing Paleozoic, Mesozoic, Pliocene, and Eocene outcrops that have been eroded elsewhere and do not out crop in the Titus Canyon area. (See **Box 2.1** and **Appendix A.**). For example, Reynolds found clasts that were limestone pebbles containing fossils from the Ordovician through the Devonian and fossils from the Permian. Furthermore, note that the clasts in the conglomerate are well rounded, highly polished, and fractured. They are rounded because they may have been a) recycled from previous conglomerates and transported limited distances or b) transported a long distances from the north. The former seems more likely. Fracturing occurred during crustal extension (13 My to present). Some fractures healed due to precipitation of silica and carbonate in the fractures. The sandstone matrix will vary in color from tan to dark red at different locations. For additional information on the Titus Canyon Formation, go to **Appendix C-5,6**.

> **Mile 10.13 - Looking down into eastern drainage channel into Titanothere Canyon**
>
> **N36° 49' 45.4" W117° 00' 33.8"**

Figure 5.9, is a great view looking down the canyon.

> **Mile 10.47 - Another drainage channel into Titanothere Canyon**
>
> **N36° 49' 53.3" W117° 00' 49.7"**

Skull Rock **Figure 5.10**, greets the motorist approaching this milestone. Note the different colored layers of ash.

Geology

We drove over another small pass that is between two of Titanothere Canyon's tributary drainage channels. Once over this pass, the Titus Canyon Formation contains less conglomerate and more mudstone and siltstone. These are flood plain deposits. You can see the layering in the rocks. Most of the layers or bedding planes **dip** approximately 45 degrees. In other words, they are tilted or inclined 45 degrees downward (measured in a vertical plane) from their original horizontal position. Strike of these bedding planes is northward (measured in a horizontal plane).

Figure 5.11 should help to clarify the definitions of dip and strike.

10.56 Miles - Honey mesquite, downhill (left) side of road
N36° 49' 50.9" W117° 00' 53.9"

Along the downhill side of this steep road is **Western honey mesquite** (*Prosopis glandulosa torreyana*), Legume family, **Figure 5.12**. This **deciduous tree** can grow from fifteen to twenty-five feet tall. It is a phreatophyte, which means it taps into permanent groundwater. Where it grows, water may be no deeper than 30 to 60 feet. However, before grabbing your shovel to get water, some roots have been measured at over 250 feet in length. Mesquite has many branches with numerous very sharp thorns. The thorns will provide you with a memorable experience if you carelessly grab some branches. Flowers appear in spring and attract many bees.

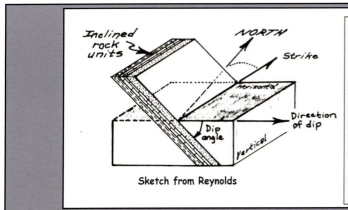

Figure 5.11 Geologists use strike and dip to define how rock beds are oriented. This information is included on their geologic maps that also contain data on rock composition.

Figure 5.12 Honey mesquite is seen growing along the downhill side of the road.

Figure 5.13 Desert Milkweed has pale cream colored flowers.

The seedpods look like lumpy string beans. Native Americans ground the pods and baked them for bread. Coyotes use the pods as a large portion of their food supply. (*Prosopis*, L., "catkin flowered", referring to the cylindrical spikes.)

> **10.68 Miles - Parking area**
> **N36° 49' 47.3" W117° 00' 59.6"**

Many years ago this was the site of a gate. During summers when there were heavy rains, the gate was closed. Rain made this part of the road very slick and impassable. If it wasn't closed, people could drive to the bottom and find they couldn't drive up the slick road. They could not get back over either White Pass or Red Pass. They were just "stuck in the middle". Today, the road is gated near the park boundary and information about possible road closure is provided by the Death Valley NPS [(760) 786-3200], as noted on the Introduction.

This is a large pullout area. It is a good place to take a lunch break or look around. This area has had many Prince's plumes and milkweeds alongside the road.

Geology

Near here you can see the reddish color of the rocks exposed along the road as it switchbacks up to Red Pass. All of these rocks comprise parts of the Titus Canyon Formation.

Plants

Besides having an exceptional display of Prince's plume and Arizona Lupine near this stop, **Desert milkweed** (*Asclepias erosa*), Milkweed family, **Figure 5.13, CP-HH**, grows in the loose soil of the washes and fans. These plants are two to four feet tall. They have six-inch long, opposing, white-green leaves that are ruffled and saw-edged at the margins. These **perennial herbs** appear to be coated with white lint. Flowers are pale cream or greenish-white. It grows in washes and dry slopes at 500-5500 feet elevation. Native Americans rubbed the milky white juice on warts. (*Asclepias*, Gr., Asklepios ancient Greek father of medicine; *erosa*, L., awl shaped.)

Animals

The **Western tanager** (*Piranga ludoviciana*) is a colorful, summer visitor to the area. The male, in **Figure 5.14**, has a brilliant flame-red head; yellow underparts and rump; black tail, back, and wings; and yellow, double wing bar.

Figure 5.14 Colorful male Western tanager is red and yellow.

Figure 5.15 Six to eight foot long blocks of megabreccia from the Bonanza King Formation are found at roadside.

> **10.89 Miles-Megabreccia- large fragments of Bonanza King Formation**
> **N36° 49' 44.9" W117° 01' 10.1"**

Geology

To the left (where the road bends sharply to the right) are large, angular blocks (**Figure 5.15**) of the

Figure 5.16 Slickenside surface indicates motion along a fault plane.

dark gray Bonanza King Formation. Although the megabreccia consists of the Cambrian Bonanza King, the fragmentation into megabreccia occurred after the Titus Canyon Formation was deposited. Reynolds noted this by observing that the megabreccia rests on the tilted and deformed beds of the Titus Canyon Formation. You will see more and larger outcrops of this megabreccia. It will be discussed further where it is exposed on the west side of Red Pass.

To the right, is the deep reddish, maroon mudstone that is part of the Titus Canyon Formation. In this mudstone, Don Curry, National Park Service, found the fossil remains of a titanothere in 1934.

To the right, is a brownish slickensided rock, **Figure 5.16**, that shows a surface ground smooth as rocks ground along each other on a fault.

11.0 Miles - Folded rock layers and fractured rocks
N36° 49' 42.1" W117° 01' 16.2"

We are almost in the west tributary channel of Titanothere Canyon. We cross the nose of a broad **anticline** that lies to the south (left) of the road. An anticline is a fold in rock that bends upward (convex) as seen in **Figure 5.17** The **syncline** is a fold that bends downward (concave). Keep these two terms in mind because we will use them frequently as we progress on the tour.

Down the canyon to your left, you will notice that the rock layers on the east (left) side of the stream channel are dipping to your left and to the right side of the stream they dip to the right. The center, highest part of the anticline has been removed by erosion. **Figure 5.18** provides a simplified sequence of events leading to this feature.

You will see more of the lower Titus Canyon Formation exposed on the north (right) side of the road, **Figure 5.19**. Note the concave pockets in the matrix. Erosion has, once again, resulted in separation of these Paleozoic (and later) clasts from a conglomerate's matrix. Note the rounded clasts and how some of them are fractured. Also, the matrix is fractured. Note the orientation of the clasts parallel to the fractures in the clasts. Analyses indicate the clasts were fractured mainly by shear during rotation in the matrix as the entire region was extending and large blocks rotating concurrent with the Miocene extensional faulting.

Mile 11.44-12.0 - Reddish brown part of Titus Canyon Formation
N36° 49' 35.1" W117° 01' 30.1"

Near a bend in the road, the color of the Titus Canyon Formation changes to reddish brown. It is sedimentary breccia that is the basal part of the Titus Canyon Formation. You will see it from here up to Red Pass. The breccia contains some rounded clasts and it is bedded.

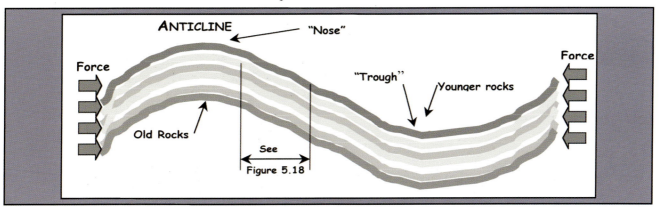

Figure 5.17 Anticlines and synclines are formed when rocks are subjected to compressive forces.

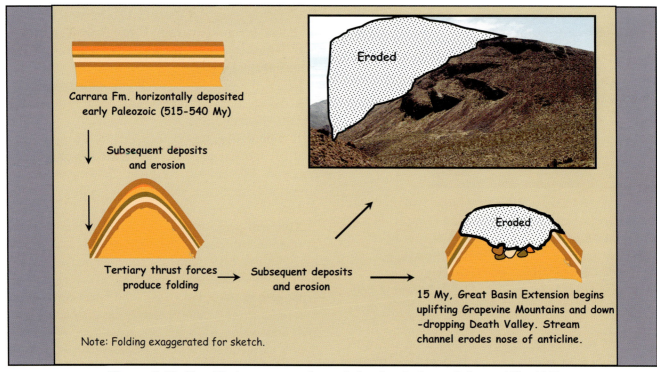

Figure 5.18 Simplified sequence of events leading to the anticline at Mile 10.7

Figure 5.19 Rounded and fractured clasts of the Titus Canyon Formation are aligned with fractures in the matrix. (Author's hat for scale)

Mile 11.9 - Looking back (east) to White Pass
N36° 49' 34.1" W117° 01' 41.6"

This is an excellent spot to pause and look back at some of the ground you covered. **Figure 5.20** identifies some highlights. Do not block the road.

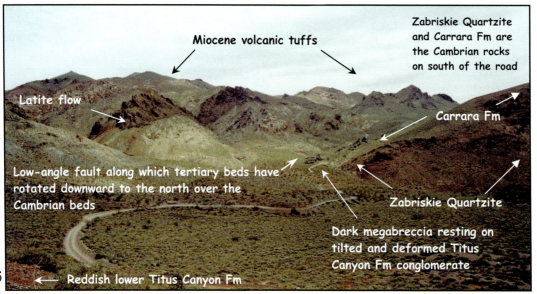

Figure 5.20 This is a spectacular view looking east back towards White Pass. Note that the colorful volcanic rocks and the reddish brown Titus Canyon Formation through which the road winds upward to Red Pass.

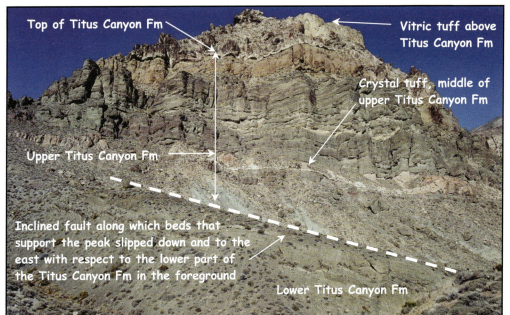

Figure 5.21
The multi-colored beds of the Titus Canyon Fm are crowned by tuff.

Mile 12.0 - View of Titus Canyon Fm. at Red Pass, Look Back at the Figure 5.20 View
N36° 49' 35.1" W117° 01' 47.4"

This is a good view of the Titus Canyon Formation and its tuff crown. **Figure 5.21** identifies specific items of interest. Note the distinct white marker bed that identifies the middle of the upper part of the Titus Canyon Formation and another white marker bed identifying the top of the Titus Canyon Formation. Geologists and visitors can use distinct features like these to help identify formations from one area to another.

Figure 5.22
A small footpath passes below and east of eroded sentinels (hoodoos) of sandstones and conglomerates interbedded with volcanic rocks.

Mile 12.43 - Red Pass
N36° 49' 43.4" W117° 01' 56.6"

The red in Red Pass (Bloody Gap) is the Titus Canyon Formation. On the east side of Red Pass a small footpath leads off to your right (eastward). The path follows the approximate top of the Titus Canyon Formation, **Figure 5.22**. As you walk along the path, you can see ahead of you a thin, white layer near the top of the red beds. This is the "marker" bed, discussed at Mile 11.7, near the top of the Titus Canyon Formation. Above the Titus Canyon Formation are more sandstones and conglomerate beds that are Miocene (5-24 My). They are interbedded with volcanic rocks and are eroded into monolith like structures.

From Red Pass you can look northwest into the drainage system of Titus Canyon, **Figure 5.23**. From here to Leadfield, the large canyon is called "Lost Canyon" (possibly called Welsh Canyon in the Leadfield days). On the far skyline ridge, almost all the rocks you can see are the Cambrian Bonanza King and Nopah formations. Still farther north are more marine sedimentary rocks that are Ordovician, Silurian, and Devonian in age. These rocks were originally deposited across the then flat Titus Canyon area during most of Paleozoic time and were later eroded from the area. In the distance are three high peaks. The peak due northwest from and closest to Red Pass is Mount Palmer (6,710 ft elevation) that is comprised of Silurian Hidden Valley Dolomite. The farthest from Red Pass, and due north of Mount Palmer is called Grapevine Peak (8738 ft) and is comprised of Timber Mountain tuff. Wahguyhe Peak (8628 ft) is north-northwest of Red Pass and is closer than Grapevine Peak but farther away than Mount Palmer. Looking northerly from the pass, **Figure 5.23**, you can see the red stained rocks of the Titus Canyon Formation extending beyond Leadfield. In the lower right foreground, are reddish rocks of the Titus Canyon Formation overlain by the variegated (tan, gray, pale green, reddish brown, and dark red) Miocene volcanic rocks from the Timber Mountain Caldera. Note the landslide and fault to your right

Looking back down the road we just came up (southwest), we can see the steep, dark cliffs of the Bonanza King Formation. The megabreccia you will see on the north side of the pass originated from this area.

Figure 5.24 shows a fault contact we passed just before reaching the turnout for parking. It is on the south facing wall of the roadside.

Do not fail to look back towards Titanothere Canyon and see the spectacular view of the area we just crossed, **Figure 5.25**. The view here emphasizes the point that throughout the tour you should continually stop and look in all directions. If you don't, you will miss some fantastic scenery.

Plants

Threadleaf snakeweed (*Gutierrezia microcephala*) (Resin-weed, Turpentine weed, Sticky snakeweed, Matchweed, Yellow-green matchweed)), Sunflower family, **Figure 5.26** can be seen along the side of the road. You will notice this **shrub** (*stem succulent*) in summer and fall when it forms a yellow dome about two-feet high and two or more feet wide. The yellow flowers are tiny but dozens combine into one head with hundreds of heads comprising a plant. The leaves are narrow and have a resinous odor. The plant is most abundant from 3,000-6,000 feet elevation. It will be in disturbed soil (roadside) up the alluvial fan, at Red Pass, and down to Leadfield. Native Americans used the leaves for teas in treating stomach ailments and rheumatism, poultices for snakebite, and as brooms. Along with Rabbitbrush, it is one of only a few plants that provide color in the summer and fall. (*Gutierrezia*, refers to a noble Spanish family with the surname Gutierrez.)

Desert pricklepoppy (*Argemone munita* ssp. argentea), Poppy family, **Figure 5.27, CP-II** has large, white flowers that seem to wave to you as they fold and sway in the breeze. This **perennial herb's** leaves are large and spiny. Plants are two to three feet tall and are found from 3,000-4,500 feet elevation. Desert pricklepoppy grows beside the road on the way to Leadfield and in the upper washes of Titus Canyon. (*Argemone*, Gr., ocular cataract, which supposedly was cured by sap from other plants with this name.)

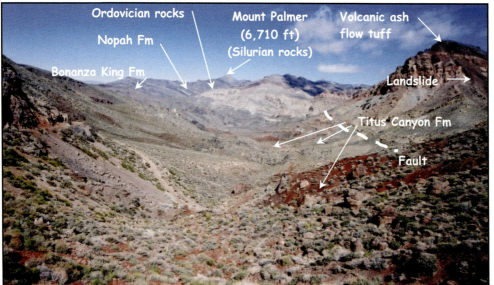

Figure 5.23 The view north from Red Pass towards Titus Canyon offers one of the most colorful panoramas in DEVA.

Figure 5.24 Fault contact in Titus Canyon Fm. is seen at Red Pass.

Figure 5.25 This is a fine view from Red Pass looking southeast across the upper part of Titanothere Canyon.

Figure 5.26 Snakeweed has many, tiny, clustered, yellow flowers.

Figure 5.27 Desert pricklepoppy has large white flowers.

> **Mile 12.43 To Leadfield - Down from Red Pass, into Lost Canyon and along Chuckwalla Road**
>
> N36° 49' 43.4" W117° 01' 56.6"

We have taken it upon ourselves to give the name "Chuckwalla" to the road leading down to Leadfield because of so many chuckwalla lizards sightings. It was "New Road" in Leadfield days. Also, we use "Lost Canyon" in reference to the canyon that leads from Red Pass down to Leadfield because of its use in a 1926 USGS paper and because Reynolds used it when he mapped the region.

You will see outcrops of dark megabreccia left of the road and crossing the road farther down. The Titus Canyon Formation generally will be to your right.

USE LOW GEAR

Geology

Along Lost Canyon, from the north side of Red Pass at Mile 12.7 to Leadfield, the principal rocks exposed along the road are outcroppings of the dark megabreccia. Outcrops of Zabriskie Quartzite and Carrara Formation are also seen as shown in **Figure 5.28**. At mile 14.42, the megabreccia is exposed on both sides of the road.

You have already seen smaller blocks of this megabreccia when you were driving in a drainage channel of Titanothere Canyon (Mile 10.6). The dark megabreccia here is monolithologic (comprised solely of blocks of one rock type) derived from the Cambrian marine Bonanza King Formation. There are two forms of megabreccia in this area. Huge, homogeneous megabreccia blocks (e.g. two-hundred foot blocks) are found near abandoned mines shafts southeast of Leadfield. An even larger block is found in the west fork of Titus Canyon. A second form of breccia, **Figure 5.29**, consists of fragments (from few inches to feet) of the Bonanza King cemented together by a matrix of calcite.

Figure 5.28 View west of road (left), north of Red Pass, includes blocks of megabreccia in foreground and outcrops of Zabriskie Quartzite and Carrara Fm. in the background.

How and when did these huge fragments come to be here? In his study of the geology of Titus and Titanothere Canyons, Mitchell Reynolds described the megabreccia and discussed its possible origin. Reynolds postulated that during the Oligocene time (24-37 My) the Bonanza King Formation that formed the megabreccia was exposed on the west side of a fault; the rocks failed and gravity induced the blocks to slide downhill.

From Red Pass to Mile 14.42 where the megabreccia occupies both sides of the road for roughly 1/2 -mile, the Titus Canyon Formation will be directly right of the road.

Figure 5.29 This boulder from the Bonanza King megabreccia is comprised of large angular fragments.

Titus Canyon Region Animals - 37 My and Present

Titanotheres grazing on savanna, Late Eocene (37 My).

Hyracodon, early rhinoceros, 37 My.

Mesohippus, 3-toed horse, 37 My.

Coyote

Chukar

Desert Bighorn

Gamble's Quail

Horned Lizard

Burrowing Owl

Chuckwalla

Indian paintbrush

Rocklady maurandya

Shredding evening primrose

Hop-sage

Grape soda lupine

Silver cholla

Fishhook cactus

Royal desert lupine

Desert pricklepoppy

Desert purple sage

Cliff-rose

Golden evening primrose

Desert fivespot

Apricot mallow

Red Pass, elevation 5,250 feet, looking north into Lost Valley and towards Leadfield.

Ghost town of Leadfield.

Red Pass "Hoodoos."

Optical illusion in layered beds of Bonanza King Formation

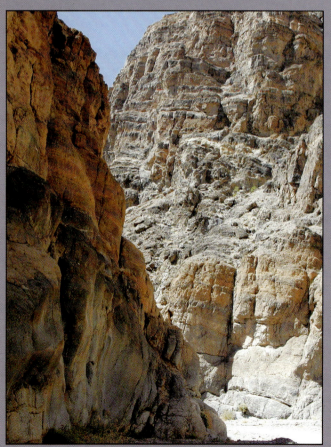
Steep, high walls in lower Titus Canyon

Jigsaw puzzle, Titus Canyon walls

Folded (180° Anticline) Bonanza King Fm. in Titus Canyon.

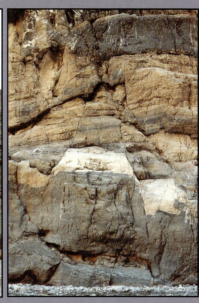
Normal Fault in Bonanza King.

Zabriskie Quartzite: purple with bedding planes.

Titus Canyon Fm: rounded, bruised, cracked clasts.

Carrara Fm: Gray siltstone, trilobite fragments.

Travertine along Titus Canyon walls.

Plants

In the spring, there are numerous flowers along this route. We have already discussed many of them. Prince's plume is prevalent in the late spring. Grape soda lupine makes a particularly outstanding visual display. Eriogonum will be in the middle and on the side of the road. In the fall, the roadside will be bordered with the yellow snakeweed and the Lost Canyon wash will be full of yellow blooming Rabbitbrush.

Just as you start downhill, from Red Pass you will see **Desert rock goldenbush** (*Ericameria cuneata var. spathulatu*), (Cliff goldenbbush), Sunflower family, **Figure 5.30**, a low growing resinous **shrub** on the uphill side of the road. It favors cracks in rock walls allowing it to get some shade. The flowers are creamy or pale yellow-white and bloom in October. The leaves are dark green, glossy, and very noticeable.

Grape soda lupine (*Lupinus excubinus*), Legume family, **Figure 5.31, CP-V**, grows one to two-feet high with generously spaced, plentiful, light blue (with shades of pink) oblong, one-inch flowers. Leaves look somewhat like palm fronds because they are compound leaves (divided into distinct parts) that are palmate (radiate from a single point). This **perennial** is quite an impressive plant when in full bloom. Even when not in bloom, the plant is easily identifiable as a lupine by its palmate leaves. You will find it near washes. (*Lupinus*, L., wolf, plant was thought to rob the soil; *excubinus*, L., vigilant.)

Figure 5.30 Desert rock golden bush has glossy, green leaves and creamy flowers. It grows from cracks in cliffs.

Figure 5.31 Grape soda lupine has numerous light blue flowers along each stem.

Animals

Figure 5.32 shows some of the many chuckwallas we have seen along this road. They are the largest lizards in the Death Valley region..

Figure 5.32 Three different Chuckwallas on Chuckwalla Road.

Figure 5.33 Skeleton weed grows in one plane.

Figure 5.34 This Pagoda eriogonum appears to grow in two different planes.

Figure 5.35 The Birdnest eriogonum derives its common name from its many, dense branches.

Chuckwalla (*Sauromalus obestus*), **Figure 5.32**, is sometimes confused with the poisonous Gila monster that received a lot of notoriety in cowboy movies from the 1950's and does not reside in Death Valley National Park. In the mornings, the chuckwalla emerges from its rocky habitat to sun itself. It is primarily a vegetarian. It stores fat in its tail and water in lymph glands along the sides of its body. When frightened, it dives into a crack in its rocky surroundings and wedges itself with its muscular legs and tail and by inflating its lungs. Native Americans used a sharpened stick with a hook on the end to deflate the chuckwalla's lungs and pull it from its hole. It made a tasty meal.

Mile 13.02 Very dark megabreccia overlain by reddish brown Carrara Formation
N36° 49' 50.4" W117° 02' 02.3"

Mile 13.52 - Eriogonums on and alongside the roadbed
N36° 50' 03.9" W117° 02' 08.1"

There are many kinds of eriogonums growing in the Titus Canyon area and in the encompassing Death Valley region. They vary in shape, size, and flower color and can be found from the valley floor up to Telescope Peak. The Desert trumpet, which we discussed previously, and the following three eriogonums represent a small portion of those in the region.

Skeleton weed (*Eriogonum brachypodum*), (Parry's buckwheat), Buckwheat family, **Figure 5.33**, looks like a flat-topped tree that grows on the African veldt. However, this eriogonum is only three to four-inches tall and twelve inches in diameter. You might have seen some of these earlier on the tour because they tend to grow beside a road or other disturbed soil. When this **annual** blooms in the springtime, it has extremely small white flowers clustered underneath its branches. In the fall it is reddish in color and helps to liven an almost colorless landscape. It grows at elevations above 500 feet. (*Eriogonum*, Gr., wooly joint or angle referring to hairy nodes that some members of the buckwheat family have; *brachypodum*, L., "turned down" referring to upper branches.)

Pagoda eriogonum's (*Eriogonum rixfordii*) (Rixford eriogonum, Rixford's buckwheat, Pagoda buckwheat), Buckwheat family, **Figure 5.34** - most distinguishing characteristic is that this annual grows in a number of flat surfaces resembling a pagoda. It grows six to twelve-inches tall and is limited to the Death Valley region and proximity. In the fall, the branches appear reddish. (*Eriogonum*, Gr., wooly joint or angle; *rixfordii*, G. P. Rixford.)

Bird nest eriogonum (*Eriogonum heermannii*) (Heermann Buckwheat), Buckwheat family, **Figure 5.35** can be found growing alongside Pagoda eriogonum in the disturbed soil along a roadside. This **shrub's** many and dense branches make it appear to be a bird nest. (*Eriogonum*, Gr., wooly joint or angle; heermannii, Dr. A. L. Heermann, collector on the Williamson Survey in 1853.)

> **Mile 14.05 - Turnout for exploration and hiking to megabreccia**
> **N36° 50' 13.8" W117° 02' 33.9"**

This is a good place to stop and look around. Park your vehicle in the turnout and hike to the megabreccia. Look for plants and animals.

> **Mile 14.42 Megabreccia on both sides of road, desert-rue, hedgehog cactus**
> **N36° 50' 13.5" W117° 02' 46.4"**

Plants

Mojave desert-rue (*Thamnosma montana*), (Turpentine broom), Rue family, **Figure 5.36, CP-LL** has dull green round stems and grows twelve to eighteen-inches high. The flowers are very deep purple in color. The resin on its two-lobed fruit can be a serious irritant to your skin. This **shrub** is related to citrus. Native Americans crushed the stems and used them as an aid to healing wounds. (*Thamnosma*, Gr., odorous shrub; *montana*, L., montane (mountain).)

Hedgehog cactus (*Echinocereus engelmannii*) (Calico cactus, Engleman's hedgehog cactus), Cactus family, **Figure 5.37, CP-MM** looks like a group of loosely clustered, hairy cucumbers with their ends stuck in the ground. This **shrub** (*stem succulent*) has ribs that run the length of the stem. The long spines are of various colors from which it derives the "calico" nickname. The flowers are a showy pale magenta. Native Americans ate its red fruit. (*Echinocereus*, Gr., hedgehog candle; *englemanii*, Dr. G. Englemann, 1809-1884, famous botanist.)

Figure 5.36 Mojave desert-rue has purple flower petals.

Figure 5.37 Hedgehog cactus looks somewhat like hairy cucumbers. Flowers are pale to dark magenta.

Figure 5.38 Dry waterfall is a witness to past deluges. Adit is from Cadalack Group of claims.

Mile 14.55 Hairpin curve, dry waterfall, old mine
N36° 50' 10.9" W117° 02' 48.5"

Figure 5.39 This sign was stolen before publication of this book. Old mines/prospects can pose a hazard to today's visitors. This mine (actually an adit) runs horizontally back to a drift. It does not use timbering because it is a "hard rock" mine cut into dolomite. It is a standard 5' x 7' with arched ceiling. It is one of two adits on the New Road claim. The other adit is back, up the road and has drifts.

Geology

Across the wash, to your left, is a dry waterfall, **Figure 5.38**, cut into the megabreccia. Past rains provided water to transport sand and rocks to erode this now dry waterfall.

At the base of the fall is an old mine adit (horizontal passage from the surface into a mine) dating back to the active days of mining at Leadfield. This effort failed to find lead in sufficient quantities to be profitable.

Mile 15.06 Prospect and hazard sign
N36° 50' 22.0" W117° 02' 57.2"

At this curve in the road, was a "Mine Hazard" sign, **Figure 5.39**. Throughout DEVA the National Park Service puts up signs to warn visitors about mine openings, particularly vertical or steeply inclined shafts. Take these signs seriously because mine hazards can include toxic gases, unseen and very deep pits, cave-ins, and rattlesnakes. Stay out of the mines!

The sign is a leftover from World War II when it was used to warn of the presence of the type of mine that exploded.

Figure 5.40 Male Black-collared lizard warms itself on reddish volcanic tuff down the road from the adit.

Figure 5.41 This Brush lizard was beside the path to the lower adit.

Animals

Black-collared lizard, (*Crotaphytus insularis*), **Figure 5.40**, hunts in the daytime and feeds on insects and smaller lizards. It grows to thirteen inches. The distinguishing characteristic is the collar on the back of the neck. The males have blue-green throats with a black center.

The **Brush lizard** (*Usasauraus gracious*), **Figure 5.41**, grows to a length of seven inches. The tail is twice the length of the body. Males have bluish patches on the side of the body. They are often found in branches (e.g. creosote bush) hunting insects.

> **Mile 15.66, 15.80, 16.03, 16.10 - Drainage channels feeding into Titus Canyon**
> N36° 50' 35.6" W117° 03' 15.6"

You are crossing into a series of drainage channels eroded by intermittent streams. These channels drain the terrain northwest of Red Pass into the main drainage channel, Titus Canyon. In the fall, these channels are colored yellow with blooming rabbitbrush. Following one of these channels to Leadfield, you will also see creosote bush, desert rue, prince's plume, and Stansbury cliff rose.

> **Mile 16.14 - Leadfield ghost town**
> N36° 50' 54.3" W117° 03' 33.5"

History

The 1904 discovery of gold in the nearby Bullfrog Hills and the ensuing gold rush drew prospectors into the Grapevine Mountains. Two of these prospectors, W. H. Seaman and Curtis Durnford (or a "Barney McCann") staked claims in 1905 on nine copper and lead sites in the vicinity of what was to become Leadfield in 1925. They sold their claims to the Death Valley Consolidated Mining Company that was a consortium fronted by Clay Tallman. The company immediately started development. Ore was shipped to smelters by May of 1906; however, high freight rates and other costs made the operation unprofitable. It folded by the end of 1906.

After nearly eighteen years, two prospectors from Rhyolite, Ben Chambers and Frank Metts, who were grubstaked by Lawrence Christiansen came to Titus Canyon in 1924. In March, they staked claims on lead prospects in the area previously abandoned in 1906 as unprofitable.

In March of the following year, 1925, John (aka Jack) Salsberry and others (including W. E. "Ed" Staunton and Jacob "Jake" Berger) bought the claims from Chambers and his partners despite the fact that little development work had been done in the previous year. It is believed by some that Berger consulted Charles Courtney Julian prior to the purchase.

On August 19, 1925, Salsberry, Berger, and Staunton formed the Western Lead Mines Company (WLMC) and issued 1,500,000 shares for sale at ten-cents per share.

We cannot continue the story of Leadfield without first discussing Charles Courtney Julian, who was born in Manitoba, Canada in 1885. After starting his career selling newspapers, he drifted to the southern California oilfields. In 1920 he started his own drilling business. By 1922, he brought in a few gushers that spring-boarded him into forming the Julian Petroleum Company. He proved to be adept at raising funds to form the company and at skimming two million dollars off of the top. Unfortunately for his investors, his other management skills were not up to running the company. He was forced to resign in 1924. Julian cast about for a new career. There seems to be two schools of thought regarding Julian. One school of thought says he was a scapegoat who *"did not start the Leadfield boom, and had plenty of help in supporting the boom once it started"*. The other school says *"he was a flamboyant hayseed huckster with a pungent but disarmingly folksy style...a sly fox, thin, wiry, and shrewd with a long vulpine nose and close set eyes."* Now let's return to the events surrounding Leadfield.

October 27, 1925, Julian took over WLMC as president and an additional 500,000 shares of WLMC were issued for sale. It appears that Julian received the majority of the stock for putting up development money and acting as president. He also convinced the other promoters to lock their stock in a bank vault for two years while he sold his shares for development expenses.

By December 1925, WLMC had expanded its holdings with additional claims, completed a road up Titus Canyon from the Death Valley floor to Leadfield, and started a road (surveyed by E. S. Giles) from Leadfield northeast to Beatty. **Figures 5.42** to **5.46** are photographs of Leadfield in February 1926. **Figure 5. 47** is later in 1926.

Figure 5.42
Leadfield, February 1926. Road to left leads down a dry gulch graded into a road. To the right is the main road. View is north-westerly.

Death Valley National Park

Figure 5.43
Upper east side of Leadfield, February 1926. View is to west. Building under construction (left), numerous tents, road in distance leads to diggings on March Storm No. 1 claim, owned by WLMC.

Death Valley National Park

Figure 5.44
Leadfield, February 1926. Gap leading into Titus Canyon is in center of photograph. View is north-westerly.

Death Valley National Park

Figure 5.45 Leadfield in February 1926. Truck and tents. Snow is visible in the mountains in the background.

Death Valley National Park

Figure 5.46 Leadfield in February 1926. Alice and Billy Van Allen, Joe Rek, and the girl's baby burro. West side of town.

Death Valley National Park

Figure 5.47 North end of Leadfield looking to the southeast in general direction of Red Pass. Seen in the foreground is where the two roads converge.

Nevada Publications, Stan Paher.

In January 1926, the name "Leadfield" was officially bestowed, six additional mining companies were in the area, a pipeline to supply additional (other springs were in the Leadfield area) water for Leadfield from Klare spring was started, Julian hired *"the foremost Engineers and Geologists of America"* who managed to determine that none of the ore samples assayed out to less than thirty dollars a ton, and WLMC was offered to the public on the Los Angeles Stock Exchange on January 30, 1926.

By the end of February 1926, Julian was very visible to the public as WLMC's leader, WLMC had 140 employees and completed the road to Beatty, and the California State Corporation Commission started investigating WLMC. Some say the Commission persecuted him while others say that they had already begun to catch on to him. Also, Julian's advertising kicked into high gear. His advertising was soon to include:

"Let's go, folks, on 'Western Lead,' because it's time to twist her tail, and every day you postpone placing your 'BUY' order is costing money."

"She's a 'High Stepping Baby' and I don't mean maybe..."

"Shut your eyes, say here goes nothing, and...mail your checks direct to me...C. C. Julian."

Additional headlines were to include: *"Chloroform Me"*, *"Cut That Grass"*, *"Here's A Hot One"*, and the soul stirring *"Hot Doggie"*. One handbill showed a picture of a steamboat carrying lead ore from Leadfield to Las Vegas via the Amargosa River (flows underground for long stretches). The one school of thought said Julian warned people who couldn't afford to take a risk while the other school referred to it as *"an outrageous new string of cornpone ads"*.

In March 1926, additional theatrics ensued but none surpassed Julian's masterstroke of bringing a trainload (340 out of 1,500 applicants) of enthusiastic investors, **Figure 5.48,** to Leadfield on March 14, for free food, free music, tours, and, above all, speeches. An additional eight hundred visitors showed up. The next day, WLMC was up to $3.30 per share. On March 15, the Commissioner of the California State Corporation Commissioner announced an investigation of WLMC and the stock dropped to $1.55 per share.

Figures 5.49 and **5.50** show Leadfield during the festivities and **Figure 5.51** is later in 1926.

Figure 5.48 Scenes at Beatty, Nevada as T&TRR, "Julian Special" unloads potential investors in Western Lead Mines Company (WLMC).

Figure 5.49 Panoramic view of Leadfield in 1926. View is looking to the southeast and Red Pass. March festivities for the 340 potential investors, and another 800 who showed up. Note the numerous cars on the lower road (Berger Street). *Death Valley National Park*

Figure 5.50 As it would later turn out, much ado about nothing at Leadfield, March, 1926. Those who are about to invest their money in worthless mines got entertained, fed, and fleeced by C. C. Julian. *Death Valley National Park*

In April and May 1926, the Commission continued its hearings. Julian's experts lost credibility under scrutiny. Ore found at the site was of small amount and poor quality. Also, there were irregularities in the manner in which his stock was listed and the price driven up. Consequently, on May 27, 1926 WLMC stock was stricken from the Los Angeles Stock Exchange and the Exodus began, His partners still had all their stock locked up in the bank vault.

United States Mineral Surveyor Edward L. Haff conducted USMS 5883 from which we can gain a partial understanding of WLMC's claims and development work, as seen in **Figure 5.52**.

In June, Julian offered to buy back his stock ($2.00 per share) via his personal note that would be payable in two-years. This was quite a stroke because he only gave out notes for approximately 90,000 shares. He had sold about eight times that amount. It is not known if any of the notes were ever paid off. He kept two dozen men "developing" and tunneling along to the "promised ledge."

In September, Julian formed Julian Merger Mines Incorporated which was also banned by the Commission. A second blow occurred in October when WLMC penetrated the ledge that its geologists said would contain the best deposits. That rock was found to contain far too little lead for profitable operations. That was essentially the end. Near death, Leadfield is seen in **Figure 5.51** A watchman stayed until the next summer when the last of the machinery was hauled off.

The Leadfield post office had missed most of the excitement for it opened August 25, 1926. Virginia Thomas Costello was the first and only postmaster that Leadfield ever had. "I opened the office on August 25, 1926, with mail in the racks for two hundred persons," she told C. B. Glasscock. "Five months later only one person called for mail. That was January 15, 1927. That was the day the post office closed."

Other fraudulent Julian mining activities followed and failed. He then moved to Oklahoma and returned to the oil business where fraudulent activities ensued and were exposed. After jumping bail, he completed his career in Shanghai with a fatal dose of amythal.

Mineral Survey 5883 indicated that there was lead in Leadfield; however, there was not enough lead to support a massive mining effort. Geologist Mitchell Reynolds, who had done a geological mapping of Titus and Titanothere Canyons, had chemical analyses done on mine samples and performed detailed inspections of the "mines." No lead or silver values were found higher than normal for carbonate rocks.

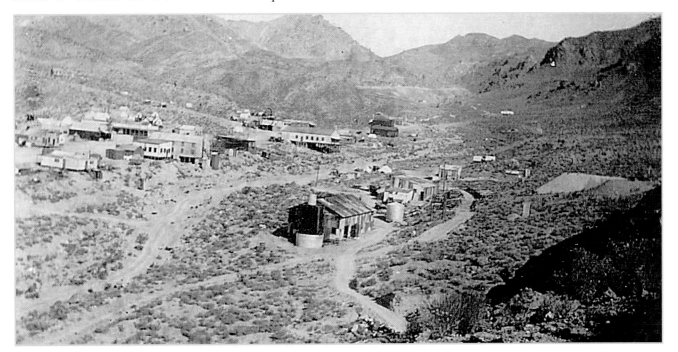

Figure 5.51 Panoramic view of abandoned or nearly abandoned Leadfield (late or post 1926). Photo shows the probable maximum extent of building that had occurred. There are few people and cars on the streets. View is looking to the southeast and Red Pass. March Storm No. 2 claim buildings and waste rock pile in center-right.

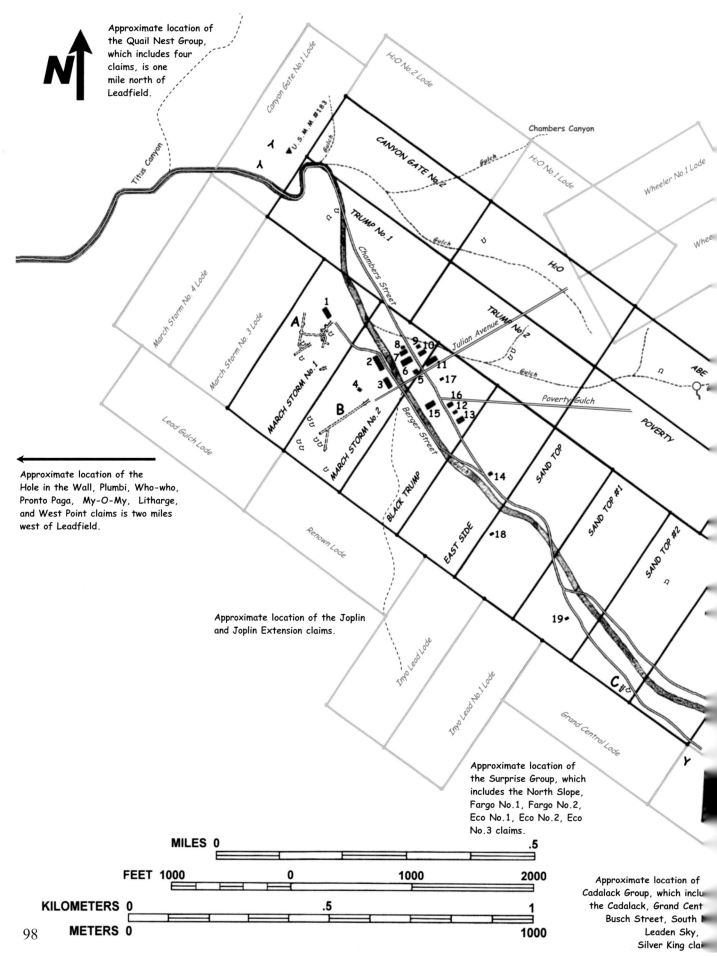

Figure 5.52 Leadfield Workings Circa August 1926

No.	Buildings
1.	Frame and Iron **Compressor and Engine Room** (40' x 120'). Claimant WLM.
2.	Frame and Iron **Compressor and Engine Room** (40' x 120'). Claimant WLM.
3.	Frame and Iron **Warehouse** (30' x 80'). Claimant WLM.
4.	A Frame and Iron **Blacksmith Shop** (30' x 20'). Claimant WLM.
5.	Frame and Iron **Assay Office** (20' x 30'). Claimant WLM.
6.	**Bunk House** (40' x 90'). Claimant WLM.
7.	Frame and Iron **Boarding House** (30' x 60'). Claimant WLM.
8.	Frame **House** (18' x 24'). Claimant WLM.
9.	Frame **House** (18' x 24'). Claimant WLM.
10.	Frame and Iron **Store** (30' x 60'). Claimant WLM.
11.	Frame and Iron **Office** (30' x 100'). Claimant WLM.
12.	Frame **House** (20' x 30'). Claimant WLM.
13.	Frame and Iron **Boarding House** (40' x 60'). Claimant WLM.
14.	Frame **House** (24' x 26').
15.	Frame and Iron **Store** (40' x 80'). Claimant Unknown.
16.	Frame and Iron **Garage** (30' x 40'). Claimant Unknown.
17.	**Cousin Jack**. Claimant Unknown.
18.	**Cousin Jack**. Claimant Unknown.
19.	"**Big Rock Camp site**". Claimant Unknown.
20.	"**Corrugate Cousin Jack and Shed**". Claimant Unknown.
21.	**Mine Building**. Claimant WLM.

NOTES:		
1.	Claims with gray boundaries are unsurveyed.	
2.	Underground operation locations.	
	A.	Tunnels and drifts totaling ~1,000'.
	B.	Tunnels and drift totaling ~ 660'.
	C.	5' x 7' 20' Timbered Shaft.
	D.	Tunnel total ~ 620'.
	E.	Northern tunnel and drifts totaling ~920'. Southern tunnel and drift totaling ~330'.
	F.	Unknown.
3.	Ω	Denotes an open cut for exploration.
4.	Y	Denotes an adit of unknown dimensions.
5.	X	Denotes a shaft of unknown dimensions.
6.	= =	Denotes underground.
7.	■	Denotes buildings.
8.	Q	Denotes springs.
REFERENCES:		
1.	USMS Map No. 5883 1926.	
2.	USGS "Thimble Peak" Quadrangle Chart.	
3.	1926 CA State Mineralogist Report.	
4.	Field Notes.	

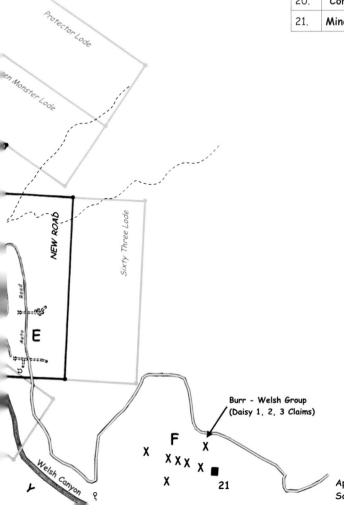

Approximate location of the South Dip Group of claims.

Map design by *Danny Ray Thomas*

Leadfield Today

Gone are all the hard working miners, the sound of music, laughter, and clinking of glasses in the bars, the trucks grinding up to Red Pass and down into Leadfield, the shopkeepers, the smell of diesel used to run compressors for the pneumatic drills and air for the miners, muffled explosions as a miner fires his shot, and the ubiquitous investors followed by those so ready to sell them stock. But, they weren't in Lost Valley long enough for the surrounding hills to get used to them. For nine months, ten at the most, Leadfield flowered. Besides the people going elsewhere, the machinery and most of the building materials were hauled off to "elsewhere" and mines in Arizona.

Holes in the ground, remnants of buildings, mine waste rock, outlines of tent campsites, occasional piles of debris, boundary markers, and faint roads and paths remain. They all contribute to the story of Leadfield when hopes were high and money was to be made. The visitor to this are can look around and try to understand the story of Leadfield and the people that wrote it. When you look around, you will realize that it was hard work and not easy living in those days.

Figure 5.53 through **5.62** are pictures of the remnants of Leadfield including cousin jacks, tent campsites, an old automobile, Western Lead Mine Company buildings, etc.

Figure 5.53 The builder of this cousin jack was fortunate enough to obtain enough lumber for the front of the exterior and some interior walls. The builder still dug into the side of the mountain and used rocks to build up the exterior side walls. It was probably warm in the winter and relatively cool in the summer. It is on what was once the East Side claim.

May 2008

Figure 5.54 This was an extensive tent campsite with various rock walls used to build up a level area. The large rock must have provided some protection from the wind and sun. There were some window framing and broken glass suggesting there was also some framed building in the area. It is on the Sand Top No. 1Claim.

May 2008

Figure 5.55 "Cousin Jack", built in to side of hill to save building materials. The builder had just enough lumber to frame the door and some walls. He found some corrugated metal sheets for the roof and probably the door. For insulation, dirt was piled on the corrugated metal roof.

May 2008

Figure 5.56 Remnants of old automobile beside the road.

May 2008

Figure 5.57 Western Lead Mine building on March Storm No.1 claim, Leadfield.

2001

Figure 5.58 Western Lead Mine building on March Storm No.2 claim, Leadfield.

2001

Figure 5.59 Remnants of building made of corrugated metal sheets. This builder had quite a supply of corrugated metal sheets but likely could have used more lumber for framing.

May 2008

Figure 5. 60 Flooring of building with corners propped up and leveled with readily accessible boulders.

May 2008

Figure 5. 61 Pole for telegraph / telephone lines providing communication with Beatty, Nevada.

May 2008

Figure 5.62 Building on March Storm No. 2 claim.

2001

Geology

Besides the obvious historical significance of this stop, the surrounding mountains provide interesting geological features. An overview of the geologic formations is seen in **Figure 5.63.** On the road behind us (south), the colorful Titus Canyon Formation crops out on both sides. On the right (east), is a fault, **Figure 5.64**, between the Titus Canyon Formation and the overlying mid Miocene volcanic rocks. This fault is present at Red Pass, east of the scenic view. Also to the right (east) is a normal fault, **Figure 5.65**, in the Titus Canyon Formation. To our left (west), folded beds of the Bonanza King Formation, **Figure 5.66**, are behind remaining Leadfield buildings. Looking north down the road, we see the green conglomerate member overlying the colorful variegated member of the Titus Canyon Formation, faults and minor landslides. **Figure 5.67** shows one of the faults down the road.

Figure 5.64 Fault between Titus Canyon Formation and Miocene volcanic rocks.

Figure 5.65 A normal fault is on the right (east) side of the road. Note how the light colored bed on the left has appeared to slide upward along the fault plane… or the right side slide downward… or both sides slid.

Figure 5.63 Geologic formations in the vicinity of Leadfield.

Danny Ray Thomas per Mitchell W. Reynolds

€c: Carrara Formation (Fm) (grey, red limestone with some trilobytes, oolites)	Ŧtg: Titus Canyon Fm, green conglomerate facies (rounded clasts in matrix)
€bus: Bonanza King Fm, striped unit of upper member (dark and light gray stripes)	Ŧtv: Titus Canyon Fm, variegated facies (pale red, reddish brown, yellow-orange, pale green)
€z: Zabriskie Quartzite (purple, fine beds)	Ŧtbr: Titus Canyon Fm, sedimentary breccia facies
€bl: Bonanza King Fm, lower member (carbonate)	Ŧtc: Titus Canyon Fm (undifferentiated)
Twd: Densely welded tuff	Ql: Landslide deposits Qt: Talus Qog: Older gravels
Tmb: Monolithologic megabreccia	Q1: Unconsolidated alluvium in canyon and wash bottoms
Tclt: Crystal lithic tuff	r: Red pass Limestone member of Carrara Fm.
Tt: Vitric tuff and associated sedimentary rocks	g: Girvanella Limestone member of Carrara Fm.
Strike and Dip: Strike east-west, dip 30° north	Strike north-south, dip 30° west
Thrust fault, sawteeth on upper plate	t: Crystal tuff marker bed in green conglomerate facies of Titus Canyon Fm

Figure 5.66 Behind (west of) Leadfield. The Bonanza King Formation is folded from thrust forces that occurred during the Mesozoic.

Seen in the lower left are two adits and a Western Lead Mines building on the March Storm No. 1 claim.

2001

Figure 5.67 Fault contact between Bonanza King and Titus Canyon Formation, looking north from Leadfield.

Transition to Segment 3 of the tour

We have seen the Titus Canyon Formation, climbed up to Red Pass, cast our eyes over broad vistas, and have seen new plants. In Segment 3, we bid farewell to the Titus Canon Formation, proceed along a constantly descending road until we near sea level, look far upwards at the towering canyon walls, and see more new plants.

Begin Segment 3... Down the drain and through Titus Canyon

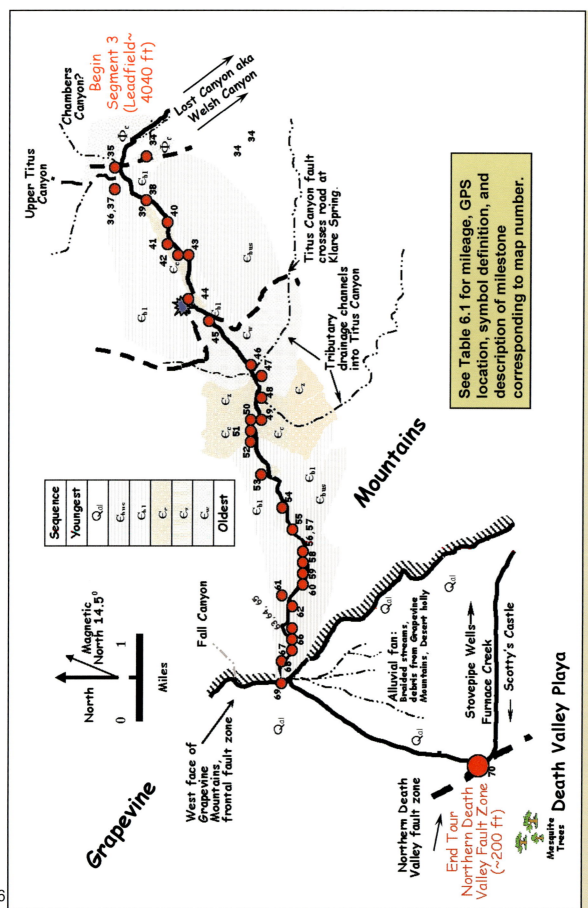

Figure 6.1 Segment 3 Titus Canyon route with geologic overviews along roadside (Length: 10.4 miles, Maximum Altitude 4040 ft. and Minimum Altitude 200 ft.)

Table 6.1 Segment 3 Milestones (MS) of Titus Canyon Tour - Odometer Mileage and GPS Locations

MS	Miles	GPS	Description	MS	Miles	GPS	Description
34	16.14	N36° 50' 54.3" W117° 03' 33.5"	Leadfield Ghost Town	53	21.90	N36° 49' 32.2" W117° 07' 44.9"	Syncline
35	16.51	N36° 51' 10.8" W117° 03' 44.7"	Optical Illusion	54	22.46	N36° 49' 19.7" W117° 08' 12.4"	Begin narrows
36	16.71	N36° 51' 10.1" W117° 03' 52.0"	Mine Prospect	55	22.59	N36° 49' 21.9" W117° 08' 20.0"	Titus Canyon Stairway
37	17.24	N36° 51' 11.3" W117° 04' 00.4"	Entering Titus Canyon	56	22.94	N36° 49' 12.4" W117° 08' 37.4"	Anticline
38	17.53	N36° 51' 04.2" W117° 04' 14.9"	The Big Tilt	57	23.16	N36° 49' 12.1" W117° 08' 49.7"	Fold in the Bonanza King
39	17.80	N36° 50' 58.3" W117° 04' 18.4"	Boundary between Bonanza	58	23.27	N36° 49' 09.5" W117° 08' 56.2"	Fold and Calcite to left
40	18.00	N36° 50' 50.2" W117° 04' 25.9"	Drainage into Titus Canyon	59	23.35	N36° 49' 08.6" W117° 09' 00.7"	Mass wasting and smooth walls
41	18.38	N36° 50' 40.5" W117° 04' 41.6"	Talus cone	60	23.39	N36° 49' 09.1" W117° 09' 02.9"	Fold and Fault to right
42	18.60	N36° 50' 38.6" W117° 04' 54.5"	Distinct white band	61	23.67	N36° 49' 13.9" W117° 09' 16.0"	Lower Narrows
43	18.71	N36° 50' 34.6" W117° 04' 58.2"	Large Talus cone	62	23.73	N36° 49' 16.1" W117° 09' 16.9"	How did these beds shift?
44	19.20	N36° 50' 28.3" W117° 05' 26.3"	Klare Spring/Wood Cyn. Fm	63	23.96	N36° 49' 18.9" W117° 09' 28.2"	Normal Fault—Great Basin
45	19.78	N36° 50' 08.6" W117° 05' 53.0"	Escarpment	64	24.06	N36° 49' 19.9" W117° 09' 34.6"	Reverse fault
46	20.49	N36° 49' 44.8" W117° 06' 27.9"	Titus Canyon anticline	65	24.51	N36° 49' 16.7" W117° 09' 52.7"	Mosaics, colorful travertine
47	20.60	N36° 49' 42.6" W117° 06' 33.8"	Begin Zabriskie Quartzite	66	24.74	N36° 49' 18.1" W117° 10' 01.0"	What came first? Ancient life
48	20.86	N36° 49' 40.9" W117° 06' 48.2"	Begin Carrara Formation	67	24.85	N36° 49' 19.0" W117° 10' 05.8"	Canyon narrows
49	21.17	N36° 49' 40.2" W117° 07' 06.6"	Ripple marks	68	25.17	N36° 49' 26.0" W117° 10' 16.5"	Titus's washbasin
50	21.27	N36° 49' 44.2" W117° 07' 09.8"	Fold, fault, and contact	69	25.38	N36° 49' 19.7" W117° 10' 24.8"	Mouth of Titus Canyon
51	21.37	N36° 49' 42.6" W117° 07' 16.2"	Passing Carrara to BK	70	28.01	N36° 47' 18.3" W117° 11' 28.8"	Death Valley Fault
52	21.60	N36° 49' 40.2" W117° 07' 30.0"	Fold in Carrara diving				

Mileages are based on GPS readings with accuracy within 25 ft.

Legend

- Q_{al} - Alluvial fan debris (boulders, cobbles, gravel, sand) eroded from Grapevine Mountains.
- $Ͼ_c$ - Titus Canyon Fm, Oligocene (24-37 My), conglomerate, red, brown, yellow, pale green.
- $Ͼ_{bus}$ - Upper Bonanza King Fm, late Cambrian (~515 my), alternating dark dolomite, gray limestone.
- $Ͼ_{bl}$ - Lower Bonanza King Fm, late Cambrian, same as upper Bonanza King except banding thinner.
- $Ͼ_c$ - Carrara Fm, early and middle Cambrian (~540 my), primarily dark limestone.
- $Ͼ_z$ - Zabriskie Quartzite, early Cambrian, grayish purple to brownish gray, forms ledges.
- $Ͼ_w$ - Wood Canyon Fm, upper member (Cambrian) (~570 my) is dolomite; lower member (Proterozoic) is quartzite and conglomerate with some dolostone.

Viewing the Titus Canyon anticline

(Starting at MS 44, sequence in which formations are encountered along the roadside)

1.	$Ͼ_w$	MS 44	Oldest
2.	$Ͼ_z$	MS 47	
3.	$Ͼ_c$	MS 48	
4.	$Ͼ_{bl}$	MS 51	
5.	$Ͼ_{bus}$	MS 54	Youngest

6.0 Segment 3... Down the "drain" and through Titus Canyon

Mile 0.0/16.14 – Leadfield drain
N36° 50' 54.3" W117° 03' 33.5"

Segment 3 of this tour starts at Leadfield and continues .4-miles north to an optical illusion at the upper narrows. Next, the tour goes into and down Titus Canyon for approximately 8.8-miles. The last 2.6-miles of the tour is down the "western" alluvial fan to the intersection with the Scotty Castle road on the floor of Death Valley. Milestones and geologic overviews are noted and described in **Figure 6.1** and **Table 6.1**. While driving down the canyon, you will see four formations in the following order: lower Bonanza King, upper Bonanza King, Carrara, Wood Canyon, Zabriskie Quartzite, Carrara, lower Bonanza King and finally upper Bonanza King. Wood Canyon is the oldest and upper Bonanza King is the youngest. The order is significant. As we pass through these Proterozoic and Cambrian marine sedimentary rocks, you will see how they have been folded ("bent"), faulted ("broken and shifted"), overturned, and eroded. An important fact to remember is that, west from Klare Spring to the mouth of Titus Canyon, the rock formations along the side of the road are "overturned". That is, the older rocks are on top of the younger rocks.

We will see varieties of plants growing in environments that include desert wash, canyon wall, and one riparian (permanent water). You will see many of the plants you have already seen on the preceding segments of the tour as well as new ones. We have already crossed some desert wash environments. However, the yet to be seen canyon wall and riparian environments provide the resources for some plants we haven't seen. Also, for the first time, we will be traveling down (west) to an elevation near sea level. We started this tour at an elevation of 3,400 feet. We may see new plants associated with lower alluvial fans and playas.

Not all odometers measure exactly the same. If you have noticed an increasing discrepancy with your mileage and the mileage at each milestone, herein, reset your odometer at the flat spot in Leadfield (near the highpoint) and use the alternate mileage markers from here on. Missing the exact location by 30 or 40 feet will make no difference on the milestone mileages. The mileages given herein are per GPS readings within 20-25 feet accuracy.

Geology

We call this stop the "Leadfield Drain" because we are at Leadfield and this drainage is one of three tributary drainages, in the immediate area, that converge to form the mainstream channel that is Titus Canyon. Two smaller channels meet the channel we are in .4-miles down the road (north). The main channel comes in from the right (north), .8-miles from here. It is the "official" beginning of Titus Canyon as designated by a National Park Service sign. Other tributary drainage channels will be encountered as we progress farther down Titus Canyon.

The discussion in the Geology text sections can become very involved. Unless you are very interested and conversant in the language of geology, it might behoove you to only pay attention to the mileage and picture captions.

Plants

If you look to your left as you leave Leadfield, you will see that the wash that drains the upstream region has the gnarled, shaggy "barked" rabbitbrush growing in it. It is typical of a desert wash plant community. To your right (east), are greenish creosote bushes that signify the creosote scrub plant community. If you look carefully you may see something staring back at you or sneaking off into the brush, (**Figure 6.2**).

Figure 6.2 Photographed near Leadfield, this Desert bighorn ram and ewe were partially hidden by the brush and shadows and acutely aware of the photographer.

Animals

The **Desert bighorn sheep** (*Ovis canadensis nelsoni*) live in the mountains surrounding Death Valley and specifically in the Titus Canyon region. Sightings are a memorable experience for both the first time and frequent Death Valley National Park visitor.

These muscular sheep, (**Figure 6.3**) are a medium shade of brown with white on their belly, rump, back of legs, and muzzle. The rams have massive "C" shaped horns that continue to grow with age and proclaim their status. Their lifespan is ten to fifteen years. Some of their average statistics are defined in **Table 6.2**.

Table 6.2 Desert bighorn sheep average statistics			
Sex	Weight (lbs)	Shoulder Height (inches)	Body Length (inches)
Ram	160	36	59
Ewe	100	32	56

They inhabit desert areas with rocky cliffs and are excellent climbers. Sheep leap from rocky ledge to rocky ledge with an astounding display of agility. They are active feeders during the day except when hot summer days cause them to feed at night. In the summer, they usually visit a water hole about every three days. Winter's moist, green vegetation allows them to greatly increase their watering interval. Desert bighorn sheep can function properly with twice as much loss of body water as can a human. They live at the higher altitudes during the hot summer months and migrate downward during the fall's cooler months.

The dominant ewe leads the herd. Fall is the breeding season with rams engaging in head-butting contests that may last twenty-four hours.

Their diet is varied for it includes grasses, non-woody flowering plants, shrubs, and trees. During this tour, you have seen some of the plants they feed on. These plants include Desert holly, Desert trumpet, Golden and Brown-eyed evening primrose, Mojave aster, phacelias, eriogonums, and others. Predators include mountain lions, bobcats, and coyotes. Golden eagles may prey on lambs.

Figure 6.3
Left, ram and ewe browse on the shady side of the hill. The male on the right may sport impressive horns, which he uses during breeding season contests with other rams, but it is the dominant ewe that leads the herd.

> **Mile .4/16.51 - Optical illusion at the "upper (canyon) narrows"**
> **N36° 51' 10.8" W117° 03' 44.7"**

Geology

An Illusion?

When you get to the "upper narrows," **Figure 6.4**, you can see some layers (beds) of the Bonanza King Formation that seem to be bent. Is this a syncline? Are the rock beds bent? Stop and look at them. The layers appear to be bent or folded rock beds but they are not. The beds are actually inclined north away from us (geologically speaking - they dip north). They are not folded at all. It is quite a good optical illusion. Furthermore, depending on where an observer stands in relation to the Bonanza King Formation beds, he can "see" different things. Move to position b) and c) as depicted in **Figure 6.5** and you will see tilted or horizontal beds, respectively as depicted in **Figures 6.6** and **6.7**. Three different positions can yield three different interpretations of what you see.

What it really is.

Now let's see what it really is and how it became that way. **Figure 6.8** describes the sequence of events that led to this optical illusion. Ocean bed deposits laid down horizontally hundreds of millions of years ago, began tilting 15-million years ago, and, recently, drainage channels eroded a section out of the beds.

Now go back to where you first saw these rock layers and convince yourself it is an illusion... really.

This illusion is an exception to what you will see on the remainder of the tour. Farther down Titus Canyon you will see many folds (bends. Synclines or anticlines) in the rocks...particularly in the Bonanza King Formation. We will point out many of them. Look for them on your own.

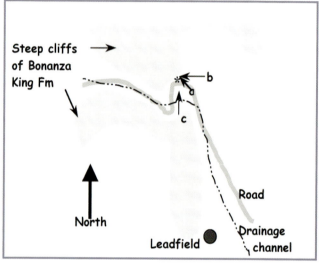

Figure 6.5 Viewing Bonanza King Fm "bent" beds from 3 positions.

Figure 6.4
At position (a) in the upper narrows, the highly visible beds of the Bonanza King Formation appear to be bent.

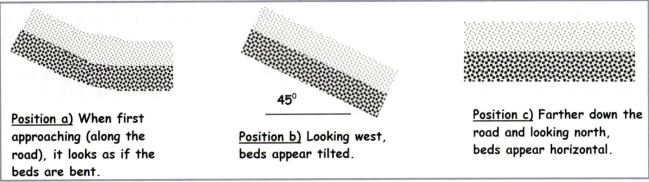

Figure 6.6 Different viewing positions yield different interpretations of what is seen.

Figure 6.8 The "illusion" at Titus Canyon's upper narrows started forming approximately 530 My when Cambrian oceans deposited the Bonanza King Formation. Great Basin extension and erosion helped to produce today's illusion.

Faults in the beds

Examine the rock beds a little closer. Look at the cliff face to the right (north). It is comprised of dipping beds of Bonanza King Formation. This has thinner beds (inches) than the previously seen Bonanza King that had beds tens of feet thick. Note that locally the bands are displaced vertically. A small fault, **Figure 6.9**, has vertically displaced beds of the Bonanza King.

Figure 6.9 Striped Bonanza King Formation shows vertical displacement along a fault.

Battered rocks from the Titus Canyon Formation

While in this area, look at some of the rounded clasts found in the tributary drainage channels and mainstream channel. You should see ones that have been fractured and/or have rounded areas that appear pock marked or damaged from some impact as seen in **Figure 6.10**. Most of these clasts have been eroded from the matrix of the Titus Canyon Formation. The fractures and pockmarks resulted when these and other clasts were in the Titus Canyon Formation and were being pressed against each other by the overburden. However, some fractures did occur from rolling around in flooded stream channels. Reynolds noted that some of the Bonanza King and Carrara limestone clasts found in Titus Canyon show impact scars from transport in turbid (disturbed or stirred up) flow down canyon. Another interesting clast you may see is one that was fractured while in the Titus Canyon Formation and "healed" or welded back together by calcite. **Figure 6.11** is an example of such a clast. Note that it fractured again subsequent to the "healing process."

Figure 6.10 Clasts from the Titus Canyon Fm. are fractured and pock marked.

Figure 6.11 This clast from Titus Canyon Fm. has been fractured "healed" and fractured again.

Plants

As you drive down the road (north) from Leadfield, you will see numerous gnarled, thick-branched, 5 to 6 foot high shrubs with greenish, needle like leaves growing in the washes that drain into Titus Canyon. These shrubs are called **Desert rabbitbrush** *Chrysothamus paniculatus*), (Blackbanded rabbitbrush),

Figure 6.12 Gnarled desert rabbitbrush's appearance in the spring and summer changes in the fall when it leafs out and masses of small yellow flowers bloom.

Sunflower family, **Figure 6.12**. They grow in sand and gravel of many canyon washes in the Death Valley region. They do not bloom in the spring. In the fall they have dense masses of small yellow flowers and thread-like, light green, resinous leaves. It is said that Native Americans knew that Piñon Pine nuts were ready for gathering when the rabbitbrush was in bloom. (*Chrysothamus*, Gr. Golden shrub; *paniculatus*, panicled.)

Animals

While looking around this area or elsewhere on the tour, you may notice a snake quietly gliding away from your presence, **Figure 6.13**. Given the opportunity, snakes would rather avoid you than take any aggressive action. Respect their privacy. Again, look where you step, look where you put your hands, and leave them alone.

Figure 6.13 Snakes quietly glide off to avoid contact with much larger humans... unless they rattle as a warning.

Figure 6.14 Entrance to prospect. It is now barred to protect bats from curious humans.

Mile 1.1/17.24 Entering Titus Canyon Main Channel

N36° 51' 11.3" W117° 04' 00.4"

Finally, we have arrived at Titus Canyon, proper. The "headwaters" are approximately eight miles due north of here in the higher peaks of the Grapevine Mountains. The drainage channel we have been driving down merges with this channel, **Figure 6.15,** to form Titus Canyon. After passing Red Pass, we were driving along a southern tributary drainage channel. Notice that we are still in the Bonanza King Formation (erosion resistant carbonate rocks that form steep walls and narrow canyon). The canyon is much wider where it crosses rocks that are less weather resistant in the desert environment (e.g. Wood Canyon Formation).

.57/16.71 - Mine prospect and waste pile to your right

N36° 51' 10.1" W117° 03' 52.0"

Figure 6.14 shows the entrance to another prospect (site of <u>potential</u> mineral deposits) that failed to become a profitable mine. The waste rock is visible from the road. You will have to walk up the trail to your right to see the horizontal entrance. A horizontal entrance into a mine is called an adit. It is not a tunnel because a tunnel is open at both ends. Horizontal side passages following a vein are called drifts. A vertical entrance is called a shaft. As with many other prospects in the area, it probably represents a lot of hard, physical work with no financial reward.

Figure 6.15 The upper reaches of the main Titus Canyon drainage merges in from the north and joins a smaller southern drainage channel (the channel we have been in). Together they form the Titus Canyon main stream channel.

> **Mile 1.39/17.53 "Big Tilt"**
> **N36° 51' 04.2" W117° 04' 14.9"**

This, **Figure 6.16**, is part of the tilted lower Bonanza King Formation. Erosion has made it mistakenly look somewhat like a slab that slid down from above. Note how the surrounding beds are tilted. The tilt or dip is due to Great Basin extension.

> **Mile 1.66/17.8 - Boundary between the Bonanza King Fm and the older Carrara Fm**
> **N36° 50' 58.3" W117° 04' 18.4"**

In the foreground, beside the road, we begin to see the upper member of the Carrara Formation cropping out on both sides of the road. **Figure 6.17** shows you where the boundary between the two formations is on the right (north) side of the road. A fault separates the Carrara and Bonanza King Formations here. This fault is on both sides of the road here and will be to your right all the way to Klare Spring. **Figure 6.18** shows you a close-up of an outcropping of the thin-bedded limestone of the Carrara Formation (left side of the road). This limestone was deposited in a shallow sea during Middle Cambrian time (530 My). Read about the Carrara Formation in **Appendix C-3**.

Farther and higher off of the road, we still see the steep, striped cliffs of the Bonanza King Formation.

Plants

One spring, we made an arbitrary stop here to examine what kind of plants grow here. If we had sped by at 30 mph, we would have missed seeing three types of cactus (cotton top, prickly pear, and hedgehog), Death Valley sage, desert tobacco and annuals such as prince's plume, Death Valley phacelia, golden evening primrose, and shredding evening primrose.

Desert tobacco (*Nicotiana obtusifolia*), Potato family, **Figure 6.19**, CP-NN is a perennial herb that grows up to 2-feet near the bases of cliffs and banks in canyons or washes. Often the plant appears to grow out of the canyon walls. The dark green leaves of this many-stemmed plant are also green in the fall. The white tubular flowers bloom in the spring. The Yuma and Havasupai cultivated and smoked it. It is very toxic to livestock (and people). (*Nicotiana*, refers to

Figure 6.16 Tilted Bonanza King Fm.

Figure 6.17 Bonanza King/Carrara Fms contact is to right.

Figure 6.18 Thin limestone beds of upper Carrara Fm are seen to the left. A camera lens cap was used for scale.

Figure 6.19 Desert tobacco has white tubular flowers.

Figure 6.20 Death Valley Phacelia has lavender flowers.

Jean Nicot (1530-1600) who is said to have introduced tobacco to Europe)

Death Valley Phacelia (*Phacelia vallis-mortae*), Waterleaf family, **Figure 6.20**, CP-OO is similar to Fremont's Phacelia except its flowers are all pale lavender. This annual is weak-stemmed and therefore grows in conjunction with other desert shrubs for support. Its height ranges from 8 to 24 inches. The leaves are longer than they are wide and are parted into leaflets. It is one of a number of phacelias that

Figure 6.21 The chukar is a handsome gray partridge that has adapted to the Death Valley region.

grow in the Death Valley region. (*Phacelia*, Gr., cluster; *vallis-mortae*, L., of Death Valley).

Animals

Chukar (*Alectoris chukar*, Red-legged partridge), **Figure 6.21** can be seen in large coveys in the Titus Canyon area. On numerous occasions we have seen them on the streets of Rhyolite. One April, we saw a small covey crossing the road at this location. The bird in **Figure 6.21** was a member of that covey. Chukar prefer arid mountainous areas, canyons, and grassy slopes with rock outcroppings. Chukar are not indigenous to the area. This gray partridge is native to Eastern Europe and Asia. Males and females are similar in appearance. They are gray with distinctive red legs and beaks and alternating black and white stripes on their sides. When spooked they will run, then take flight and then glide to a new location. It can also be seen singularly or in very large coveys. It is about twice the size of a Gamble's quail. As with quail, you can hear this bird calling to its compatriots. Its call is a harsh "chuk-karr." Its loud calls are easily heard and will often draw your attention to its presence long before you see this bird. If you decide to follow some Chukar, they will easily outdistance you because they may run uphill and fly downhill.

Mile 1.86/18.0 Drainage into Titus Canyon from south
N36° 50' 50.2" W117° 04' 25.9"

Geology

On the left (south) is another small drainage channel that funnels rainfall from the adjacent hills into Titus Canyon. Here and in many other places down the canyon, you see where waterfalls spill into the canyon during heavy rains. As seen in **Figure 6.22**, runoff has been inadequate to erode these smaller tributary channels to the level of the main Titus Canyon channel.

On the skyline to your left are cliffs of the Bonanza King Formation. It is separated from the Carrara Formation beneath by a fault. Up the channel, you can see the purple cliffs of the Zabriskie Quartzite faulted upward against the Carrara Formation.

Figure 6.22 Tributary channel drains rainfall from hills to the south into Titus Canyon.

Figure 6.23 Talus forms into a cone.

Figure 6.24 The middle of Carrara Fm has a distinct white band topping its Red Pass Limestone member.

The formations are in the correct stratigraphic sequence. That is, the youngest formation is the Bonanza King and it is on top. The oldest formation of the three is the Carrara and it is on the bottom. When we get to Klare Spring, we will begin to see "overturned" formations (the oldest is on top and the youngest is on the bottom).

> **Mile 2.24/18.38 Talus cone on right (north) side**
> **N36° 50' 40.5" W117° 04' 41.6"**

Here you can see talus (coarse and angular rock fragments of various sizes lying at the base of a cliff) derived by weathering of the cliffs above. Talus creep is the slow downslope movement of talus that is caused by mass wasting (gravity) and erosion (transportation) by water. Note the conical shape in **Figure 6.23**.

> **Mile 2.36/18.6 Distinct white band in Red Pass Limestone**
> **N36° 50' 38.6" W117° 04' 54.5"**

Figure 6.24 is a close-up of what you originally saw from White Pass when looking towards Thimble Peak. The middle part of the Carrara Formation is exposed here. Note the distinct, horizontal white band that extends towards Klare Spring. This "marker bed" helps to identify the top of the Red Pass Limestone member of the Carrara Formation. Beneath the white band is a darker gray band of limestone. Above the white band are slopes comprised of siltstone, dolomite, and limestone.

Because this horizontal white band or marker bed is so distinct, geologists and visitors can use it to identify these geologic units from one area to another. Recall **Figure 5.21** and our discussion on marker beds in the Titus Canyon Formation.

> **Mile 2.57/18.71—Large talus cone and cacti on left**
> **N36° 50' 34.6" W117° 04' 58.2"**

Geology

On the left (south) there is a much larger version of the talus cone we just passed. The talus consists of alluvium deposits transported downslope by streams and colluvium deposits moved downslope by gravity. Note the braided stream channels cutting though the talus cone, **Figure 6.25**. They are analogous to those we crossed on the alluvial fan of Segment 1 and illustrated in **Figure 4.1**.

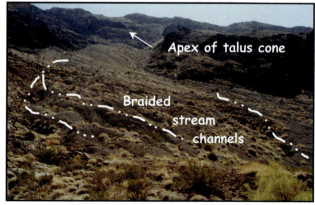

Figure 6.25 The large talus cone has braided stream channels and various cacti.

Figure 6.26 This cluster of cottontop cactus will bloom with yellow flowers in the middle of summer.

Plants

On the slopes are hedgehog, cottontop, and beavertail prickly pear cacti.

Ribbed, foot-high clusters of **Cottontop cactus** (*Echinocactus polycephalus*), Cactus family. **Figure 6.26**, CP-PP are scattered on the talus cone. This shrub (**stem succulent**) can have as many as forty to sixty heads in a cluster. At one time, a cluster on Highway 190, west of Death Valley Junction and near the 3,000-foot elevation sign, had approximately one hundred heads in the cluster. Unfortunately, the cluster has since disappeared. The name cottontop is in reference to the white tufts of cotton-like hairs that surround the yellow flowers on the top of each head. Yellow flowers do not appear until July-August, which makes them the latest blooming cacti in the region. Native Americans used the seeds for food. (*Echinocatus*, Gr., hedgehog cactus; *polycephalus*, many headed.)

> **Mile 3.06/19.20—Klare Spring, Titus Canyon fault, riparian plant community, and petroglyphs**
> **N36° 50' 28.3" W117° 05' 26.3"**

This is a very good place to stop and spend time looking around. Klare Spring supplies the water for the only riparian community on the tour, the Titus Canyon fault crosses here, the Wood Canyon Formation is exposed here, and there are nearby petroglyphs.

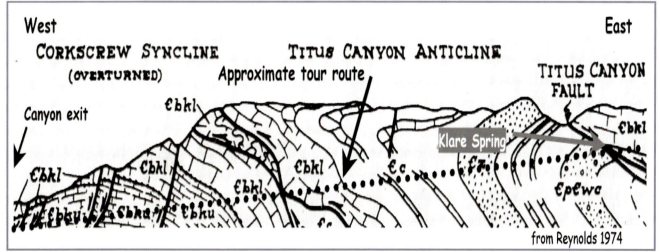

Figure 6.27 Cross section showing formations and structure along Titus Canyon tour. Note the order of formations and the Titus Canyon fault and how the anticline has rotated and produced overturned formations along the north side of the tour's route. Where: ЄpЄwc - Wood Canyon Fm, Єz - Zabriskie Quartzite, Єc - Carrara Fm, Єbki - lower Bonanza King Fm, Єbku - upper Bonanza King Fm.

Figure 6.28 Folds in Wood Canyon Formation at Klare Spring, north canyon wall.

Geology

Formations and structures to be seen as we travel down Titus Canyon

Down the canyon (west) from Klare Spring, the canyon cuts through the Wood Canyon Formation, Zabriskie Quartzite, Carrara Formation, and Bonanza King Formation. We will also get a better view of the Titus Canyon anticline, **Figure 6.27**, farther down the road. Examine and note the order of formations, the Titus Canyon fault, and how the anticline has rotated and produced overturned formations along the tour's northern roadside.

Titus Canyon Fault

From Leadfield to near Klare Spring, we have traveled in a steep-walled canyon cut mainly in the carbonate rocks of the Bonanza King Formation. The canyon widens here because we will enter the Wood Canyon Formation which erodes more easily in a desert environment than the carbonate rocks. Klare Spring issues from rocks that are faulted… the Bonanza king Formation faulted above the Wood Canyon Formation. Down canyon (west) from the spring we enter the wider channel cut into the Wood Canyon Formation. The fault is late Miocene (less than ten million years) in age and formed during Great Basin extension. The huge mass of the lower Bonanza King Formation that lies north of the road was transported from west to east along this fault. Near the spring is not a good spot to view the fault because we are too close to see it well. However, near the spring we can see some folds in the Wood Canyon Formation beneath the fault, **Figure 6.28**.

Figure 6.29 Travertine at Klare Spring indicates a previously higher location for the spring.

Travertine - Spring Deposits

The pale brown to tan rock mass, **Figure 6.29**, above and alongside the petroglyphs is travertine. It is $CaCO_3$ (calcite) similar to the limestone (also $CaCO_3$) in the surrounding Bonanza King Formation. However, unlike the limestone that was formed on a sea floor, this $CaCO_3$, called travertine, was formed by chemical precipitation from the calcite rich water from Klare Spring. Colors are usually brown, cream, or white.

Figure 6.30 Desert globemallow has grenadine or apricot petals.

Figure 6.31 Groundsel has yellow flowers and brilliant green herbage.

You can see from the height of the travertine that the spring water was once at a higher level than it is today. Travertine is common around hot springs, in limestone caves, and at springs derived from water percolating through mountains composed principally of limestone rock.

Plants

You have seen and will continue to see quite a bit of rabbitbrush in the canyon.

When **Desert globemallow** (*Sphaeralcea ambigua*), (Apricot mallow, Desert mallow), Mallow family, **Figure 6.30, CP-QQ** is in bloom, you might have noticed it from the start of the trip and with great frequency, particularly along the drive up the eastern alluvial fan in segment one of the tour. You will see this **perennial** from Klare Spring to the mouth of the canyon. We discuss it here because excellent examples of this shrub are near the spring. The flower's five petals have been described as grenadine, apricot, salmon, and reddish -orange. The stamens are a lighter color. Star-shaped hairs cover the stems and the three-lobed leaves. The lower stem and base are stiff and woody while the upper stem is more flexible. Renowned botanist Edmund Jaeger called it a "shrubby" perennial. Other sources refer to it as a perennial herb. It is aptly named. (*Sphaeralcea*, Gr., round mallow; *ambigua*, ambiguous.)

Groundsel (*Senecio mohavensis*), (Mojave groundsel, Mojave ragwort), Sunflower family, **Figure 6.31, CP-RR** grows to 18-inches. The yellow flowers are rayed and appear in mid-spring. Herbage is a bright green. This annual grows in the limey soils of washes below 3,000 ft elevation.

Figure 6.32 Pygmy cedar has dark green leaves and will bloom with small yellow flowers. With its thick, woody stems and greenish leaves, this member of the sunflower family fools many into thinking it is a juniper. It is a refreshing, definite dark green along the canyon floor or walls.

(*Senecio*, L., "old man", referring to the venerable pappus; *mohavensis*, L., of the Mojave.)

Pygmy cedar (*Peucephyllum schotti*), (Sprucebush, Desert fir), Sunflower family, **Figure 6.32** has vivid dark green needle-like leaves that are bright green even in summer. Yellow flower heads appear after a winter rain. This **shrub** grows from three to six feet high. Although it looks like a juniper, it belongs to the sunflower family. You will commonly see this plant in washes and growing from cracks in the canyon walls. (*Peucephyllum*, Gr., fir leaf; *schotti*, Arthur Schott, one of the naturalists of the Mexican Boundary Survey.)

Around Klare Spring is an isolated riparian plant community that survives due to the small, but steady flow of water from the spring. Plants such as stream orchids, cattails, and arroweed grow at this and no other location on the tour.

Figure 6.33 Stream orchids have small reddish-brown flowers.

Figure 6.34 Cattails rely on the wind to disperse their seeds.

Figure 6.35 Bighorn sheep tracks are seen at Klare Spring.

Figure 6.36 Tarantula hawk seen at the edge of Klare Spring's stream.

Stream orchids (*Epipactis gigantea*), Orchid family, **Figure 6.33, CP-SS** only occur at perennial seeps and springs. This **perennial herb** grows three feet high. Flowers are shaped like orchids, about 1-inch across, and brown-red in color. Flowers grow from the nodes (where the leaf meets the stem) of the upper leaves. The large, green leaves are very conspicuous.

Cattail (*Typha latifolia*) (Broad-leafed cattail), Cattail Family, **Figure 6.34** is another member of this riparian community that lives in marshes, ponds, and lakes (below 6,000 ft) in California, North and Central America, Eurasia, and Africa. Perhaps this **perennial herb's** most distinguishing feature is the brown pistillate stalk comprised of dense, white, hair-like seeds, which are dispersed by the wind. Youngsters have been known to call these "punks" and ignite the tip to use the smoldering "punk" to drive off insects and provide a source of entertainment.

Animals

Bighorn sheep visit Klare Spring for water. If you look around this area, you will probably see some of their scat or tracks, **Figure 6.35**. If you are trying to sight some sheep, look up above yourself and you might see some looking down at you.

Water from Klare Spring will commonly flow alongside the road. Look there for insects such as butterflies. You might see a one-inch long, orange-winged wasp, called a **Tarantula hawk** (*Hemipepsis* spp.), **Figure 6.36**. This wasp has evolved to specialize in eating tarantulas and trap-door spiders. It prowls the desert floor until it finds a tarantula's burrow and web. It then disturbs the web and the spider emerges to do battle. The Hawk stings the spider and thereby paralyzes the spider. The Hawk drags it into a burrow and lays an egg on it. The egg becomes a white larva in a few days. The larva feeds on the still living spider for approximately thirty days. The larva then pupates with the adult wasp emerging the following year.

History

Rock art

Native Americans left behind three types of rock art: pictographs, geoglyphs, and petroglyphs. Pictographs are rare in Death Valley National Park; however, geoglyphs and petroglyphs are relatively abundant.

Pictographs are rock paintings. Colors were obtained from naturally occurring materials such as hematite (an oxide of iron) for red and charcoal for black and mixed with a fluid medium such as blood or animal fat. The mix was then used to "paint" images on rock surfaces. There are a number of pictograph sites in the Death Valley region. However, you will not see any pictographs on the Titus Canyon tour.

Geoglyphs are rock arrangements or scrapings in the desert floor. Rock arrangements are cobbles or boulders arranged into straight or curved lines. Some of these can be as simple as a single straight line. Other may be arranged with many curved and straight lines, **Figure 6.37,** into a complex design whose meaning or form is not readily decipherable. Another method is to scrape the desert surface to create a design. A circle with the debris from scraping piled in the center , **Figure 6.38**, is an example. You will not see any geoglyphs on the Titus Canyon tour.

Petroglyphs are made by utilizing various tools to peck dots or scratch designs through the dark desert varnish that coats rocks. This is the rock art form seen at Klare Spring. By examining the degree of revarnishing , the relative age of petroglyphs can

> **Please do not touch or deface these artifacts**

Figure 6.37 Cobbles arranged in lines.

Figure 6.38 Legendary Southern Paiute, George Ross near circular rock scrapings.

Figure 6.39 Klare Spring petroglyphs include Desert bighorn sheep. (Photo contrast is computer enhanced.)

Figure 6.40 Additional petroglyphs include shaman (?), snakes (?), lizard (?) and geometric designs.. (Photo contrast is computer enhanced.)

mean. That is not such an easy question to answer. Petroglyphs left behind by Native Americans in one region of the country do not necessarily have the same meaning as in another region. The question of "what" they are has to be resolved before we can interpret what they mean. Explanations of what petroglyphs are include:

a) Some form of magic to provide successful hunts for game,

b) Boundary or route markers providing directions,

c) Graffiti by someone who had too much time on his hands,

d) Sites for astronomical observations during the summer and winter solstices,

e) Illustrations of myths,

f) A form of communication to record significant events, and

g) Sites of supernatural power to which shaman (priests who use magic to cure the sick, to divine the hidden, and to control events) went to obtain some of that power for themselves.

be determined. Methods for absolute age are not accurate Archaeologists have estimated that the Klare Spring petroglyphs are less than one thousand years old. Let's take a close look at what we see "engraved" in the rock. Unfortunately, Leadfield miners or later day vandals have provided some modern graffiti. The miner or vandal's graffiti will appear to be fresh (lighter colored) or completely out of place. Focusing on the petroglyphs we see what appear to be human stick figures, bighorn sheep, possibly a lizard, and a host of geometrical designs that include zigzags, diamonds or squares strung together, a nested curve, and parallel lines. Concentrate on the area depicted in **Figures 6.39** and **6.40** and count the different figures that you see. There are approximately thirty different figures, not including the modern additions such as the perpendicular line and some hippie's peace symbol.

You may be wondering what all these figures

Let's pursue the explanation that says a petroglyph site is a location of power, where a shaman came to experience a self-induced trance (tobacco weed, jimsonweed) such that he could leave this world and enter the supernatural. Shaman did this to get spirit helpers, talismans, songs, and ceremonials that gave them the power to cure illnesses, cause illnesses, make it rain, combat other shaman, cure snake bites, and so on. After the trance, the shaman would record his visions on the surrounding rocks in order to keep them for posterity and as a visual reminder to himself. The human figures might be the shaman himself, someone who the shaman was trying to help or hurt, or a spirit helper. Animal figures could be bighorn sheep for rainmaking, rattlesnakes (zigzags) for curing snakebite, or lizards for carrying messages between the shaman's world and the supernatural world. Some of the geometric designs might be some type of object headdress or bag) that the shaman saw as a source of power. Some that appear to be nothing more than geometric patterns (nested curves, parallel lines) are difficult to interpret because the shaman who recorded them may be the only one to know their meaning. Some of these geometric patterns are the types of things the shaman might see in the initial stage of his induced trance.

Miners at Klare Spring

It is said that when Leadfield was starting, an enterprising individual at Klare Spring mounted a 50-gallon drum on a platform and marked it with a sign advertising showers for twenty-five cents. Miners would stand below the pipes at the bottom of the platform while the owner would release enough water for a very brief shower. In order to increase the flowrate of water at Klare Spring, miners excavated into the rock and enlarged the opening. In January of 1926, a pipeline from Klare Spring to Leadfield was started. It had been called Hidden Spring until changed to its current name by the National Park Service.

> Mile 3.06-4.35 /19.2-20.49
> Wood Canyon Fm - A record of the transition of life forms
> N36° 50' 28.3" W117° 05' 26.3"

Geology

Exposures of the Wood Canyon Formation, **Figure 6.41**, begin at Klare Spring and continue on for another 1.3 miles until it transitions to the younger Zabriskie Quartzite. West of Klare Spring and beside the road is the lower part of the Wood Canyon Formation. Note the reddish carbonate beds higher in the formation. In the background, to the west, are the steep, rugged cliffs of the Bonanza King Formation. Typically the Wood Canyon forms monotonous dark brown or gray slopes. Because it erodes easily, the canyon is very wide where the Wood Canyon Formation crops out.

Figure 6.41 Slopes of the lower part of the Wood Canyon Fm, cliffs of the Bonanza King Fm, and traces of the Titus Canyon fault are visible at Klare Spring.

Look at **Figure 6.41**, and northward at this milestone, to see the Titus Canyon fault, a detachment fault, along which the big block of Bonanza King Formation slid eastward to overlie the deformed beds of the Wood Canyon Formation.

As we drive down (west) the Titus Canyon road, to our right (north) we first see the oldest part of the Wood Canyon Formation and progress on to younger beds of the Wood Canyon. They are "overturned". Higher up, the members are not overturned. **Figure 6.27** shows the arrangement of the formations and their beds, the Titus Canyon fault, and the Titus Canyon anticline. We will discuss the Titus Canyon anticline and why the beds are overturned at a better view, Mile 3.7.

> **Major Point:**
>
> The Wood Canyon Formation and the subsequent Zabriskie Quartzite, Carrara Formation, and Bonanza King Formation are overturned, along the road side, from Klare Spring to the mouth of Titus Canyon.

Ancient animals

The boundary between the Proterozoic and the Cambrian period is found within the Wood Canyon Formation. The boundary is scientifically defined as the change from the Proterozoic metazoan ediacaran (*first animals*) to the many and more sophisticated *first shelly and skeletal life* forms of the Cambrian. The period to the right of this boundary has been referred to as the "Cambrian Explosion". Whether this occurred as a result of a major mass extinction influenced by planet-wide environmental phenomenon or simply by natural evolution is under study. Some geologists also debate exactly where that boundary lies. It is debatable whether trilobites or soft-bodied organisms, such as found in the 500 (?) My, Burgess Shale (British Columbia), initially typify the boundary. In stratigraphic sense, the top third of the Wood Canyon Formation contains Cambrian fossils as compared to the bottom two-thirds that does not.

So, the rocks of the Wood Canyon Formation witnessed early, major paths on the evolutionary trail to today's animals. The first definite animals appeared and were replaced by the first animals with shells or skeletons. **Figure 6.42** summarizes these animal changes. Pursue this in more depth in **Boxes 6.1-6.3**.

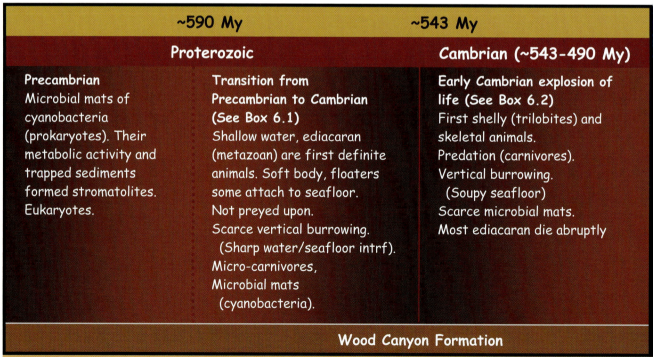

Figure 6.42 The Wood Canyon Formation witnessed dramatic changes in animal life forms.

Box 6.1 Transitioning of life forms

Long before the Wood Canyon Formation was deposited, life was dominated by prokaryotes (organisms lacking membrane bounded nuclei) called cyanobacteria. The primitive organisms left behind forms called stromatolites. Stromatolites are layered, structures formed by the trapping of sedimentary particles and precipitation of calcium carbonate in response to the metabolic activities and growth of matlike colonies of cyanobacteria and some other prokaryotes. Some stromatolites look somewhat like mushrooms when viewed from the side. When cut perpendicular to the longitudinal axis, they look like deformed concentric circles. Stromatolites are found in Precambrian rock formations in the Death Valley region. During the Late Proterozoic, the microbial mats were sharing the shallow passive margin with eukaryotes (living cell containing a nucleus enclosed within a membrane) and there was some minor burrowing on the sea floor.

During the end of the Late Proterozoic, metazoans (multicellular animals that have more than one kind of cell and have their cells organized into tissues and organisms) appeared (~700 My (?)) in shallow waters, such as the area where the Wood Canyon Formation was being deposited. These first animals were soft-bodied (no internal skeleton or external shell) and floated near or attached to the bottom. Sparse burrowing in the sea floor occurred. There were some micro-carnivores but none threatened the ediacaran. See **Box 6.2** for additional information.

Then a major change occurred in the form of the "Cambrian Explosion". It was now to become the time of the animal with the shell or skeleton. Predation blossomed and spread. Vertical burrowing, possibly in search of food and/or to avoid the predators, made the sea floor soupy. Microbial mats became scarce while new animals like trilobites flourished. The top third of the Wood Canyon contains Cambrian fossils. See **Box 6.3** for additional information.

Precambrian stromatolites from the Death Valley region include (top to bottom) side view in Crystal Spring Fm, circular pattern in Beck Spring Dolomite, and fluid vents in Noonday Dolomite.

Box 6.2 Looking back: a slice of time from the Late Proterozoic ~ 590 My

First animals-bizarre shapes existed in the seas.
(Lower part of the Wood Canyon Fm)

The region that was to become Titus Canyon was offshore from a continent that is now called Laurentia. This continent and its coastal waters were on a tectonic plate that had drifted into the southern latitudes. Earth was cooler than it is today. Inland, there was no plant or animal life, only the barren landscape and glacial ice sheets. It would be nearly another 100-million years before the first land plants would take root, 200-million years before the first amphibians crawled ashore, 400-million years before the age of dinosaurs would be in full swing, 515-million years before the age of mammals would begin, and approximately 580-million years before homo sapiens would build the Visitor Center at Furnace Creek. The continent's margin was quiet with little or no volcanic activity or earthquakes and had been both above and below the ocean waters due to rising and falling sea levels or cooling and subsidence of the continental margin. During Wood Canyon Formation deposition, the Titus Canyon area was below sea level. The seas did not teem with fish as they do today. Instead, life had recently evolved from single cell blue-green algae to multicelled life (metazoans) called Ediacaran. The ediacaran had no bones and lacked teeth or any other offensive weapons with which to attack their fellow metazoans. Some looked like jellyfish, huge blobs, fried eggs, threads, pancakes, ribbons, worms, or plantlike organisms. The sea was full of weird shapes. Some floated while others may have been attached to the bottom. A few miles away, an undersea landslide might have buried some of the ediacaran. The low oxygen content environment created by the landslide would have helped fossilize the impressions they left on the soft sediment. It would be 580-million years later that their fossils or trace fossils (marks made by an invertebrate creeping feeding, hiding, or resting in soft sediment) could be found near Titus Canyon in Boundary Canyon between the Funeral and Grapevine Mountains. One of these was a trace fossil, Cloudina, that was tube shaped and characteristic of the end of the Proterozoic eon. (After 20 My. the ediacaran, in turn, disappeared abruptly near the beginning of the Cambrian Explosion with its shelly and burrowing animals, **Box 6.3**.

 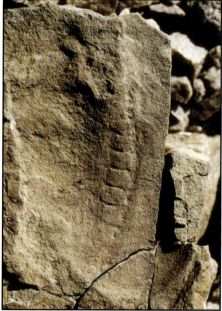

Trace fossils Cloudina (left) and Swartpuntia (right) depict life found during deposition of the lower Wood Canyon Formation, Late Proterozoic 580 My. Photos: J. W. Hagadorn

Box 6.3 Looking back: a slice of time from the Early Cambrian ~565 My

First animals with shells and skeletons

(Upper Wood Canyon Formation)

The ediacaran are no longer living in the seas. Whether or not they had been killed off in a major extinction event or evolved into the Cambrian life forms will long be debated. The Late Precambrian continent had been drifting north from its presumed location in the southern latitudes. It was not at the equator but it would reach and pass it before the end of the Cambrian. The environment started to warm up and some of the glaciers inland on Laurentia are disappearing. The land still has no plant and animal life. The Titus Canyon region had recently been above the waves but the sea level has risen so that now it was well beneath the waves. This is the beginning of the Cambrian Explosion that would yield many new life forms. In the beginning of the Cambrian Period there are invertebrate animals that are leaving behind small shelly fossils that looked like tiny tubes, spines, cones, or plates, some sponges, starfish, and many others. The upper Wood Canyon Formation would some day yield a 30-centimeter long trace fossil (Plagiogmus) of a large, soft-bodied organism that had moved within a sedimentary bed in what was to become part of nearby San Bernardino County. A trilobite came to rest on the sea floor and produced the impression for the trace fossil called Rosophycus. A 4-centimeter trace fossil would be found in the upper Wood Canyon Formation in the nearby Montgomery Mountains, Nevada. A helically coiled 2-centimeter long trace fossil, Harlaniella, formed in the Funeral Mountains. A 3-centimeter long cone-shaped fossil called Volborthella formed in the upper Wood Canyon Formation.

Plagiogmus

Volborthella

Photos: J. W. Hagadorn

Rosophycus

Harlaniella

Mile 3.64/19.78-Escarpment in young stream deposits (right)
N36° 50' 08.6" W117° 05' 53.0"

An escarpment is a cliff or steep wall created by erosion or faulting. The Titus Canyon stream channel has eroded deposits of earlier flooding events to create this escarpment ("scarp"). Note the different layers formed by abrupt changes in sediment size, **Figure 6.43**. As we pointed out at Mile 6.0, large fragments are transported by high-energy environment from heavy flooding and fine sediments are from lower energy events. How many events can you count? Can you identify any of the rock fragments? Are they angular or rounded? What difference does it make if they are rounded or angular?

Mile 4.35/20.49 - Titus Canyon anticline (right)
N36° 49' 44.8" W117° 06' 27.9"

Geology

Recumbent anticline

Park here and look northward at the big fold of the Zabriskie Quartzite striking north across the stream channel, **Figure 6.44**. It bends and turns to your right (east) to outline the recumbent anticline. Look how, in Titus Canyon, the anticline lies on its side with its axial surface dipping eastward 10-15

Figure 6.43 Eroded "scarp" defines flood events.

degrees. The overturned beds below the nose make us first view the old and then the young beds as we move down the canyon (west).

The folding in the Wood Canyon to Bonanza King Formation is evident. Note the trace of the Titus Canyon fault as it heads towards and through Klare Spring. The fault is inclined east (up canyon) and continues to the south side of the canyon. Remember, the large block of Bonanza King Formation slid eastward to overly older formations.

Look to the south (left) at the gray carbonate rocks high on the canyon wall. These carbonate rocks overly the Titus Canyon fault.

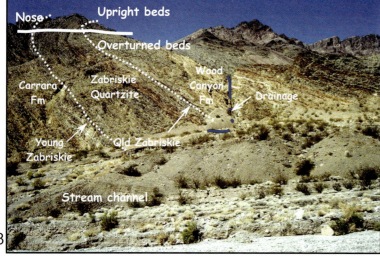

Figure 6.44
Folded Zabriskie Quartzite highlights the shape of the recumbent anticline. Beds below nose of anticline are overturned.

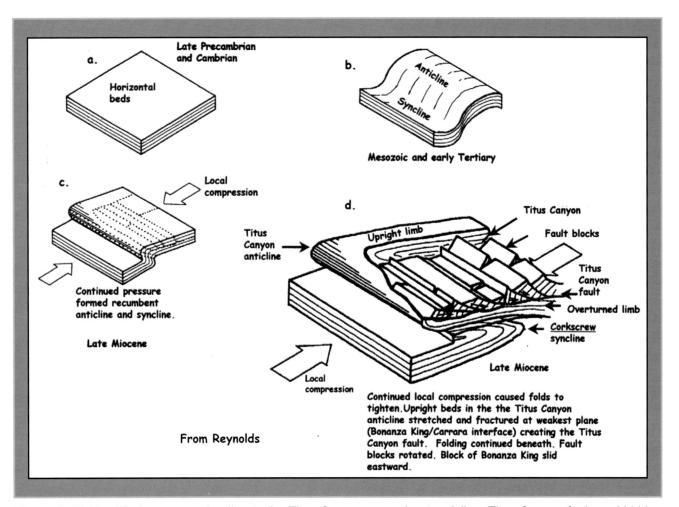

Figure 6.45 Simplified sequence leading to the Titus Canyon recumbent anticline, Titus Canyon fault, and hidden Corkscrew syncline is as follows: a) horizontal beds of Wood Canyon Fm, Zabriskie Quartzite, Carrara Fm, and Bonanza King Fm are deposited, b) beds are initially folded into broad anticline and syncline, c) extreme local folding during basin and range deformation caused the anticline to become recumbent, d) continued local compression with stretching of rock units results in tight recumbent folds and upright beds fracturing creating fault blocks and the Titus Canyon fault.

Figure 6.45 explains how the Titus Canyon recumbent anticline and Titus Canyon fault (**Figures 6.27** and **6.41**) developed. After the formations were deposited on the Precambrian and Cambrian seafloor, an anticline formed during the Mesozoic or early Tertiary. Later, likely in Late Miocene time, extreme local compression and folding during Great Basin extension, caused the anticline to lie on its side and be "recumbent." Continued compression stretched the rock units and made the recumbent anticline's folds even tighter. Stretching continued and upright beds broke along the Titus Canyon fault. The aerial view, **Figure 6.46**, provides a better overall perspective of the recumbent anticline.

Flooding events

Six ledges, (**Figure 6.47**) here mark the high water of some floods that have rampaged down Titus Canyon. Number six is the oldest preserved record of the many flooding events. The remaining ledges resulted from progressively smaller floods until we reach number 1. Ledge six also contains debris from higher surrounding cliffs.

Titus Canyon is not the place to be in the event of a summer flash flood. This should give you an appreciation for why the Rangers sometimes close Titus Canyon to visitors.

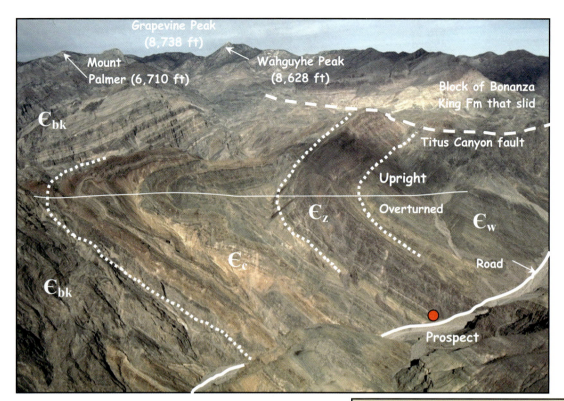

Figure 6.46 Aerial view (north) shows Titus Canyon anticline and fault.

Where:

$\mathbb{C}_w$ - Wood Canyon

$\mathbb{C}_z$ - Zabriskie Quartzite

$\mathbb{C}_c$ - Carrara

$\mathbb{C}_{bk}$ - Bonanza King

Photo by Marli Miller

Plants

Woody forget-me-not (*Cryptantha racemosa*), (bushy cryptantha), Borage family, **Figure 6.48** has small, 5-petaled, white flowers in clusters that may appear to be surrounded by hairy leaves. This **perennial herb** grows one to two feet high. There are numerous stems. Main stems are woody.

Figure 6.47 Flooding events are numbered on the south side of the canyon.

Mile 4.46-4.72/20.6-20.86 Zabriskie Quartzite
N36° 49' 42.6" W117° 06' 33.8"

Geology

At a distance, the Zabriskie Quartzite looks like nearly vertical, purple cliffs. When you get closer, the quartzite sparkles in the sun and has distinct thin beds. On even closer inspection, the observer might see trace fossils. The trace fossils look like tubes, perpendicular to the bedding, filled with light colored sand. Also present could be ripple marks. **Figure 6.49** shows the thin bedding and trace fossils found in a piece of Zabriskie Quartzite found at this location. **Figure 6.50** shows lighter colored sand filling worm burrows.

Figure 6.48 Woody forget-me-not has small white flowers surrounded by "hairy" leaves.

Mile 4.72-5.23/20.86-21.37
Carrara Formation
N36° 49' 40.9" W117° 06' 48.2"

Geology

Near the prospect on the right (north) side of the road is the contact between the older Zabriskie Quartzite and the younger Carrara Formation below, **Figure 6.51**. Once you pass the purplish outcrops of the Zabriskie Quartzite, you drive through the Carrara Formation. On the north wall of the canyon, you can clearly see the different types of rock in the Carrara. They are siltstone and limestone. There are nine members that are siltstone or limestone deposited by transgressing and regressing seas. One feature that is common in the Carrara Formation along the south wall in this canyon, are oncolites. Oncolites are algal masses that formed on the sea floor but weren't cemented to sea floor. They rolled around. Fossils of bits and pieces of trilobites, **Figure 6.52**, can be found in siltstone of the lower Carrara. Oncolites appear as dark, circular nodules in the limestone of the Carrara as can be seen in **Figure 6.53**.

See **Appendix C-2** for detail on the Zabriskie Quartzite and **Appendix C-3** for the Carrara Formation.

Figure 6.49 Purple, thin-bedded Zabriskie Quartzite has trace fossils noted by circles.

Figure 6.50 Fossilized worm burrows are found in the upper Zabriskie Quartzite.

Figure 6.51 This contact between Zabriskie Quartzite and the Carrara Formation is near a mine prospect. Beds are overturned so that the oldest Zabriskie overlies the youngest Carrara Fm.

Figure 6.52 Fossilized fragments of trilobites, "trilobite hash," are found in Carrara Fm, Titus Canyon.

Figure 6.53 These once round oncolites in the Carrara Fm. have been flattened by overburden.

Animals

Northern oriole (*Icterus galbula*) is a summer visitor who ranges over much of the U. S. The male, on the left in **Figure 6.54**, has a black back and gold breast and face with a white wing patch. The female, on the right, has a brownish back and paler gold breast.

Figure 6.54 The Northern Oriole is a summer visitor.

Mile 5.03/21.17 - Ripple marks in Carrara Fm to left
N36° 49' 40.2" W117° 07' 06.6"

Ripple marks are small ridges formed on the surface of a soft, particulate sediment layer by moving wind or water. They form perpendicular to the direction of motion. Usually, symmetrical ripple marks are caused by waves with a forward and backward motion (beach) while one-directional water currents (stream) cause asymmetrical ripple marks.

These ripple marks, **Figure 6.55**, are symmetrical. This limestone formed in a shallow marine environment. When viewed in detail with a hand lens, this limestone consists of recrystalized oolites, small fragments of fossil shells, carbonate pellets, and silt-and sand-sized carbonate and silica rock fragments. This limestone is part of the Red Pass member of the Carrara Formation.

Figure 6.55 These ripple marks were formed by waves in shallow marine environment (Carrara Fm. Titus Canyon).

Mile 5.13/21.27 Fold, fault, and contact between the Carrara and Bonanza King Fm
N36° 49' 44.2" W117° 07' 09.8"

See **Figure 6.56.**

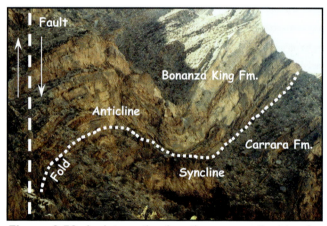

Figure 6.56 An interesting location on south side of Titus Canyon displays folding, faulting, and the contact between the Carrara and Bonanza King Fms.

Mile 5.23/21.37 - Passing from Carrara Fm to Bonanza King Fm... overturned contact
N36° 49' 42.6" W117° 07' 16.2"

Geology

At the point where the road makes a sharp left turn, we pass through the multi-colored Carrara

Formation and return to the rather dull gray, monotonous Bonanza King Formation. Here we enter the narrows cut into Bonanza King Formation. A detailed description of both formations can be found in **Appendix C-3** and **C-4**. The beds along the road are overturned.

> ### Mile 5.46/21.6 - Fold in Carrara dives beneath Bonanza King Fm
> N36° 49' 40.2" W117° 07' 30.0"

Figure 6.57 highlights how the Carrara Fm folds and dives beneath the Bonanza King Fm.

> ### Mile 5.76/21.9 - Syncline to right
> N36° 49' 32.2" W117° 07' 44.9"

> ### Mile 6.32/22.46 - Begin narrows
> N36° 49' 19.7" W117° 08' 12.4"

Geology

Near this point we drive across a poorly exposed and complex fault zone. West (down the canyon) of the fault, the canyon walls continually expose strata of the Bonanza King Formation that are overturned in a huge fold, as depicted in the previously discussed **Figure 6.27** cross section. From here to the mouth of Titus Canyon, the upper member (younger) of the Bonanza King Formation will be along the roadside while the lower member (older) will be visible high up on the canyon walls. **The strata are upside down!** Geologically speaking this is an antiformal syncline (a syncline that looks like an anticline). It is an impressive feature. Many geologists and geology students visit Titus Canyon just to see the details of this feature.

On most folds, the limbs of the fold contain small, subsidiary folds as illustrated in **Figure 6.58**. They are usually formed by slippage between bedding planes during development of the main folds. Many such parasitic folds are exposed in the canyon walls downstream from this point.

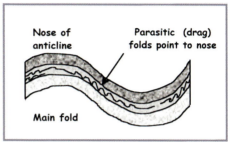

Figure 6.58 Parasitic faults are formed by slippage between bedding planes.

> ### 6.45/22.59 - Titus Canyon Stairway
> N36° 49' 21.9" W117° 08' 20.0"

Geology

Look down the canyon and you will see what looks like a tilted stairway for a giant, **Figure 6.59**. At certain times of the day, the sun makes the stairway shine. The stairway is comprised of eroded beds of the Bonanza King Formation.

Figure 6.57 Bonanza King and Carrara Formations are overturned and in fault contact. Drag folding is seen in the Carrara Formation.

133

Figure 6.59 When coming around a bend, these eroded beds of Bonanza King Fm often are seen shining in the distance. They look somewhat like a giant's stairway.

Mile 6.8/22.94 - Anticline to left
N36° 49' 12.4" W117° 08' 37.4"

Mile 7.02/23.16 - Fold in the Bonanza King Fm to left
N36° 49' 12.1" W117° 08' 49.7"

A parasitic fold, **Figure 6.60**, is on the left (south) wall of the canyon. It is in the form of an anticline that appears to plunge into the ground and lie on its side. This parasitic fold can be envisioned to be a fold within a larger fold. Per our discussion at Mile 6.3, when sedimentary beds are folded, their sides slip along each other and minor folds form within the weakest, or least "competent" bed. **Figure 6.58** illustrates folds formed within the least competent bed. Note that in **Figure 6.58** that the steep sides of the parasitic or "drag" folds point toward the nose of the anticline and away from the lowest part of the syncline.

Downstream from this point, the lower parts of the canyon walls are polished (scoured) by sediment carried through the canyon by runoff from intense rainstorms in the headwater areas. The boulder laden runoff water is a very effective erosive agent. It smoothes the walls by impact. If it is a mudflow, you can see many places where mud (usually tan) has splashed upon the canyon walls and is preserved beneath overhanging segments of the canyon wall.

Mile 7.13/23.27 - Fold and calcite to left
N36° 49' 09.5" W117° 08' 56.2"

Geology

There is a very nice parasitic fold on the left (south) side of the canyon. Also, there is a lot of white calcite ($CaCO_3$) filling what were once open spaces in the Bonanza King Formation. We are now beginning to enter the narrower part of the canyon. The canyon walls here are resistant to erosion; therefore, they are narrow.

Mile 7.21/23.35 - Mass wasting and smooth walls
N36° 49' 08.6" W117° 09' 00.7"

Geology

No, this rock fall, **Figure 6.61**, did not occur yesterday or even last week. We estimate these rocks surrendered to the force of gravity between twenty to fifty years ago. Eventually a super flood will move this material down the canyon. Note the smoothness of the left (south) wall. How far above road level are the walls smooth?

Figure 6.60 A parasitic fold in the Bonanza King Fm. appears to be an anticline lying on its side.

Mile 7.17/23.39 - Fold and fault to right
N36° 49' 09.1" W117° 09' 02.9"

Geology

On the right (north) side of the canyon we see a recumbent fold, **Figure 6.62**, with its nose pointing up canyon (east). Compression forces folded the Bonanza King Formation into an anticline, which was later laid on its sides. Note that on the lower limb, the beds are overturned. Look at the fault shown in **Figure 6.63**. Note the relative motion across the fault plane.

Mile 7.53/23.67 - "Lower narrows"
N36° 49' 13.9" W117° 09' 16.0"

Geology

At mile .4/15.6 we entered Titus Canyon's "upper narrows". Here, the canyon becomes very narrow again and we refer to it as the "lower narrows", **Figure 6.64**. This is a good location to review some interesting data about this portion of the tour. For example:

a) the strata are overturned with the older Bonanza King Fm rocks above the younger rocks,

b) the canyon is 15-40 feet wide,

c) the floor to top of the walls is as much as five-hundred feet, and

d) water has eroded and smoothed the walls forty feet above the canyon floor.

History

When the town of Leadfield was beginning, freight wagons came up from Death Valley and through the lower and upper narrows to supply the town. The road climbed 4,000 feet in the 10.8 miles from the floor of Death Valley to Leadfield. A 1926 road to Leadfield via White and Red Passes replaced the supply route thought the narrows. That newer route is the one you drove on for 16-miles to get to Leadfield.

Figure 6.61 A portion of the canyon wall has succumbed to gravity.

Figure 6.62 A recumbent fold has its nose pointing towards the east.

Figure 6.63 A vertical fault plane.

Mile 7.59/23.73 - How did these beds shift?
N36° 49' 16.1" W117° 09' 16.9"

Geology

You have seen many faults in the canyon. Try to figure out how and why the beds in **Figure 6.65** shifted to their current positions.

Mile 7.82/23.96 - Miniature Great Basin
N36° 49' 18.9" W117° 09' 28.2"

Geology

The left (south) wall shows a normal fault, **Figure 6.66** that occurs when strata are subject to tensional forces. The center portion has risen while the two sides appear to have dropped. This normal fault in the canyon wall is a miniature of what is occurring throughout the Great Basin. The Great Basin is undergoing tensional forces (extension), the cause of which is being debated. The result is mountain ranges and adjacent basins that trend northwest. A satellite view of Nevada looks like a herd of caterpillars all heading northwest. If you were to start in California and drive eastward through Nevada into Utah, you would repeatedly cross over mountain ranges (horsts) and dip down into and though basins (grabens).

Mile 7.92/24.06 - Reverse fault
N36° 49' 19.9" W117° 09' 34.6"

Geology

A reverse (thrust) fault on the left canyon wall (south) (**Figure 6.67**) is caused by compression. The hanging wall (from which a miner could hang his lamp) rises while the footwall (on which a miner could walk) drops. This is opposite of what occurs in the case of a normal fault (tension) as seen at Mile 22.3.

Although this particular fault is late Tertiary, it serves as a reminder of what occurred in this region long before then. During the Mesozoic and early Tertiary, when the west coast was subjected to tectonic forces causing subduction (oceanic plate diving under continental plate), compressive forces were transmitted inland to what was to become the Great Basin. It was not until the middle Miocene (15 My) that the Great Basin was subjected to extension (resulting from tensional forces) and the Mile 22.3 normal faulting occurred on a vast scale.

Mile 8.37/24.51 - Puzzle of the mosaics, scouring the canyon walls, and travertine
N36° 49' 16.7" W117° 09' 52.7"

Figure 6.64 Steep walls of Bonanza King Fm. rise high above the canyon floor. Note the vehicle to lower left.

Geology

This is quite an interesting area and merits getting out of your vehicle and looking around. Because the road is very narrow, park your vehicle in a manner the next vehicle coming down the canyon will be able to pass.

Canyon wall mosaics

Perhaps the first things that will catch your eye are the canyon walls, which appear to be mosaics, **Figure 6.68**. The dark, angular fragments are the carbonate rocks of the Bonanza King Formation (BK). The white is crystalline calcite (calcium carbonate). It is quite natural to immediately wonder about how the mosaic formed. Correspondence with Reynolds solved this puzzle. Study the mosaics and you will arrive at the following observations:

a) dark, angular fragments of BK appear to be suspended in the white calcite,
b) BK fragments have flat sides many of

Figure 6.65 How did the "white" bed(s) get into this arrangement?

Figure 6.66 Normal faults result from tensional forces.

    which appear like they can be fitted back together (right side of Figure 6.67),
c) BK fragments aren't heaped in a pile,
d) calcite is coarsely crystalline and does not show horizontal bedding planes,
e) and small tongues of white calcite penetrate large fragments of dark BK as if in the process of splitting them (right side of Figure 6.67).

These observations led Reynolds to think that a likely explanation is that the mosaic formed under severe stress, perhaps while an antiformal recumbent syncline was developing, when the physical state of the limestone was on the threshold between

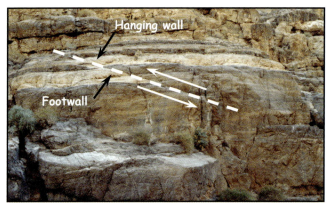

Figure 6.67 A reverse (thrust) fault caused by compressive forces.

Figure 6.68 Angular fragments of dark Bonanza King Fm are supported by white calcite to create canyon walls that resemble mosaics.

fracturing and melting with attendant material flow under extreme pressure. The host rock (BK) was fracturing concurrently with intrusion of the carbonate (calcite) derived by pressure solution of the host rock.

Scouring the canyon walls

The "cave", **Figure 6.69**, seen at the bend in the road is really not a cave in the true meaning of the word. Rather the canyon wall has been scoured out and undercut by erosion caused by debris-laden waters as they encountered this turn in the canyon. Still, it is a cool spot on a hot day.

Note how high above the canyon floor that the walls have been smoothed by erosion, **Figure 6.70**. It is another reminder of what can occur here during a flash flood. Also, note the veins of calcite intruding the Bonanza King.

Travertine

Also at this milestone, the canyon walls have some colorful travertine on the right (north) side. **Figure 6.71** shows some of the many cavities that festoon the walls and a relatively flat area of red, purple, tan, yellow, and white travertine.

Plants

You might have already spotted some **Death Valley sage** (*Salvia funerea*), (Wooly sage), Mint family, **Figure 6.72, CP-TT**, as soon as you entered Titus Canyon; however, now you should see quite a bit of it because we are in its favorite habitat of shady areas at low elevations near bases of canyon walls and hanging from cliffs. The leaves and branches are white and the leaves are spine tipped. When in bloom, this shrub is very noticeable due to the small violet-blue or purple flowers that seem to be floating in a bed of white wool. This **shrub** is found only in canyons that drain into Death Valley. It is endemic (confined naturally) to this region. (*Salvia*, L. "to save for medicine"; funerea, funeral referring to Funeral Mountains.)

We are also getting into the principal range of **desert holly** (*Atriplex hymenelytra*), Goosefoot family, (Saltbush), **Figure 6.73**. The holly is a low, rounded **shrub** that is salt tolerant so that it can grow close to saltwater basins in the valley. (Pickleweed and salt grass are plants that will grow closer to saltwater basins.). It tolerates a salt environment by excreting salt from its small leaves. The leaves resemble those of the holly you make into wreaths at Christmas time. The leaves are pale green in the spring, later a pinkish tinge, and later a silver color to better reflect the sun's rays. Its leaves also tend to remain vertical so that they avoid the sun's rays. As you would guess by now, desert holly is an extremely drought tolerant plant. (*Atriplex*, Gr. "not" + "to nourish", because it robs the soil; *hymenelytra*, Gr. membrane-covered, referring to the broad membrane like fruiting bracts.)

Figure 6.69 Erosion has undercut a canyon wall where the canyon makes an abrupt right turn.

Figure 6.70 Erosion has smoothed the surfaces high up the canyon wall. Calcite veins have intruded surrounding rock. Geologist Bennie W. Troxel provides scale and a smile.

Figure 6.71 Colorful travertine adorns the canyon walls.

Mile 8.6/24.74 - What came first...? and Signs of ancient life.
N36° 49' 18.1" W117° 10' 01.0"

Geology

What came first...?

By now you may have seen many cavities in the canyon walls filled or partially filled with travertine (**Figure 6.71** and **6.74**). Were the cavities filled with travertine before or after the area's beds were overturned? The cavities that are not completely filled with travertine provide useful information about when the area's rocks were overturned. Because partly filled cavities contain horizontal layers of travertine at the bottom of the cavities, the travertine was deposited after the rocks were overturned. The exact age of the travertine cannot be determined.

Signs of ancient life

Five hundred and twenty million years ago, below the tidal banks, shallow banks only a few meters deep, or in lagoons where the water is quiet and the bottom is carbonate mud, the marine worms burrowed, fed, and stirred up the mud sediments in a process called bioturbation. When they died, the worms soft bodies did not become fossilized. Instead this evidence of churning and stirring of the sediments is left as a mottled, variation in the color of the rocks as shown in **Figure 6.5**.

Plants

Coyote melon (*Cucurbita palmata*), (Palmleaf gourd, Coyote gourd), Gourd family, **Figure 6.76** is found on alluvial fans and washes throughout California, Nevada, and Arizona deserts. This particular specimen is anchored to the floor of the wash with one of its tendrils creeping up the Bonanza King Formation rock walls.

Figure 6.72 Death Valley sage grows along cliff walls and blooms in the spring with small purple flowers.

Figure 6.73 Desert Holly leaves resemble leaves on Christmas holly wreathes.

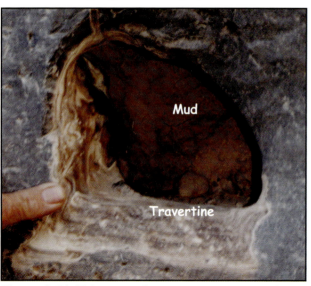

Figure 6.74 This travertine cavity is partially filled with sediments deposited during past flooding events.

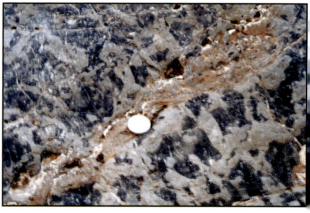

Figure 6.75 Paleozoic worms stirring ocean bottom sediments (bioturbation) caused this mottling in Bonanza King Formation.

This **perennial herb** (vine) has palmate leaves that are separated into five distinct parts. The six-petalled, yellow flowers should be familiar to gardeners who grow cucumbers or squash. The round, dull green to yellow, mottled fruit is three to four inches in diameter. According to Jaeger, the unpalatable gourds are called "coyote melons" because Native Americans said, "they are [only] good enough for coyotes". If you see some broken gourds, they were broken by rodents, which have fed on the gourds. (*Cucurbita*, L., of the gourd; *palmata*, palmate, referring to the leaf pattern.)

Arrow-leaf (*Pleurocorinis pluriseta*), Sunflower family, **Figure 6.77** can be found growing out of rock crevices in the canyon walls. This **subshrub** is weak-stemmed and intricately branched. The leaves are narrow and greenish. The discoid head has many, small whitish flowers. **Figure 6.77** shows it growing in proximity to **Death Valley sage**. (*Pleurocorinis*, Gr., side crown.)

Mile 8.71/24.85 - Canyon narrows with sculpted walls
N36° 49' 19.0" W117° 10' 05.8"

Figure 6.76 Tendril of Coyote melon creeps up canyon wall. It will bloom with yellow flowers,

Figure 6.78 Sediment laden waters have sculptured the canyon walls.

Figure 6.77 Arrow-leaf grows from rock crevices and has composite flowers or many whitish flowers in a single head.

Figure 6.79 Colorful travertine bowl has trapped rainwater.

Figure 6.78 shows sculpted walls on the right (north) side of the canyon. The canyon is very narrow with steep, high, walls comprised of erosion resistant Bonanza King Formation. Because the road is so narrow here, you will have difficulty providing room for a down-canyon (west) motorist.

```
Mile 9.04/25.17 -
Titus Canyon "washbasin"
N36° 49' 26.0"  W117° 10' 16.5"
```

Geology

On the left (south) wall of the canyon, there is a "washbasin", **Figure 6.79,** It is eroded travertine creating a bowl-like depression. Rainwater sometimes fills this depression giving it the look of an expensive, marble washbasin. The manner in which the layers of travertine have been eroded leaves colorful and intriguing patterns in the "washbasin.

Plants

Desert rocknettle (*Eucnide urens*), (Stingbush, Desert bush nettle), Loasa family, **Figure 6.80**, is a **subshrub** that grows two-feet high and spreads along the canyon floor and ledges. There are long sharp bristles on stems and leaves. The flowers are pale

Figure 6.80 Desert rocknettle's bristle laden leaves and creamy white flowers can be seen along the canyon walls and floor.

Figure 6.81 The Titus Canyon mouth is a "wineglass" and provides a view across Death Valley.

yellow with a greenish tinge. The plant grows at the base of canyon cliffs in alluvial gravels and from cracks in the canyon walls. It is quite profuse in Titus Canyon. Despite the bristly armament on the leaves and stems, bighorn sheep feed on it. (*Eucnide*, GR., true sea-nettle; L., *urens*, burning or stinging.)

> **Mile 9.24/25.38 - Mouth of Titus Canyon**
> **N36° 49' 19.7" W117° 10' 24.8"**

The mouth of the canyon is an exit for us. For hikers who have left their vehicles in the nearby parking lot, it is an entrance.

Geology

The mouth of the canyon, **Figure 6.81**, provides an excellent view across Death Valley to the Cottonwood Mountains and their alluvial fans.

The strata at the mouth of Titus Canyon have been overturned through 210-degrees down toward the valley, yet within a mile north of here (near Fall Canyon), the strata are upright again.

The mouth of Titus Canyon is a large example of a feature common to many canyons on the east side of Death Valley, especially between here and Shoreline Butte many miles to the south. The narrow canyon mouth forms the stem of a typical wine glass, the wide upper walls form the bowl, and the alluvial fan forms the base. This giant Titus Canyon wineglass must be seen from the air. Small canyons south of Natural Bridge Canyon on

Figure 6.82 Afternoon sun highlights the shape of a wineglass canyon south of Natural Bridge. Titus Cyn. is also a wine glass but not as dramatic.

Highway 175 (south of Furnace Creek, north of Badwater) provide excellent examples, **Figure 6.82**, of wineglass canyons and can easily be seen from the roadside. The stem is indicative of rapid uplift while the bowl indicates slow or no uplift.

> **Mile 9.24/25.38 to 11.9/28.0 - Down the western alluvial fan**

Geology

The **Figure 6.83** aerial view affords us the opportunity to make some pertinent observations.

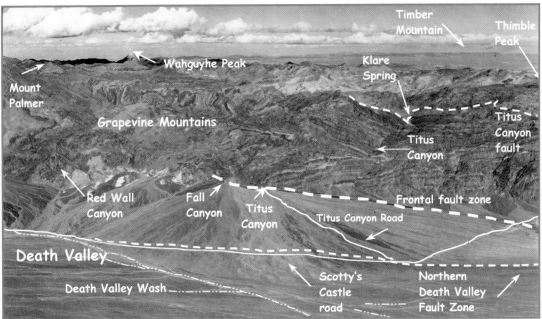

Figure 6.83 This aerial view (looking east) of the Grapevine Mountains shows the mountains, canyons, faults, and other features Surrounding Titus Canyon.

Photo by John H. Maxson

In the text we discussed Great Basin extension and how, as a result, mountains rose and valleys fell. Extension has been going on in the Death Valley region for approximately 15 My. Mountains continue to rise and valleys continue to fall…even today! As you drive down the fan, stop, and look back (east) at the steep and rugged western face of the Grapevine Mountains. The steep face is a fault escarpment ("scarp") along which the range has risen as much as **8,000 feet** relative to the valley floor in the last five million years. **Figure 6.82** identifies the frontal fault zone along which this **vertical motion** is occurring.

Figure 6.83 also identifies the northern Death Valley fault zone. Movement on this fault is right lateral meaning that when you are standing on one side of the fault, everything on the other side is shifted relatively to the right. Movement along this fault zone has been occurring since the middle Cenozoic (~30 My). Evidence of Quaternary (0 to 2 My) faulting is seen along the west front of the Grapevine Mountains. Estimates of total lateral motion or offset occurring since the middle Cenozoic range from a **few miles to scores of miles**.

The alluvial fans of Titus, Fall, and Red Wall Canyons record the amount of material that flowed through the canyons. The largest and oldest fan comes from Fall Canyon. The surface material also records the rock types that are exposed in the canyons' drainage area. The size, degree of rounding, and distance from the mountain front or source of the rock material, are a record of the energy required to transport the material. Note the braided stream pattern in **Figure 6.82**. Walk on the fan and note the different rocks washed down from the various formations in the Grapevine Mountains. Can you identity some of the rocks?

Plants

Desert fivespot (*Eremalche rotundifolia*), (Falsemallow, Lantern flower, Chinese lantern), Mallow family, **Figure 6.84, CP-UU** is one of the prettiest **annual** flowers in the region. It grows at lower elevations in washes and bajadas. Its leaves are round and purplish red. The 5-petaled flower is shaped like a globe and is rose pink to lilac with a red spot near the base of each petal. (*Eremalche*, Gr., lonely mallow; *rotundifolia*, L., round-leaved.)

Gravel ghost (*Atrichoseris platyphylla*) (Tobaccoweed, Parachute plant), Sunflower family, **Figure 6.85, CP-VV** grows to two-feet high. Its leaves are broad, bluish, brown spotted, and at the base of this **annual**. The flower is white with purplish tinge on the ends of the petals, is about 1-inch wide, has many petals that are saw-toothed on their ends, and has a vanilla-like aroma. The flower is perched atop a slender, erect, leafless stem that makes it appear like a ghost or a parachute floating above the gravel. Tobacco-like leaves lie flat on the ground (basal). Gravel ghost grows in desert valleys and washes. (*Atruchoseris*, Gr., chicory like plant; *platyphylla*, Gr. wide-leaved.)

Figure 6.84 Desert fivespot has five lavender petals each of which has a distinct red spot near the stem.

Figure 6.85 Gravel ghost "floats" above the sands. Flowers have white petals yellowing toward the stem.

Figure 6.86 View southeast, shows Northern Death Valley fault zone (right lateral).

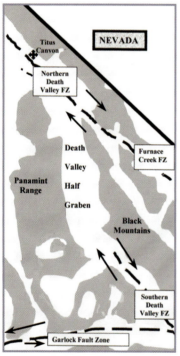

Figure 6.87 There are major faults in the Death Valley region

Figure 6.87. This fault zone is one of a number of faults in the region. **Figure 6.86** identifies some of the other major faults.

Look at **Figure 6.83** and then look eastward and try to identify a) the frontal fault scarp, b) the upright rocks of the Bonanza King Formation that slid eastward, along the Titus Canyon fault, and covered the overturned rocks of the Titus Canyon anticline and c) the steep alluvial fans. Note how the mouth of Titus Canyon has been lost to view along the range front.

Plants

Note the mesquite that grows in the washes and anchors the dunes in the alkali sink. This plant is a "champion". Measured at over 200 feet, they have the longest root system of any desert plant.

Animals

The coyote (*Canis latrans* [*barking dog*]), **Figure 6.87** is just as likely to be seen walking along a highway as in Titus Canyon. If you see a coyote alongside the road, do not feed the coyote. An adult coyote is twenty-six inches high at the shoulder and if measured from the tip of its nose to the black tip on its

---

Mile 28 - Death Valley Fault…end of tour

N36° 47' 18.3" W117° 11' 28.8"

Geology

Here we cross the northern Death Valley fault zone. Recent faulting is evident at this junction with Scotty's Castle road (**Figure 6.86**) and as shown in

tail it might reach five feet. Weight in the Death Valley region would be twenty-five to thirty-five pounds. In the winter, coyotes grow heavy coats that make them look larger then they really are. In the summer, they shed fur. The coat is reddish gray, the legs, feet, and ears are trimmed in rust, and the under parts are whitish. The female has a litter of four to eight pups in April to May. Often coyotes run in loosely knit packs but do not have the teaming skill of their larger cousins, wolves. They have a widely varied diet that includes rabbits, rodents, insects, fruit including mesquite beans, and anything else they can catch or find that is edible. More often than not, the scat he leaves behind will contain vegetable matter, particularly seeds or seedpods from mesquite trees.

Figure 6.88 Coyotes can be seen watching passing motorists on Scotty's Castle road.

Appendices

A - Formations and major geologic events in the development of Death Valley

B - Native animals common to Death Valley

C - In Greater Depth...

    C-1 Wood Canyon Formation

    C-2 Zabriskie Quartzite

    C-3 Carrara Formation

    C-4 Bonanza King Formation

    C-5 Titus Canyon Formation

    C-6 Miocene Volcanics

    C-7 Late Eocene Fauna in the Titus Canyon area

A - Formations and major geologic events in the development of Death Valley

Era (My)	Period/Epoch	[1] Unit/Thick. (ft)	Major Events
Cenozoic 0-66	Quaternary — Holocene Epoch (0.0-0.1)	Surface Deposits – 100'	Topography is shaped by Great Basin extension producing mountains, valleys, and volcanoes; right lateral plate motion; and erosion.
	Quaternary — Pleistocene Epoch (.01-2.)	Surface Deposits – 2000'	
		Funeral Fm – 1000'	
	Tertiary — Pliocene Epoch (2-5)	Funeral Fm	
	Tertiary — Miocene Epoch (5-24)	Copper Canyon – 10000' / Furnace Creek-5000' / Artist Drive-5000'	Transition to DV extension and lateral plate movement begins approximately 16-15 My
	Tertiary — Oligocene Epoch (24-34)	Titus Canyon Fm-3000'	
	Tertiary — Eocene Epoch (34-58) - Paleocene Epoch (55-66)	Deposits lost to erosion	
Mesozoic 66-245	Cretaceous Period (66-144)	Erosion removed DV Mesozoic deposits except for granitic plutons	As a result of subduction throughout Mesozoic and Early and Middle Cenozoic, DV region sees thrust faulting and rhyolitic arc volcanics
	Jurassic Period (144-206)		
	Triassic Period (208-248)	Butte Valley Fm – 8000'	Transition from passive margin to subduction during Triassic
Paleozoic 245-570	Permian Period (248-290 My)	2) Owens Valley-2000'	UNCONFORMITY. DV region is underwater on a "passive continental margin" in a marine environment, with rising and falling shallow seas. Extensive carbonate deposits. DV is above sea level during middle Ordovician when the Eureka Quartzite was deposited.
		2) Tihvipah Fm-200'	
		2) Keeler Canyon Fm-300'	
	Pennsylvanian Period (290-323 My)	2) Keeler Canyon Fm / Resting Spring Shale-750'	
		Lee Flat Limestone-650'	
	Mississippian Period (323-354 My)	Perdido Fm-350'	
		Tin Mt. Limestone-1000'	
	Devonian Period (354-417)	Lost Burro Fm-2000'	
		Hidden Valley Dol. 1000'	
	Silurian Period (417-443)	Hidden Valley Dolomite	
	Ordovician Period (443-490)	Ely Springs Dolomite-700'	
		Eureka Quartzite-350'	
		Pogonip Group-1500'	
	Cambrian Period (490-543)	Nopah Fm-1300'	
		Bonanza King Fm-1000'	
		Carrara Fm-1000'	
		Zabriskie Quartzite-150'	
		Wood Canyon Fm-2500'	Continental rifting results in DV region being in a marine environment by early Cambrian
Proterozoic – Eon 570-2500	Precambrian Period (543-2500) Upper (Late) (800-543)	Wood Canyon Fm	Rifting of Rodinia begins in late Proterozoic
		Stirling Quartzite-2000'	
		Johnnie Fm-4000'	
		Ibex Fm-1000'	
		Noonday Dolomite-1000'	
	Middle (1600-800)	Kingston Peak Fm- 200-3000'	UNCONFORMITY. Glaciers
		Beck Spring Dolomite- 1000'	
	Lower (Early) (2500-1600)	Crystal Spring Fm- 200-3000' / Crystalline Basement	DV Region on continent of Rodinia

Archaen (3800-2500) and Hadean (4600-3800) eons. No rocks of these eras found in DV

1) Thicknesses are only representative. 2) Not on passive margin, NE DEVA.

B - Native animals common to Death Valley

Mammals (50)

13-Bats (California Myotis, Western Pipistrelle, Hoary Bat, Silver-Haired Bat, Western Red Bat, etc.)

3-Rabbits (Nuttal's Cottontail, Desert Cottontail, Jackrabbit)

12-Mice (Great Basin Pocket, Desert Pocket, Brush, Deer, Canyon, Piñon, Cactus etc.)

6-Rats (Desert Woodrat, Bushy-Tailed Woodrat, Desert Kangaroo Rat, Panamint Kangaroo Rat, etc.)

4- Ground Squirrels (White Tailed Antelope, California, Round Tailed, and Mojave)

3-Carnivores (Mountain Lion, Bobcat, Desert Shrew)

4-Omnivores (Coyote, Badger, Kit Fox, Gray Fox)

4-Herbivors (Nelson Bighorn Sheep, Mule Deer)

Others: Panamint Chipmunk, Porcupine, Ringtail

Birds (100's)

There are hundreds of birds that range from rare and irregular visitors (accidental or not seen in some years) to birds that are common for their appropriate season and habitat. Common birds include: Mallard and American Widgeon Ducks, Pied-Billed Grebe, Turkey Vulture, Red-Tailed Hawk, Gamble's Quail, Chukar, Roadrunner, Poorwill, White-Throated Swift, Western Kingbird, Ash-Throated Flycatcher, Say's Phoebe, Violet-Green Swallow, Tree Swallow, Barn Swallow, Cliff Swallow, Common Raven, Mountain Chickadee, Plain Titmouse, Rock Wren, American Robin, Starling, House Sparrow, Western Meadowlark, Yellow-Headed Blackbird, Red Winged Blackbird, Brewer's Blackbird, House Finch, Savannah Sparrow, White Crowned Sparrow.

Reptiles (38)

Desert Tortoise

17-Lizards and Skinks (Desert Iguana, Chuckwalla, and Zebra-Tailed, Collared, Leopard, Whiptail, Alligator, etc. Lizards)

19-Snakes (Panamint Rattlesnake, Mojave Rattlesnake, Mojave Desert Sidewinder, and Constrictors (California King Snake, Great Basin Gopher Snake, Rosy Boa, Desert Night Snake, etc.))

Fish (6)

5-Pupfish (Amargosa, Saratoga, Devil's Hole, Salt Creek, and Cottonball Marsh)

Western Mosquito Fish, Snails

Insects

Harvester Ants, Scorpions, Tarantulas, Termites, Grasshoppers, Bees, Butterflies, Moths, Beetles, etc.

Ila Ross photo

Tabular data derived from DEVA NPS Website. *Lengner photos*

C - In Greater Depth…

C-1 The Wood Canyon Formation

What is the Wood Canyon Formation?

In the Titus Canyon region, the Wood Canyon Formation is approximately twenty-nine hundred feet thick. It is comprised of two carbonate members, a conglomerate quartzite member, and three siltstone and quartzite members. It grades into the Zabriskie Quartzite above it and is separated from the Stirling quartzite below it by a fault. The order in which these members were deposited can be seen in the accompanying sketch. Nolan applied the name "Wood Canyon" to outcroppings in the Spring Mountains in 1929. Mitchell W. Reynolds geologically mapped and studied the Titus and Titanothere Canyon region in the 1960's.

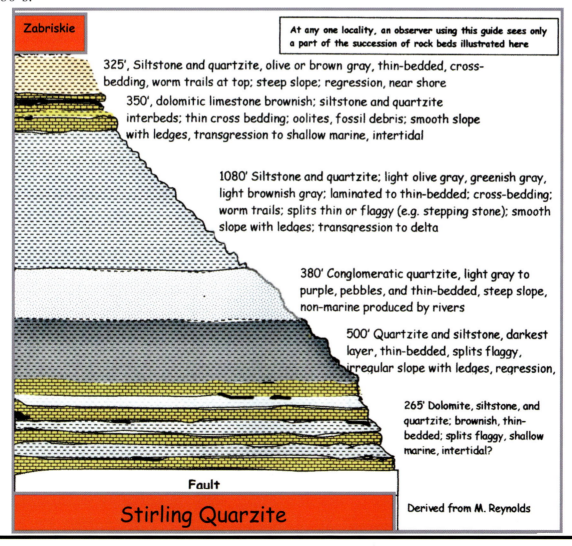

Derived from M. Reynolds

Wood Canyon Formation

How can you identify the Wood Canyon Formation?

Looking at the Wood Canyon Formation as a whole, you can see that it slopes and is quite unlike the steep walled Bonanza King Formation. The Wood Canyon Formation is more easily eroded than the Bonanza King Formation; hence, it forms the wider part of the canyon. It does not have the very distinct stripes or bands of the light and dark Bonanza King Formation; however, the composition of its members vary so you will see some color variations. The two carbonate members are a yellow brown and form ledges. The upper carbonate member has scolitus (wormlike trace fossils that appear to be narrow, vertical, straight tubes), oolites and fragments of fossilized trilobites, brachiopods, and pelmatozoans. The conglomeritic member is near the center of the formation, contains rounded pebbles, and forms a light gray slope. Study the preceding sketch for details.

Where can you find the Wood Canyon Formation?

In the Titus Canyon region, it extends from Klare Spring west for about a mile and a half and southeast from Thimble Peak. It is also found in the Nopah and Resting Spring Ranges, Funeral Mountains, the Panamint and Argus Ranges, southern Last Chance Range, other parts of the Grapevine Mountains, and southwest Great Basin.

What is the origin of the Wood Canyon Formation?

We know that the formation was deposited from the late Precambrian though the early Cambrian and that it spanned the timeframe in which life took a new and more complicated form. During the deposition of the Wood Canyon Formation, the Titus Canyon area was on a shallow continental margin. Sea levels would transgress or regress depending on glacial events and margin subsidence. The depositional environments included fluvial (river), delta, and shallow marine. For the majority of the time, the Wood Canyon deposits accumulated in a near shore environment with a terrigenous source. See the preceding sketch of the Wood Canyon Formation.

C-2 The Zabriskie Quartzite

What is the Zabriskie Quartzite?

In the Titus Canyon region, the Zabriskie Quartzite is about eight hundred and thirty feet of quartzite. It is not subdivided into members. It grades into the Carrara Formation above and the Wood Canyon Formation below. It was originally named for some crops out in the Resting Spring Range by Hazard (1937) and later raised to formation status by Wheeler (1948) when he determined it was widespread.

How can you identify the Zabriskie Quartzite?

It is between the Wood Canyon Formation on the bottom and the Carrara Formation on the top. It weathers a dark reddish-brown or purplish but when broken up by a fault, it is white or pink. It is course to fine grained with well-rounded grains. Bedding is laminated or very thin with some cross bedding. It splits flaggy, forms ledges, and is more erosion resistant then the Wood Canyon Formation beneath it. There are no fossils; however, there are worm-like trace fossils that look like tubes filled with finer sediments are found in the lower 110 feet of the formation. Current (symmetrical) ripple marks are found in the top of the formation. Along the road in Titus Canyon, the quartzite is overturned.

Where is the Zabriskie Quartzite?

It is found in the Grapevine and Funeral Mountains, Panamint, Resting Spring, and Nopah Ranges, and the Nevada Test Site. In the Titus Canyon region, it is found southeast of White Pass, behind (west) Leadfield below the Bonanza King and Carrara Formations, beneath Thimble Peak, and 1.3 to 1.6 miles down (west) the road from Klare Spring.

When and what is the origin of The Zabriskie Quartzite?

The Zabriskie Quartzite was deposited on a broad, shallow continental margin during the Early Cambrian approximately five hundred and forty million years ago. The environment was intertidal or lower where currents could sweep the sand into symmetrical ripple marks.

Purplish, thin-bedded Zabriskie Quartzite has a fine sandpaper like texture and where fractured sparkles with pin pricks of light.

C-3 The Carrara Formation

What is the Carrara Formation?

Cornwall and Kleinhampl first used the name "Carrara" in 1961. It comes from an abandoned town, south of Beatty, that owed its temporary existence to a marble quarry. The Carrara Formation's upper sixty percent is primarily limestone and the lower forty percent is primarily siltstone. It can be divided into nine members that represent the transition from Early Cambrian continental quartzitic sedimentation to Middle Cambrian marine carbonate sedimentation. The accompanying sketch depicts the Carrara Formation. It is derived from Reynolds' map and measured section data from Titanothere Canyon. The following sketch is not to scale. Remember the Carrara Formation along the roadside from Klare Spring is overturned and faulted. It is 1,560 feet thick.

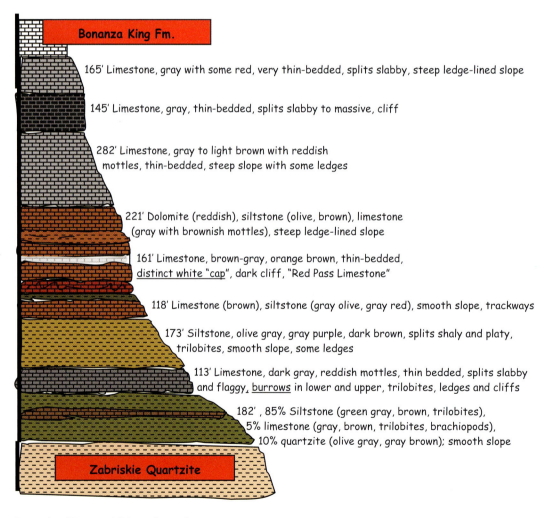

Bonanza King Fm.

165' Limestone, gray with some red, very thin-bedded, splits slabby, steep ledge-lined slope

145' Limestone, gray, thin-bedded, splits slabby to massive, cliff

282' Limestone, gray to light brown with reddish mottles, thin-bedded, steep slope with some ledges

221' Dolomite (reddish), siltstone (olive, brown), limestone (gray with brownish mottles), steep ledge-lined slope

161' Limestone, brown-gray, orange brown, thin-bedded, distinct white "cap", dark cliff, "Red Pass Limestone"

118' Limestone (brown), siltstone (gray olive, gray red), smooth slope, trackways

173' Siltstone, olive gray, gray purple, dark brown, splits shaly and platy, trilobites, smooth slope, some ledges

113' Limestone, dark gray, reddish mottles, thin bedded, splits slabby and flaggy, burrows in lower and upper, trilobites, ledges and cliffs

182', 85% Siltstone (green gray, brown, trilobites), 5% limestone (gray, brown, trilobites, brachiopods), 10% quartzite (olive gray, gray brown); smooth slope

Zabriskie Quartzite

Mapped in Titus and Titanothere Canyons
by Mitchell Reynolds

Sketch – Carrara Formation – 1560 feet

How can you identify the Carrara Formation?

It is between the distinctly striped and banded Bonanza King Formation and the dark reddish-brown Zabriskie Quartzite.

The upper sixty percent is primarily limestone so it supports either cliffs or very steep, ledge-lined slopes that are shades of gray. It contains trilobite fossils. Some reddish siltstone is present and forms intervals in the limestone. The lower middle of the Carrara is one hundred and sixty feet of limestone named the Red Pass Limestone (for the Red Pass you encountered on this tour). It is capped by a distinctive twelve-foot thick light gray bed, has reddish brown coloration in the bottom fifty-five feet, and has oolites. It reflects the time when the depositional environment had transitioned to primarily shallow marine. The lower forty percent has primarily siltstone that forms generally smoother slopes than the upper part of Carrara Formation. Slopes are an olive or brownish except for one gray limestone bed just above the basal siltstone. That limestone forms ledges and has abundant burrows. Siltstone above that limestone has trilobites and trackways and burrows. The base of the Carrara Formation grades into the top of the Zabriskie Quartzite. Do not forget that along the road in Titus Canyon, the Carrara Formation is overturned.

Where can you find the Carrara Formation?

The Carrara Formation is widespread in the Titus and Titanothere Canyon region. At White Pass we could see the Carrara beneath Thimble Peak. Looking south at the eroded anticline in Titanothere Canyon, we saw the Carrara again. It is southwest of Leadfield beneath the Bonanza King Formation. We see it in Titus Canyon after we passed through the Zabriskie Quartzite. There will be a thin slice of Carrara inside the Bonanza King Formation farther down the road.

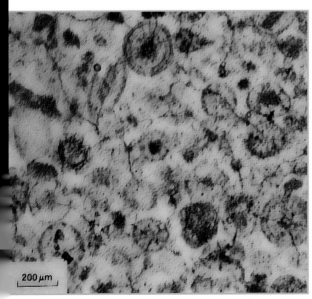

Photomicrograph of Oolites, Red Pass Limestone, Titanothere Canyon

Olenllus gilberti
Early Cambrian

Glossopleura Walcotti
Middle Cambrian

**Trilobite Fossil Fragments
Carrara Fm., Titanothere Canyon**

Photos USGS Professional Paper 1047

What is the origin of the Carrara Formation?

The Carrara Formation was deposited from the Early Cambrian into the Middle Cambrian (515 to 540 million years ago).

The lower portion of Carrara, from its base to the base of its Red Pass Limestone member, was dominantly derived by erosion of continental sediment that resulted in siltstone. The region was in shallow water as shown by the burrowing animal trackways. There were cycles of transgressing and regressing seas. When the seas transgressed toward the inner part of the North American continent, limestone deposits accumulated.

The Middle Cambrian deposits of the Carrara marked a change back to a dominantly shallow marine environment (e.g. Zabriskie Quartzite depositional environment). In other words, the upper part of Carrara (above the Red Pass Limestone) is dominated by carbonate rocks (limestone). The oolites in the Red Pass limestone attest to a shallow, agitated, marine environment.

What are oolites and why should I care?

They are distinctive, generally round carbonate particles formed where strong tidal currents flood the tidal banks everyday. They are spherical shaped grains of calcium carbonate (CaCO3) that are made up of concentric layers surrounding a nucleus like the structure of an onion. The nucleus gets coated with layers of calcium carbonate as the tides bring in cold ocean water that becomes supersaturated with calcium carbonate as it warms and evaporate on the shallow banks. Currents keep the grains rolling in the bottom or suspended in the water thereby coating them evenly on all sides as calcium carbonate precipitates from the warm water. The limit to growth of the oolites is determined by the maximum grain size that can be moved by the currents.

Arthropod feeding trail, Carrara Fm., siltstone below Red Pass Limestone, Titanothere Canyon

Hook shaped horizontal burrow, Carrara Fm., Siltstone below Red Pass Limestone, Titanothere Canyon

Photos USGS Professional Paper 1047

C-4 The Bonanza King Formation

What is the Bonanza King Formation?

The Bonanza King Formation is roughly 3600-feet thick. It is comprised of primarily carbonate (CO3) rocks. More specifically, the formation consists of interbedded limestone and dolomite with occasional sediments from the continent. Limestone is calcite (calcium carbonate, $CaCO_3$) and can be formed in quite a number of ways. Dolomite ($CaMg(CO_3)_2$) formed from limestone interacting with magnesium rich waters.

How can you identify the Bonanza King Formation?

It is the only formation that you see on this trip that beds that appear to be stripes that are different shades of gray and occasionally some shades of brown. The difference in colors results from impurities in the limestone or dolomite. Both limestone and dolomite can be different colors.

The Nopah Formation overlies the Bonanza King Formation, can be seen on the range front south of the mouth of Titus Canyon, and has very similar, but much thicker, color bands. The Bonanza King conformably overlies the upper Carrara Formation that is very similar in appearance.

The Bonanza King Formation weathers to form rugged, steep cliffs because it's limestone and dolomite are resistant to erosion in the dry desert environment. Dolomite is slightly more resistant and may appear to bulge outward or form ridges when interbedded with limestone. The lower third of the formation appears mottled. Its texture is finely to coarsely crystalline. Also, it may be very thinly bedded.

Where will you see the Bonanza King Formation?

We have seen the formation at a number of tour locations including the drainage into Titanothere Canyon, atop Thimble Peak, in the megabreccia, and on the striped, bent mountainside west of Leadfield. While we are in Titus Canyon, it will be alongside the road or in plain view in the surrounding hills for much of trip through the canyon. It is the most widespread formation in the southern Grapevine Mountains. It is found throughout Death Valley National Park and the southwestern Great Basin.

Thin beds in the Bonanza King Formation

What is the origin of the Bonanza King Formation?

It was deposited in the Middle to early Late Cambrian (~530 to 515 million years ago) above (after) the Carrara Formation and below (before) the Nopah Formation. The region was on passive continental margin covered by a warm, shallow sea, saturated with calcium carbonate. The seas transgressed and regressed due to glacial events and/or subsidence (sinking of the continental margin as it cooled). The major source of the Bonanza King limestone stems from a time when the depositional environment was offshore, slightly farther than the intertidal zone and hence, calm waters. The source of the calcite was algae (kelp, seaweed) that produced the calcite. A muddy calcite seafloor resulted in limestone that was finely textured and thinly bedded. When the seas retreated, an intertidal environment could result and yield stromatolites and thin limestone beds. If the depositional environment were closer to the shoreline, a coarser limestone would result. The mottling found in the lower portion of the BK is due to seafloor creatures that burrowed and tunneled their way through the mud. This process is called "bioturbation".

Striped beds of the Bonanza King Formation

C-5 The Titus Canyon Formation (~37-15 My(?))

Vitric Tuff

Unconformity

Green conglomerate facies
Primarily composed of well-rounded pebbles and cobbles of previous rocks (e.g. granite, Paleozoic carbonate rocks, rhyolite, silica). Beds six inches to four feet.

Some tuffaceous sandstone, limestone, and tuff beds.

Color is greenish gray to light brown. Columnar jointing and spheroidal weathering of some outcrops.

Conspicuous white to yellow crystal lithic tuff layer in the middle is a marker bed.

Unconformably overlies variegated facies.

(Crystal lithic tuff)

Unconformity

Change from rivers and lakes to rivers and increased volcanic activity.

Variegated facies
A diversity of appearance due to variety of colors and composition.

Pale red, reddish brown, yellow orange, light green. Pale and brick red dominate near top.

Siltstone, mudstone, marl, sandstone, conglomerate, limestone. Conglomerate (well rounded and fractured, quartzite, chert, carbonates quartz) and sandstone most prevalent.

Lower portion is where titanothere three-toed horse, rodent, oreodont and other fossils have been found.

Conformably overlies sedimentary breccia.

Sedimentary breccia facies
Angular fragments of earlier carbonate rocks. Pale red or yellow siltstone matrix. Bedded. Interfingers with variegated facies.

Megabreccia
Large fragments (few inches to hundreds of feet) form breccia comprised of single lithology (Bonanza King Formation). Black, dark gray.

Unconformity — 470 million year gap in sedimentary rock record in Titus Canyon

PALEOZOIC: Bonanza King or Carrara Formations unconformably underlie megabreccia and Titus Canyon Formation.

Reference: Reynolds

What is the Titus Canyon Formation?

In 1935, Stock and Bode first applied the name "Titus Canyon Formation" to some of the colorful sedimentary rocks in the region. They performed preliminary mapping of the formation as part of their primary task of finding, excavating, and studying fossils found in the lower Titus Canyon Formation. Years later, as part of his mapping of the Titus and Titanothere Canyon region, Reynolds redefined the Formation to be sedimentary and volcanic rocks which lie unconformably atop either the Paleozoic Bonanza King or Carrara Formations and which lie unconformably below Miocene volcanic rocks. That definition yields a formation that varies in thickness from approximately 1,800 (upper Titanothere Canyon) to 2,600 feet (Leadfield). The rock records immediately before and after the Titus Canyon Formation have been lost to the ravages of weathering and erosion. Reynolds divided the Formation into four groups or facies. Three of the four are illustrated in the accompanying sketch and will be discussed further herein. The fourth is not seen on this tour because it is exposed only in the West Fork of Titus Canyon.

How can you identify the Titus Canyon Formation?

The green conglomerate facies is greenish gray, pale green, and gray-brown north and east of Leadfield. It is light brown to gray orange in the upper part of Titanothere Canyon that is west of White Pass and along the road. In the center of the green conglomerate facies there is a fifty to hundred foot thick bed of white to yellow-gray, crystal lithic tuff. This acts as a marker and should draw your attention. There are well-rounded pebbles and cobbles (Paleozoic, granite, rhyolitic, silicic, etc. rocks) with some boulders to twenty inches. Some outcrops display columnar jointing or spheroidal weathering.

The variegated facies derives its name from the multiple colors and rock types that give it anything but a homogeneous appearance. Refer to the accompanying figure. Colors are mostly reds, yellows, and greens. There are some orange and gray colors seen. The upper part has some red and brick red. Conglomerate beds have medium to coarse pebbles and cobbles that are well rounded with some fractures. The various beds of sandstone, marl, limestone etc. weather differently. The marl forms knobby ledges while the limestone forms steep ledges.

The sedimentary breccia facies contains rocks of various lithologies and it is bedded. Clasts are angular to subrounded and from an eighth of an inch to eight inches in size. A pale red-yellow matrix loosely cements the clasts.

Where can you find the Titus Canyon Formation?

Besides in the Titus and Titanothere Canyon area, the Titus Canyon Formation also can be found in the northern Funeral Mountains and at Daylight Pass. At Daylight Pass you drive along a road cut through the Titus Canyon Formation. Possibly it crops out in the Lost Chance Range.

The Titus Canyon Formation will be along both sides of the road from White Pass until you enter the east fork of Titus Canyon a half mile north of Leadfield. In upper Titanothere Canyon west of White Pass, the road will cut through the variegated facies and the green conglomerate facies can be seen north of the road. East and southeast of Leadfield you can see both the green conglomerate and variegated facies. The sedimentary breccia crops out along the road from a mile and a half before Red Pass to Red Pass.

What was the origin of the Titus Canyon Formation?

In the late Eocene and early Oligocene, when the deposition of the sediments that were to become the Titus Canyon Formation began, the region was part of the continent. It was a region of low relief. In other words, the tops of the hills and bottoms of the basins were separated only by a vertical displacement estimated at two hundred and fifty feet. Lakes, rivers, and streams dotted the countryside. Parts of the region resembled a savannah upon which Titanotheres and three-toed horses roamed. The lakes were the environments where the algal limestones and marls of the variegated facies formed. Occasionally rivers swept sand, pebbles, and cobbles that were later to become sandstone and conglomerates of the variegated facies. Drainage from the hills cut a canyon through which debris was swept down toward a basin. An alluvial fan was formed that was to become the sedimentary breccia faces found on the east side of Red Pass. Early Oligocene faults created escarpments from which gravity tore loose talus and large blocks to become the dark megabreccia on both sides of Red Pass. Also in the early Oligocene, streams from the northwest transported, rounded, and eventually deposited fragments of quartzite, chert, granite, and carbonate rocks from earlier formations such as the Stirling Quartzite, Wood Canyon, Zabriskie Quartzite, Eureka Quartzite, Nopah, and Ely Springs. Siltstone and mudstone were deposited when stream banks overflowed or when they ended in shallow, broad basins like today's Death Valley floor. Sediment deposition continued in this manner further into the Oligocene and variegated facies deposits built up.

During the middle to late Oligocene, the setting and events changed. Erosion produced an unconformity. We know that after that unconformity the environment changed to be predominately rivers and streams together with increased volcanic activity. This was the time when the green conglomerate facies were deposited. Streams swept in more pebbles and cobbles to form conglomerates. Again they were well rounded and attested to the great distances they were transported from the northwest or recycling from conglomerate beds. Volcanoes spewed forth ash that fell to form tuff beds and the distinctive crystal lythic tuff in the middle of the green conglomerate facies. Buildup of the green conglomerate facies continued possibly in to the early Miocene. Again we have an unconformity and loss of the record that defined the transition into the portion of the Miocene when volcanic tuff deposits dominated.

Titus Canyon Formation conglomerate

C-6 Titus Canyon Region Miocene Volcanic Rocks

MIDDLE MIOCENE

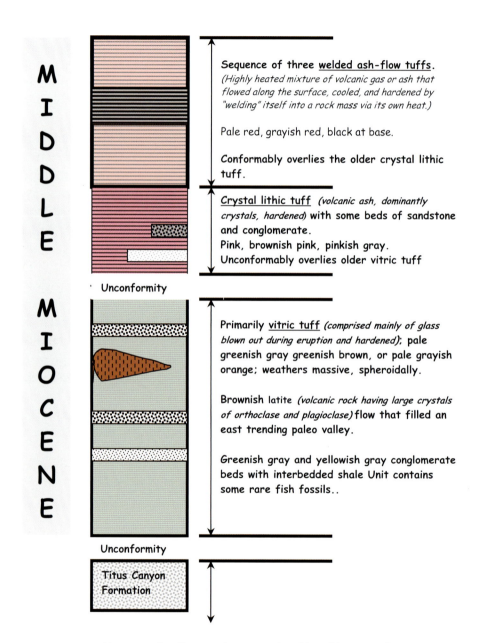

Sequence of three <u>welded ash-flow tuffs</u>. *(Highly heated mixture of volcanic gas or ash that flowed along the surface, cooled, and hardened by "welding" itself into a rock mass via its own heat.)*

Pale red, grayish red, black at base.

Conformably overlies the older crystal lithic tuff.

<u>Crystal lithic tuff</u> *(volcanic ash, dominantly crystals, hardened)* with some beds of sandstone and conglomerate.
Pink, brownish pink, pinkish gray.
Unconformably overlies older vitric tuff

Unconformity

Primarily <u>vitric tuff</u> *(comprised mainly of glass blown out during eruption and hardened)*; pale greenish gray greenish brown, or pale grayish orange; weathers massive, spheroidally.

Brownish latite *(volcanic rock having large crystals of orthoclase and plagioclase)* flow that filled an east trending paleo valley.

Greenish gray and yellowish gray conglomerate beds with interbedded shale Unit contains some rare fish fossils..

Unconformity

Titus Canyon Formation

At any one locality, an observer using this guide sees only a part of the succession of rock beds illustrated here.

Reference: M. Reynolds

Appendix C-7 Late Eocene Fauna on the Savannah of the Ancient Titus Canyon Area

The Titus Canyon area, 37 My in the late Eocene (possibly long before that), was on a savannah with streams running through it and was subject to occasional flooding. Floral environment was changing from open woodlands with trees and shrubs to grasslands as the climate became more arid. There would have been a large diversity of animal life present which would have included mainly browsers and some grazers and those who preyed upon them. Fortunately, some of these animals are identifiable by their fossilized remains found in the Titanothere Canyon area by H. Donald Curry, Chester Stock, et al. Unfortunately, only a limited amount of fossils have been found and not all of the animals roaming the late Eocene plains of the Titus Canyon area definitely known. However, many fossils of these diverse plains dwellers have been found in the western U.S. and Canada. The following table identifies the animals having left their fossils behind in Titanothere (noted as **Titus**) Canyon as well as some **contemporary** animals which left their fossils behind in nearby areas and similar environments. References: Osborn, Stock, Janis, Woodburne, Merryman, McKenna, Nyborg and Santucci.

Unshaded box denotes fossils of fauna that were found in the Titus Canon area by Stock or others.	**Gray box:** fauna **Contemporary** (time, range, environment) with but fossils not found in Titus Canyon. Very few identified herein.

1.0 Order Rodentia: Early Eocene immigrants which replaced Multituberculates as forest canopy and underbrush dwellers. The Late Eocene saw the greatest diversification of rodent families.

1.1 Order Rodentia Suborder Sciurmorpha Family Ischyromyidae Subfamily **Paramyinae**. Extinct family comprising most ancient ancestors of rodents. Subfamily was herbivore, ground dweller. Range: Canada, CA, and **Titus**

1.2 Order Rodentia Suborder Sciurmorpha Family Aplodontidae. (Stock 1949). Burrowing rodent. Thickset and heavy body. First appeared in Late Eocene and then intermittently expanded and contracted its diversity until a single species, mountain beaver, survives in the Rockies. Range: Western North America and **Titus**

> 1.3 Order Rodentia Family Castoridae. Contemporary. *Agnotocastor* Earliest(?) Beaver. Body length < 20". Late Eocene-Early Oligocene. CO, WY and SD

2.0 Order Perissodactyla: Generally odd toed. Initial immigrants to North America came from Europe during early Eocene.

2.1 Order Perissodactyla Family Equidae. Somewhere in North America, during the early Eocene (~55 MY), a single species originated this family. Approximately 29 genera resulted.

Mesohippus (Stock 1949) *("Middle horse")* Equidae. Hyracotheriinae Mid Eocene-Late(?) Oligocene. (39.5-23.0?) MY Herbivore. Three-toed (tridactyl), small, early horse, size of German Shepard dog (2' at shoulder). Browsed on tender twigs and fruits. Common throughout North America. The "fourth" in horse evolution. Very widespread. First Equidae to appear in southeast. Range: MT; ND; SD; NE; Saskatchewan and **Titus**.

2.2 Order Perissodactyla Family Tapiroidea. 50 MY the tapiroid and rhinocerotoid (Superfamily Rhinocerotoidea) lineage diverged. Today's tapirs have a stout and streamlined body, short legs, keen hearing and smell, relatively poor eyesight, low crowned teeth (browser), three toes on the front feet, four toes on the hind feet, and a prehensile nose. They are 6'-8' long.

Colodon (Stock 1949) Tapiroidea. Mid Eocene-Late Oligocene (45.9- 24(?) MY) Tapir. Medium sized to large. Range: Saskatchewan, NE and **Titus**.

> **Contemporary:** *Protapirus* Tapiroidea Late E-Early O (37.1-31.9 MY) Medium-large sized. Low crowned teeth – browser. Known exclusively from river channel deposits. Range: Saskatchewan, SD, WY, MT, NE, CO, and NV (Mineral County and Smith Valley)

2.3 Order Perissodactyla Family Rhinocerotidea. A very successful North American mammal which was the largest from the late late Eocene to Middle Miocene. They are believed to have migrated from Asia in the late middle Eocene. Most rhinos had tridactyl feet.

Teletaceras mortivallis Rhinocerotidae Mid Eocene (39.5-37.1 MY) aka *Eotrigonias mortivallis* (Stock 1949) Small. Low crowned teeth, browser. Range: OR; Mojave Desert (Ludlow), CA, **Titus**.

Undescribed rhinocerotid (Kelly 1987) and another undescribed rhinocerotid (UC Berkeley 1987). Range: **Titus.**

> **Contemporary:** *Hyracodon* "Running rhino" Rhinocerotoidea Hyracodontidae Hyracontinae. Mid Eocene-Late Oligocene (39.5-28 MY). Medium sized hyracodontid. 4' at shoulder. 8' nose to tail. 14" skull. Long, slim legs aided in running from predators. Increased hypsodont Rough browse such as twigs, buds, tough leafy vegetation. **The most common and best known of the hyracodontid rhinoceroses.** Range: SD,NE, WY, UT, MT, CO, TX, Saskatchewan, and Mexico. (Originally Stock thought the Titus Rhinocerotidea fossils represented the subfamily Hyracontidae but changed his mind in 1949 paper.)

Contemporary: *Subhyracodon* Rhinocerotidae. Late E-Late O (37.1-27.7 MY) Large size. Skull 32"-40", nose to tail 12'. Cow-sized, hornless, low crowned teeth, browsed on more succulent vegetation in riparian areas. Not found on open plains. Very common. Range: CA (San Diego and Ventura), WY, NE, ND, SD, CO, and MT.

2.4 Order Perissodactyla Family Brontotheriidea Sufamily Brontotheriinae (Titanothere = Brontothere)

General characteristics: "Medium– to very large-sized brontotheres with distinct frontonasal prominence or horn over the facial concavity…" (Brian J. Mader @ Janis). Elephant sized. Bulky, short neck, stocky body, relatively short limbs. Some with shoulder height >8 feet, 12 to 14 feet in length, and 4 to 5 tons in weight. Male's horn were up to 45-inches from the base of the skull to the tip of the horn. Contentious. Sexually dimorphic. Forefeet=4 digits, Hindfeet=3 digits. Browser. Possible lips and long tongue to grab leaves, twigs etc. Weak dentition. Cheek teeth low crowned. Failure of teeth to become high crowned and adapt to grazing may have led to its extinction.

Protitanops curryi (Curry, Stock 1936, 49) Mid Eocene (39.5-37.1 MY)) Large-sized brontothere. Relatively large horns that are roughly elliptical in cross section; widened cranial vertex (top of head) with no sagittal crest (prominent point on top of head where two skull bones meet). Range: **Titus Canyon only.**

Unnamed brontothere described by Stock as: "Menodontine?" "A poorly preserved facial portion of skull," **Smaller that** *P. curryi*. Found at different site in "stratigraphic position similar to that of *Protitanops curryi*." "Little is left of the **horn**, but they appear to have a round or rudely **triangular cross section**." "Relationship… to the menodontine titianotheres among the White River Brontotheriidae is suggested by the elongate premolars and to some extent also by the basal cross section of the horn."

A contemporary for Stock's second fossil ?
Menodontine titanothere (Stock 1936, 49) = Telmatherinae family (current family name, it was Menodontinae). Could have been 4 others contemporary with Protitanops (*Brontops, Duchesneodus uintensis, Megacerops,* and *Menodus*; all four were geographically widespread; all large to very large; 2 had long horns and 2 short horns)?

- A) ***Brontops robustus*** Late Eocene (37.1-33.4 ?MY) aka ***Brontotherium leidyl*** (Osborn). **Very large-sized.** Short, anteriorly directed horns that are **round to elliptical in cross section**. Wide, saddle-shaped cranial vertex. Range: SD, WY, UT,NE, Saskatchewan.
- B) ***Duchesneodus uintensis*** Late Eocene (39.5-37.1 MY). **Large-sized.** Small frontonasal horns that are roughly **circular in cross section**. Broad, saddle-shaped cranial vertex. Range: NM, UT, CO, TX, **CA (Ventura (Sespe))**, Saskatchewan.
- C) ***Menops*** Late Eocene (37.1-33.4 MY). aka ***Allops*** or ***Menodus***. **Very large-sized.** Horns relatively large, laterally directed, and **strongly trihedral in cross section.** Wide, saddle-shaped cranial vertex. Range: SD, NE, CO, Saskatchewan.
- D) ***Megacerops*** Late Eocene (37.1-33.4 MY). Aka **Megaceratops** or **Brontotherium** or **Titanops**. **Large to very large sized.** Horns that are long, directed laterally or forward, and roughly **elliptical in cross section**. Wide, saddle-shaped cranial vertex. Range: SD, NE, CO, MT, Saskatchewan.

No match to Stock's second brontotheres fossil. They all seem to be too large with only one with trihedral cross-section horns.

3.0 Order Artiodactyla: Immigrants during early Eocene. Even toed hoofed mammal (ungulate). (Led to earliest camels, pigs, hippos, goats, antelope, sheep, cattle, deer, etc).

3.1 Order Artiodactyla Super Family Oreodontoidea: North America only. Pig-like skeleton. Oreodonts looked like a cross between a pig and a sheep. They had enlarged canines. Long body, short legs, short neck, large head, long tail, 4 toes and digitigrade. Ranged in size from a cat to a wild boar. Family Agriochoeridae (~8 genera, browser lived in gallery forests, some clawed and arboreal, 7 of 8 genera Early to Late Eocene and 1 genera to Late O, radiation in Late Eocene.)

Agriochoerus transmontanus Agriochoeridae. Middle Eocene-Late Oligocene(45.9-23 MY) Skull 10". Nose to tail ~ 3'. Long tail. Browser. 4-toes. Clawed. Tree climber and branch walker. Inhabited gallery and savanna woodlands. Resembled a cross between a cat, dog, and horse. Range: WY, CO, UT,TX, and Saskatchewan. Several individuals of Agriochoerus were found in **Titus.**.

Contemporary: *Protoreodon transmontanus* (Nyburg) Agriochoeridae. Early-Late Eocene (46.7-35.5 MY) Most primitive of Oreodont genera. Basal stock for Oreodont descendants. Range:TX (Big Bend Area), ;UT; WY, SD, MT, and CA (Ventura and San Diego).

3.2 Order Artiodactyla Family Camelidae Ancestors to modern camels. Evolved broad foot pad, splay-toed foot and a pacing gait whereby both legs on one side were of the ground simultaneously. Evolved in NA. Not immigrants. First appeared in Mid Eocene when drying conditions were producing savannas. Relatively rare in Eocene.

Contemporary: *Poebrotherium* Camelidae. Late Eocene- Late Oligocene (37.1-27.7 MY). Early camel genera. Variable in size. 3-4 feet long. Larger size, longer neck, more hypsodont than *Poebrodon*. Range: Central and Northern Great Plains including: TX, SD, WY, MT, NE**.**

3.3 Order Artiodactyla Family Leptomerycidae. Leptomerycidae migrated from Asia to North America in the Middle to Late Eocene (40 MY). The Leptomerycidae were abundant and moderately diverse during the Oligocene, selective browsers and frugivores in forest understory and woodland settings, and the longest lived family of ruminants (Middle Eocene-Middle Miocene: 30 MY) in North America.

Leptomeryx blacki (Stock) Leptomerycidae Mid Eocene-Early Mioicene (41.3-17.5) Small and lightly built. Deer-like. Hornless. Lived in wooded environs feeding on fruits, tender shoots, and possibly insects. Very common early Oligocene Widespread Range: MT,WY, SD, ND, NE, CO, northern Mexico, Saskatchewan, and **Titus.**

Contemporary: *Hypertragulus* Mid E-Early M (39.5-18.8 MY) Notable for small size and short forelimbs. Range: NE, SD, CO, MT, and CA (Ventura and Kern Counties).

3.4 Order Artiodactyla Family Protoceratidae.
Originated in North America in middle Eocene. Started out as small and hornless browsers. Late Eocene saw some moving to hypsodont… adapting to grass.

Poambromylus robustus Protoceratidae: Originated in North America in middle Eocene. Started out as small and hornless browsers. Late Eocene saw some moving to hypsodont… adapting to grass. By Mid Oligocene, size varied from 45-770 lbs. Deer or antelope like bodies and short legs. Mid-Late Eocene (41.3-33.4 My) Range: SD, WY, UT, NM, TX, and **Titus**.

Contemporary: *Leptotragulus* Protoceratidae. Mid-Late Eocene (45.9-33.4 MY) Range: UT, WY, SD, MT, TX, NE, British Columbia, Saskatchewan, and CA(San Diego).

3.5 Order Artiodactyla Family Entelodontidae
Eocene-Oligocene North America had 5 genera. Asia and Europe also had Entelodontidae. Pig-like. Omnivorous. Bulky bodt. Short and relatively slender legs. Large canines, heavy incisors, and powerful molars. For crushing bones. Large heads with bony lump on each side. Sexually dimorphic.

Archaeotherium Entelodontidae. Mid Eocene-Late Oligocene (39.5-24 MY). Pig-like. Omnivorous. Scavenger eating carrion and plants (roots, tubers). Huge, 3' long skull with knobs and with bone crushing jaws and teeth. Elongated face. Moderate length neck. Moderate length tail. Slender limbs relative to size of body. Didactyl (walked on two digits). Species were 3-6' tall at shoulder. Most common in floodplain environments of northern Great Plains.

4.0 Order Carnivora:
Late Eocene true carnivores were represented by early Canidae (dogs), cat-like Nimravidae, and beardog Amphicyonidae predators.

4.1 Order Carnivora Family Canidae
originated in the Late Middle Eocene of North America and then greatly spread and diversified in the Oligocene and Miocene. They are thought to have originated from the miacoid carnivores of the middle Eocene. Canids varied greatly in diet, size, and social structure. Canids generally have long and slender limb bones and long tails. They are digitgrade. **Titus.**

Contemporary: *Hesperocyon* "Western dog." Canidae Hesperocyoninae. Late Eocene- Late Oligocene. Fox-sized but mongoose like: long slender body (2'-6", short limbs, 4" skull, and long tail). Forefeet were subdigitigrade and claws probably retractile. Could climb trees. May have hunted small mammals in riparian forests and adjacent grasslands. Very common. Possible ancestor to all current canines. Range: Canada, MT, WY, SD, ND, CO, and NE.

4.2 Order Carnivora Family Nimravidae
appeared in the late Eocene, blossomed in the Oligocene, and became extinct by the early Early Miocene. They were cat-like (short face, retractable and hooded claws, probably capable of climbing trees like a modern leopard, had three types of canines (scimitar-toothed, dirk-toothed, and conical-toothed).

Contemporary: *Hoplophoneus* Nimravidae. Late, Late Eocene-Early Oligocene. Predator. Dirk-toothed with fine serrations. Retractable claws. Cat-like. Robust body and relatively short legs like Smilodon but size of a mountain lion or small leopard. Range: WY, SD, ND, CO, and NE.

Contemporary: *Dinictis* Nimravidae. Late Eocene-Early Oligocene. (37-29 MY) Predator. Scimitar-toothed. Ranged in size from that of large lynx to mountain lion. Short legs.

4.3 Order Carnivora Family Amphicyonidae
(aka Beardogs) appeared in North America and Europe in the Late Eocene (~40 MY), diversified in North America in the Oligocene, and was gone from North America by the early Late Miocene (~9 MY).

Contemporary: *Daphoenus* Amphicyonidae. Daphoeninae Late Middle Eocene- Early Miocene (40-27 MY). Small to mid sized Beardog. Skull 6"-10." Coyote sized. 11-50 lbs. Small in Eocene and larger in Oligocene. Range: WY, TX, OR, and Saskatchewan. Numerous fossil sites in Central Great Plains.

4.4 Order Carnivora Family Miacoidea
were early representatives of Order Carnivora. They were of small body, typically weasel-sized, with a maximum size being that of a coyote. Locomotion for some genera may have been scansorial (capable of climbing), arboreal (capable of living in trees), ambulatory (capable of walking), and cursorial (capable of running). They are first known from the Early Paleocene in NA and peaked in diversity in the Eocene.

Contemporary: *Miacis,* Miacidae. Early Early Eocene-Late Eocene (55-35 MY) Three Sites: Brea and Tapo Canyons, Ventura County and Santiago Fm, San Diego County, CA. *Preponderance* of fossil sites are in the Central Great Plains.

5.0 Other

Contemporary: Snakes, lizards, land tortoise, aquatic turtles

Recommended Reading

"Death Valley and the Amargosa - A Land of Illusion" by RICHARD E. LINGENFELTER

"Death Valley Wildflowers" by ROXANA S. FERRIS

"Desert Wildflowers" by Dr. EDMUND JAEGER

"Guidebook: Death Valley Region, California and Nevada", by BENNIE TROXEL, MITCHELL REYNOLDS, et al.

"Jepson Desert Manual, The," MARGRIET WETHERWAX, Managing Editor.

"Leadfield, Death Valley Ghost Town," by KEN LENGNER and DANNY RAY THOMAS

"Mammalian Fauna from the Titus Canyon Formation, California", CHESTER STOCK

"Mojave Desert Wildflowers" by JON M. STEWART

"A Natural History of California" by Dr. ALLAN A. SCHOENHERR

"Tecopa Mines, Operating during 82 years of the Death Valley Region Mining Boom," by KEN LENGNER and GEORGE ROSS

References

Author(s)	Title and Publication Information
Audesirk, Teresa and Gerald	"Biology, Life on Earth, Prentice Hall, 1999.
Bates, Robert L. and Jackson, Julia A.,	"Dictionary of Geological Terms", American Geological Institute, 1984.
Benson, Lyman	"The Native Cacti of California", Stanford University Press, 2002.
Benton, Arthur R.	"The Wrong Way," Desert Magazine, April, 1961.
Berryman, Wm. Scott	"A History of Land Mammals in the Western Hemisphere," The Macmillan Company, 1913.
Bowers, Janice, E. and Wignail, Brain	"Flowers and Shrubs of the Mojave Desert", Southwest Parks and Monuments Association, 1999.
Bowers, Janice E. and Wignail, Brain	"Shrubs and Trees of the Southwestern Deserts", Southwest Parks and Monuments Association, 1993.
Byers, F. M., et al	"Volcanic Suites and Related Cauldrons of Timber Mountain - Oasis Valley Caldera Complex, Southern Nevada", USGS Professional Paper 919, 1976.
Clements, Lydia	"The Indians of Death Valley", Hollycrofters-Hollywood, 1962.
Cornwall, Henry J. and Kleinhampl, Frank J.	"Geology of Bullfrog Quadrangle and Ore Deposits Related to Bullfrog Hills Caldera, Nye County, Nevada and Inyo County, California", USGS Professional Paper 454-J, 1964.
Corsetti, Frank A. and Hagadorn, James W.	"The Precambrian-Cambrian Transition: Death Valley, USA", Geology, volume 28, number 3 and volume 33, pages 958-959, 2000.
Dodge, Natt N.	"100 Desert Wildflowers in Natural Color", Southwest Parks and Monuments Association, 1982.
Fenton, Carrol, L. and Mildred, A.	"The Fossil Book, Doubleday and Company, 1958.
Ferris, Roxanna S.	"Death Valley Wildflowers", Death Valley Natural History Association, 1981.
Glasscock, C. B.	"Here's Death Valley", Grosset and Dunlap, 1940.
Haff, Edward L.	"Mineral Survey 5883, Survey of the Mining Claims of Western Lead Mining Company, Sections 33-34, 10-11, Township 12S and 13S, Range 456E MDM; May 22 to August 19, 1926," Public Survey Office, January 1927.
Hickman, James C. (Editor)	"Jepson Manual - Higher Plants of California", University of California Press, 1993.
Hunt, Alice	"Archaeology of the Death Valley Salt Pan" University of Utah, Department of Anthropology, Anthropological Papers Number 47, October 1960.
Hunt, C. B.	"Plant Ecology of Death Valley", USGS Professional Paper 509.
Jaeger, E. C.	"A Naturalists Death Valley", Death Valley Forty-Niners, Inland Printing, Inc., 1957.
Jaeger, E. C.	"The California Deserts", Stanford University Press, 1965.
Jaeger, E. C.	"Desert Wildlife", Stanford University Press, 1961.
Jaeger, E. C.	"Desert Wildflowers", Stanford University Press, 1969.
Jahns, Richard (Editor)	"Geology of Southern California, Bulletin 170, Chapter 3, Historical Geology", California Division of Mines, 1954.

Janis, Christine M., Scott, Kathleen M., Jacobs, Louis L.; Editors	"Evolution of Tertiary Mammals of North America, Volume 1: Terrestrial Carnivores, Ungulates, and Ungulatelike Mammals," Cambridge University Press, 1998.
Kingsley, Kenneth J.	"Mammals of the Grapevine Mountains, DVNM, Thesis UNLV, 1981.
Kurzuis, Margaret Ann	"Vegetation and Flora of Grapevine Mountains, Death Valley National Monument", Thesis UNLV, 1981.
Lengner, Kenneth E. and Thomas, Danny Ray	"Leadfield… Death Valley Ghost Town," Deep Enough Press. 2009.
Lingenfelter, Richard E	"Death Valley and the Amargosa - A Land of Illusion", University of California Press, 1986.
Maldonado, Florian	"Structural geology of the upper plate of the Bullfrog Hills detachment fault system, southern Nevada", Geological Society of America Bulletin, v. 102, p. 992-1006, July 1990.
Maldonado, Florian	Map I-1985,"Geologic Map of the Northwest Quarter of the Bullfrog 15-minute Quadrangle, Nye County, Nevada, USGS, 1990.
Martineau, LeVan	"The Rocks Begin to Speak", KC Publications, 1994.
Miller, Martin G.	"Death Valley's Visible History: A New Geologic Map and Accompanying Photographs" California Geology Volume 54/Number 2, March/April 2001.
Morris, Simon Conway	"The Crucible of Creation, The Burgess Shale and the Rise of Animals," Oxford University Press, 1999.
Morrison, Roger B., and Mifflin, Martin D.	Lake Tecopa and its environs: 2.5 million years of exposed history relevant to climate, groundwater, and erosion issues at the proposed nuclear-waste repository at Yucca Mountain, Nevada, GSA, 2000.
Mozingo, Hugh N.	"Shrubs of the Great Basin, A Natural History", University of Nevada Press, 1987.
Munz, Philip A.	"California Desert Wildflowers", University of California Press, 1962.
Narbonne, G. M.	"The Ediacaran Biota: A Terminal Neoproterozoic Experiment in the Evolution of Life", GSA Today, February 1998.
Nyburg, Torrey G. and Santucci, Vincent L.	"Death Valley National Park Paleontological Survey," National Park Service. 1999.
Osborn, Henry Fairfield	"The Titanotheres of Ancient Wyoming, Dakota, and Nebraska", United States Government Printing Office, 1929.
Palmer, Allison R. and Halley, Robert B.	"Physical Stratigraphy of the Carrara Formation (Lower and Middle Cambrian) in the Southern Great Basin", USGS Professional Paper 1047, 1979.
Palmer, T. S.	"Chronology of Names of the Death Valley Region in California, 1849-1949", Borgo Press, 1989.
Plumer, Charles C., McGeary, David	"Physical Geology", Wm. C. Brown Publishing, 1993.
Ransome, Fredrick L.,"	"Preliminary Account of Goldfield, Bullfrog, and Other Mining Districts in Southern Nevada, USGS Bulletin 303, 1907.
Press, Frank and Siever, Raymond	"Earth" W.H. Freeman and Company, 1979.
Reynolds, Mitchell W.	"Stratigraphy and Structural Geology of the Titus and Titanothere Canyons Area, Death Valley, California", Unpublished Dissertation Doctor of Philosophy in Geology, University of California, Berkeley, 1959.
Reynolds, Mitchell W.	"Geology of the Grapevine Mountains, Death Valley California: A Summary", pages 91-97 of "Guidebook: Death Valley Region, California and Nevada, Death Valley Publishing Company, 1974.
Reynolds, Mitchell W.	Written correspondences to Kenneth Lengner, March 27, 2002 and August 12, 2002.
Reynolds, Mitchell W., Lengner, Kenneth E.	Oral correspondences, 2002.
Schoenherr, Allan A.	"Natural History of California, A", University of California Press, 1992.
Scott, Wm. Berrtyman	"A History of Land Mammals in the Western Hemisphere," The Macmillan Company, New York, 1913.
Stark, Milt	"A Flower Watcher's Guide", Flower Watching Publishing Company, 1991.
Stewart, Jon Mark	"Mojave Desert Wildflowers", ISBN 0-9634909-1-5, 1998.
Stock, Chester	"Mammalian Fauna from the Titus Canyon Formation, California", Carnegie Institute of Washington, Publication 582, Pages 229-244, June 22, 1949.
Stock, Chester and Bode, Francis	"Occurrence of Lower Oligocene Mammal Bearing Beds Near Death Valley California", Contribution No. 177, Proceedings National Academy of Science, October 1935.
Stoffle, R. W., Evans, J. E., and Halmo, D. B.	DOE/NV-10576-19, "Native American Plant Resources in the Yucca Mountain Area, Nevada", U. S. Department of Energy, November, 1989.
Streitz, Robert and Stinson, Melvin	"Geologic Map of California, Death Valley Sheet", California Department of Conservation 1991.
Thain, M. and Hickman, M.	"Penguin Dictionary of Biology," Penguin Books, 2000.
Twiss, Robert J. and Moores, Eldridge M.	"Structural Geology,"W. H. Freeman and Company, Fourth Printing, 1997.
University of California, Berkely	"Botanical Data Overview," U. C. Berkeley Digital Library Project, http:www.calflora.org/calflora/botanical.html.
Wetherwax, Margriet (Managing Editor)	"The Jepson Desert Manual, Vascular Plants of Southeastern California," University of California Press, 2002.

Wallace, William J. and Edith	"Ancient Peoples and Cultures of Death Valley National Monument", Acoma Books, 1978.
Wetherwax, Margeriet, Mgr. Editor	"Jepson Desert Manual, The, Vascular Plants of Southeastern California," University of California Press, 2002.
Wells, Ralph E. and Florence B.	"The Bighorn of Death Valley", NPS United States Government Printing Office, 1961.
Whitley, David S.	"A Guide to Rock Art Sites in Southern California and Southern Nevada", Mountain Press Publishing, 1996.
Woodburne, Michael O., Editor	"Late Cretaceous and Cenozoic Mammals of North America," Columbia University Press, 2004.
Death Valley National Park	Website and links found at: http://www.nps.gov/deva/

Glossary

Terms — Definitions

adit — Horizontal entrance into a mine.

alluvium — A general term for detrital deposits made by streams on riverbeds, flood plains, and alluvial fans.

angiosperm — Plant that bears true flowers, made up of two major groups, dicots and monocots.

animal — Metazoan, including vertebrates, insects, worms, jelly fish, starfish, etc.

annual plant — Plants that complete their entire life cycle (germination through death) in one year (or growing season). Essentially non-woody. Herb.

antithetic fault — Smaller-scale faults not generally parallel to the main fault but are in a conjugate orientation.

anticline — A fold, generally convex upward, whose core contains the stratigraphically older rocks. Formed within the earth where the rock layers are plastic to brittle.

antiformal syncline — A fold, which was originally an anticline in form but has been overturned to appear now as an anticline.

ash fall — A rain of airborne volcanic ash falling from an eruption cloud.

ash flow — Generally a highly heated mixture of volcanic gases, ash, crystals, and volcanic rock fragments that travel down the flanks of a volcano or along the ground.

asthenosphere — The region of the earth's outer shell beneath the lithosphere. Extends down to a depth of about 300 kilometers. It behaves plastically.

axil — The angle between the upper side of the stem and a leaf, branch, or petiole.

basal — Referring to the base of a plant or rock formation or member.

bajada — Gently inclined detrital surface formed by the coalescence of alluvial fans. Below alluvial fans and generally above playa..

biennial — Completing life cycle (germination through death) in two years or growing seasons (generally flowering only in the second) and non-woody (at least above ground), often with a radiating cluster of leaves near ground level during the first season. Herb.

bioturbation — The turning and churning of sediments by a burrowing organism.

boulder — A detached rock mass larger than a cobble, having a diameter 256 mm (10 inches) or about the size of volleyball, being rounded or otherwise distinctly shaped by abrasion in the course of transport.

brachiopod — Bivalve (double-shelled) marine invertebrates. Opposing shells are not mirror images as in petycypods (such as modern clams). Common and widespread in the Paleozoic but fewer exist today.

bract — Small, leaf- or scale-like structure associated with an inflorescence or cone. Generally substitute for a branch, peduncle, pedicel, flower, or cone scale.

braided stream — A stream that divides into an interlacing network of branching and reuniting shallow channels separated from each other by islands or channel bars, resembling in plan strands of a complex braid.

branch — An offshoot of the stem.

breccia — A coarse grained sedimentary rock with angular rock fragments.

By — Billion years ago.

calcite — $CaCO_3$. Calcium carbonate. A common rock-forming mineral that is a chief constituent of limestone, tuffa, travertine.

carbonate — Sediment formed of the carbonates (CO_3) of calcium, magnesium, and/or iron, e.g. limestone or dolomite.

caseharden — Process by which the surface of a porous rock, especially sandstone or tuff, is coated by cement or desert varnish, formed by evaporation of mineral bearing solutions.

clast — An individual fragment within a sedimentary rock.

carbonate	A mineral that contains carbon and oxygen: CO_4. Calcium carbonate ($CaCo_4$) is limestone and Magnesium carbonate ($MgCO_4$) is dolomite which is the type of rock that the Tecopa Mines lead and other metals are found in. The miners excavated in dolomite.
carpel	The female reproductive structure, which occupies the uppermost position in a flower. Which is comprised of a stigma (sticky structure for catching pollen), style (an elongated structured upon which the stigma is mounted and which connects the stigma and ovary), and ovary (inside which fruit and seeds develop).
chlorophyll	A pigment found in plants that captures light energy during photosynthesis.
claim	See lode claim or mining claim.
clastic rock	A sedimentary rock comprised principally of fragments derived from pre-existing rocks and transported mechanically to their places of deposition (e.g. sandstone, shale, or conglomerate or a limestone).
claystone	A sedimentary rock comprised of clay and hardened by pressure similar to shale but lacking the characteristic of splitting easily into flat plates.
cobble	A rock fragment between 64 and 256 mm (2 1/2 to 10 -inches) in diameter thus larger than a pebble and smaller than a boulder, rounded or otherwise abraded in the course of aeolian, aqueous, or glacial transport.
colluvium	A general term applied to loose and incoherent deposits, usually at the foot of a slope or cliff brought there chiefly by gravity. Talus is included in such deposits.
competent	Said of a bed of stratum that it is able to withstand the pressure of folding without flowage or change in original thickness.
composite flower	In the sunflower family (Asteraceae), flower head composed of multiple disk flowers, ligulate flowers, or ray flowers in combination with disk flowers.
compound leaf	A leaf divided into distinct parts.
conglomerate	A coarse grained sedimentary rock with rounded rock fragments of granule or larger size.
conjugate fault orientations	Having comparable dip angle magnitude but having different dip direction and opposite directions of shear. Example is both sides of normal faulting.
corolla	Collective term for petals; whorl of flower parts immediately inside or above calyx, often large and brightly colored.
cotyledon	Seed leaf; a modified leaf present in the seed, often functioning for food storage. Persistent in some annuals.
crassulacean acid Metabolism (CAM)	A variation of the photosynthesis process used by succulents Cacti). Stomates are opened only at night to collect carbon dioxide, which is stored., thereby reducing water loss if stomates opened during daytime. The stored water and carbon dioxide is then used during the daytime in the photosynthesis process.
crystal	A homogeneous, solid body of a chemical element, compound, or isomorphous mixture, having a regularly repeating atomic arrangement that is outwardly expressed by plane faces.
crystal lithic tuff	An indurated deposit of volcanic ash dominantly composed of crystal fragments. Contains not only crystals but also fragments of lithified volcanic rock or other rock types in a matrix of volcanic ash.
crystal tuff	An indurated deposit of volcanic ash composed of crystal fragments. Does not contain lithic fragments.
cut, or open cut	An above ground trench made for exploring the mineral wealth of a location.
detritus	Loose rock and mineral fragments produced by mechanical means, e.g. disintegration and abrasion, and removal from its place of origin.
detachment fault	A low angle fault that marks a major boundary between unfaulted rocks below and deformed and faulted rocks above.
dip	The angle that a planar feature makes with a horizontal plane, measured in the vertical plane perpendicular to the strike. Measure downward from the horizontal plane to the bedding surface in question.
disk flower	In the sunflower family (Asteraceae). 5-lobed corolla. Appears with other disk flowers in discoid head. Appears in center, surrounded by ray flowers in radiate head.
discoid head	In the sunflower family (Asteraceae). A head composed entirely of disk flowers (5-lobed corolla).
dolomite	A sedimentary rock formed from limestone when part of the calcium in the limestone is replaced by magnesium.
drag fold	A minor fold, usually one of a series, formed in an incompetent bed lying between more competent beds, produced by movement of the competent beds relative to one another.
drift	A horizontal passage underground. A drift follows the vein, as distinguished from a crosscut that intersects it, or a level or gallery, which may do either.
echinoderm	Any solitary marine bottom dweller invertebrate, belonging to the phylum Echinodermata, characterized by radial symmetry, an endoskeleton formed of plates or ossicles of crystalline calcite, and a water vascular system. Crinoids belong in this phylum.
ediacaran	The first true multi-cellular animals which appeared at the end of the Proterozoic, approximately 590 My.
endemic	Native, or confined naturally to a particular area or region; indigenous.
erosion	The removal and transportation of rocks by water, winds, and/or ice.
eukaryote	A type of living cell containing a true nucleus enclosed within a nuclear membrane, and having well-defined chromosomes and cell organelles. Life form, which appeared about 1.8 By.

extension	Refers herein to the stretching of the earth's crust. In the Great Basin region it is approximately in an east-west direction and results in the basins (e.g. Death Valley) and ranges (Panamint Range) found throughout the Great Basin.
fault	A break in the earth's crust across which rocks are displaced. {Normal (Tension), Reverse (Compression)}.
flaggy	Splits uniformly along bedding planes into thin slabs that may be suitable for terraces and walls. It is not slabby.
flower	The reproductive structure of an angiosperm plant. A sexual display that enhances a plant's reproductive success. Complete flowers consist of a central axis on which four successive sets of modified leaves (sepals, petals, stamens, and carpels) are attached. Incomplete flowers lack one or more of the four modified leaves.
fluvial	Of or pertaining to rivers, produced by the action of a stream or river.
Fm.	Formation.
fold	A bend in the earth's crust (e.g. anticline, syncline).
footwall	The rock wall beneath an inclined vein or fault.
formation	A formally defined body of rock strata that consists dominantly of a certain lithologic type or combination of types, or has other unifying lithologic features. Some formations can be subdivided into "members".
genus	The taxonomic category contained within a family and consisting of very closely related species.
geology	The study of Planet Earth, the materials of which it is made, the processes that act on those materials, the products formed, and the history of the planet and its life forms since its origin.
geophyte	Shed above ground parts during dry season.
graben	A down-dropped block bounded on both sides by conjugate normal faults.
granite	A coarse grained, plutonic rock in which quartz makes up 10-50% of the light colored minerals, which are also composed mostly of potassium and sodium rich feldspars.
granule	A coarse grained, plutonic rock in which quartz makes up 10-50% of the light colored minerals, which are also composed mostly of potassium and sodium rich feldspars.
half graben	A down-dropped and tilted block bounded only on one side by a major normal fault.
hanging wall	The rock wall above an inclined vein or fault.
herb	A plant that has little or no wood above ground. Above ground parts are of less than one year (or growing season) in age. (All plants called annual, biennial, or perennial, according to Jepson, are herbs.)
herbaceous	Lacking wood. Having the characteristics of an herb.
hoodoo	Spires of soft rock capped with harder rock.
horst	A "relatively" uplifted block bounded by two conjugate normal faults.
igneous rock	One of the three main classes into which rocks are divided, the others being sedimentary and metamorphic. Igneous rock has solidified from molten or partly molten materials (magma or lava). Intrusive (plutonic) igneous rocks cool deep within the earth's crust and contain very visible crystals (e.g. granite, diorite, or gabbro)). Extrusive (volcanic) rocks cool at or above the surface producing very fine crystals, glass, or a mixture of volcanic rock fragments and ash (e.g. obsidian, rhyolite, andesite, or basalt).
imbricate	A sedimentary structure characterized by thin flat pebbles all tilted in the same direction, their flat sides dipping upstream.
imbricate faults	Closely spaced parallel faults of the same type that either terminate against or merge with the detachment fault.
incline	Any entry to a mine that is not vertical (shaft) or horizontal (adit). Alternate: Secondary inclined opening, driven upward to connect levels, sometimes on the dip of a deposit; also called "inclined shaft".
indurated	A rock or soil hardened or consolidated by pressure, cementation, or heat.
inflorescence	An entire cluster of flowers and associated structure.
Ky	Thousand years ago.
lacustrine	Pertaining to, produced by, or inhabiting a lake or lakes.
larva	An immature form of an organism with indirect development prior to metamorphosis into its adult form; includes the caterpillars of moths and butterflies and the maggots of flies.
latite	An extrusive igneous rock (volcanic) that has large crystals of plagioclase ((Na,Ca)Al(Si,Al)Sis) and orthoclase (KalSi3O8) in equal amounts, little quartz, commonly hornblende and scattered pyroxene in a finely crystalline matrix.
lava	Molten rock that issues from a volcano or a fissure on the earth's surface.
leaf	Contains chloroplasts and creates plant food via photosynthesis. Grows from node in stem. Arrangements include opposite and alternate along stem, whorled (multiple leaves per node), and basal. Various shapes include elliptical, linear, round, and needlelike. Margins include toothed, wavy, lobed, and cleft. Simple (one leaf per petiole) or compound (multiple leaflets per petiole (palmate)) leaves.
lichen	Colorful crust on rocks and tree trunks formed by a combination of an alga and fungus living in a mutually beneficial arrangement.
ligulate flower	In sunflower family (Asteraceae). Long, 5-lobed flower that only appears with other ligulate flowers in a ligulate head.

limestone	A sedimentary rock composed mostly of calcite (CaCO3,) precipitated in shallow seawater through the actions of organisms or comprised of fragments from calcite secreting organisms or processes.	**member**	A lithostratigraphic unit of subordinate rank, comprising some specially developed part of a formation. It may or may not be formally defined or mappapable.
listric fault	A fault whose dip decreases (shallows) with increasing depth. The fault shape is concave. As the hanging wall block slips on the fault, it deforms to maintain contact with the footwall block across the fault producing a bend or convex curvature in the hanging wall block.	**metamorphic rock**	A rock having gone the transformation from a preexisting rock into a texturally or minerallogically distinct new rock as a result of high temperature, high pressure, or both but without melting in the process (e.g. marble, slate, quartzite, gneiss, schist), generally at depth in the earth's crust.
lithic tuff	An indurated deposit of volcanic ash in which the fragments are composed of previously formed rocks (e.g. sedimentary rock or pieces of earlier lava).	**metazoan**	Multicellular animals.
		mine	A site, open pit or vertical or horizontal excavation into the earth, where mineral resources are extracted for the purpose of financial or other gain.
lithologic	Pertaining to rocks. Physical characteristics such as color, mineral composition, and grains.		
lithification	The conversion of newly deposited sediments or volcanic deposits into a rock.	**mineral**	A naturally occurring (not man made) inorganic element or compound having an orderly internal structure and characteristic chemical composition, crystal form, and physical properties (e.g. borax, salt, limestone).
lithosphere	The rigid outer shell of the earth 70 to 100 kilometers thick. Consists of the earth's continental and oceanic crusts and the uppermost part of the mantle.		
lode claims	Pertaining to veins or lodes having well-defined boundaries. Described as parallelograms with the longer sides running parallel to the vein or lode. Length and direction of each boundary line must be given. Federal law limits to a maximum length of 1,500 ft along the vein or lode. The width is a maximum of 600 ft., 300 feet on either side of the centerline of the vein or lode. The end lines must be parallel to qualify for extralateral rights which involve the rights to minerals that extend at depth beyond the vertical boundaries of the claim. One person can locate lode claims 1,500 feet on each side of a tunnel site. This allows one person to claim 3,000 ft by 3,000 ft or the equivalent to 10 maximum size lode claims.	**mining claim**	Portion of land appropriated by an individual according to established rules and allowing for exclusive rights to harvest natural minerals. There are patented and unpatented mining claims. There are two types of mining claims… lode claims (Tecopa Mines) and placer claims. Claims **must be** *located* **on** *open Federal* **land.** A location notice must be filed with the appropriate county's auditor (Inyo County, Independence for Tecopa Mines) and fees paid Currently, it is required that said filing must also be done with the BLM. Claims needed to be "staked" by erecting corner posts and/or monuments (four) and post a copy of your recorded location notice.
		monolithologic	Of one lithology.
		mudstone	A sedimentary rock hardened by pressure and comprised of equal proportions of clay and silt and lacking the characteristic of splitting into thin, flat plates like shale.
marl	A sedimentary rock consisting of unconsolidated deposits of clay and calcium carbonate and usually containing rock fragments. It is generally formed under freshwater conditions but can form under marine conditions.	**My**	Million years ago.
		node	Part of the stem from which a leaf, branch, or aerial root grows.
magma	Naturally occurring molten rock material, generated within the earth.	**normal fault**	A fault along which the hanging wall block moved down relative to the footwall. Tension.
massive	Said of rocks of any origin that are more or less homogeneous in texture or fabric and do not split easily. They displaying an absence of flow layering, foliation, cleavage, joints, fissility, or thin bedding.	**nutlet**	Small, dry nut (or nut-like fruit), generally one of several produced by a single flower.
		oncolite	Formed by accretion of successive layered masses of gelatinous blue-green algae. Smaller than a stromatolite. Less than 10 cm in diameter.
mass wasting	A general term for the down slope movement of soil and rock material under the direct influence of gravity.		
megabreccia	A breccia containing individual blocks as much as 400-meters long, developed by gravity induced sliding. Some megabreccias contain blocks that are shattered but little rotated.	**oolite**	Small, rounded carbonate rock particles consisting of a nucleus (rock fragment) and concentrically layered calcium carbonate formed by accretion in calcium carbonate saturated waters of tidal flats. Look like fish eggs with a diameter of .25 to 2.0 mm.
member	A lithostratigraphic unit of subordinate rank, comprising some specially developed part of a formation. It may or may not be formally defined or mappapable.	**palmate**	Radiating from a common point. Generally said of veins, lobes, or leaflets of a leaf.

pappus	In sunflower family, the aggregate of structures such as scales, appendages, or bristles arising from the top of the inferior ovary, in the place where sepals would be expected.
parasitic fold	Folds formed due to slippage between rock beds.
passive (continental) margin	A margin that includes continental shelf, slope, and rise that generally extends down to an abyssal plain at a depth of 5-kilometers. Occurs where tectonic plates are diverging and not converging. Usually no earthquakes or volcanoes.
pebble	A rock fragment, generally rounded by abrasion, larger than a granule and smaller than a cobble; it has a diameter of 4 to 64 mm (5/32-inches to 2 1/2-inches), or a size between that of a pea and a tennis ball.
pedicel	Stalk of an individual flower or fruit.
pediment	A broad gently sloping erosion surface or plain of low relief, typically developed by running water, in an arid or semiarid region at the base of an abrupt and receding mountain range. Generally above alluvial fan, bajada, and salina.
peduncle	Stalk if an entire inflorescence or of a flower or fruit not borne in an inflorescence.
pelmatozoan	Any echinoderm, with or without a stem, that lives attached to a substrate.
perennial plant	a) Plants that grow for many years during which time they establish an elaborate root system. b) Plant that lives for an indefinite number of years. and c) Living more than two years (or growing seasons) Herb (per Jepson).
petal	The brightly colored and fragrant parts of the flower that advertise its location. They are located above the sepals.
petiole	A leaf stalk.
photosynthesis	Plant process that utilizes water and carbon dioxide with solar energy, captured by chlorophyll, to create carbohydrates and oxygen.
plate tectonics	A theory that the earth's surface is divided into large, thick plates that are moving and changing in size by collision, melting, fragmentation, and warping. Intense geologic activities occur at the plate boundaries.
platy	Splits uniformly along bedding planes. Thinner than slabby or flaggy.
pluton	An igneous intrusion (e.g. body of magma rising and forcing its way into existing rocks).
portal	The structure surrounding the immediate entrance to a mine; the mouth of an adit or tunnel.
prokaryote	Organisms that lack membrane bounded nuclei and other membrane bounded organelles. Photosynthesizing prokaryotes well established 3.5By.
prospect	Location being excavated to determine mineral wealth and economic feasibility of progressing on to mining operations.
pyroclastic rock	Any rock consisting of volcanic fragments of any size explosively ejected from a volcanic vent.
Quaternary	The latest time interval of the Cenozoic (0-65 My) and following the Tertiary (2-65 My). The last two million years (0-2 My) of geologic time.
quartzite	A metamorphosed rock, consisting mainly of quartz, that was originally sandstone (e.g. metaquartzite) or sandstone consisting of quartz grains cemented by secondary silica (e.g. orthoquartzite).
raise	A secondary or tertiary inclined opening, vertical or near-vertical opening driven upward form a level to connect with the level above, or to explore the ground for a limited distance above one level.
ray flower	In the sunflower family (Asteraceae). Long, 3-lobed flowers on the margin of radiate heads (disk flowers in the center).
recumbent fold	An overturned fold in which the axial surface is more or less horizontal.
relief	The vertical difference in elevation between a summit and lowland of a given area.
reverse fault	A fault along which the hanging wall moved up relative to the footwall. *Compression.*
reworked	Sediment, fossil, rock fragment, or other geologic material that has been removed or displaced by natural agents from its place of origin and incorporated in recognizable form in a younger rock, such as a "reworked tuff", pebble, or cobble carried by flowing water and redeposited in another locality.
rift	A major linear depression in the earth's crust formed by tension pulling apart a section of the earth's crust.
riparian	Pertaining to or situated on the bank of a body of water.
rock	An aggregate of one or more minerals or solid organic material.
Rodinia	An ancient continent. Tectonic forces assembled and disassembled this continent approximately 1.1 By and 750 My, respectively. North America was once part of Rodinia.
root	Anchors and supports plant. Absorbs water and minerals and channels them to stem. Stores plant food.
runoff	That part of precipitation appearing in surface streams.
sandstone	A sedimentary rock formed by cementation of sand size grains in a matrix of silt or clay and cemented by silica, iron oxide, or calcite. The consolidated equivalent of sand.
savannah	An open, essentially treeless, grassy plain. Usually found in tropical or subtropical regions.

sedimentary rock	Formed from pre-existing rocks (sandstone) or pieces of once living organisms (limestone). Chemical sediments or rocks form from precipitation of minerals from solution (e.g. calcium carbonate, borax, salt, gypsum). Organic sediments form from the remains of once living organisms (e.g. limestone, coal).
sepal	A modified leaf at the base of a flower. Sepals protect the flower bud as the petals, carpels, and stamens develop.
shaft	In a mine, a vertical excavation.
shale	Fine grained sedimentary rock formed by the compaction of clay, silt, or mud. It readily splits into very thin, flat layers. Deposited on lake bottoms, at the ends of rivers in deltas, and on quiet parts of the deep ocean floor.
shrub	A woody plant of relatively short maximum height, much-branched from the base.
silicate	A compound whose structure contains silicon and oxygen arranged in tetrahedron form, $SiO4$. Largest and most common class of minerals (orthoclase and plagioclase that are called feldspars, quartz, hornblende, etc.).
siliceous	Containing abundant silica ($SiO2$) such as chert, chalcedony, or quartz.
siltstone	A sedimentary rock consisting of silt sized grains. It has the same texture and composition of shale but lacks its ability to split into very thin layers. Usually splits flaggy.
simple leaf	A leaf with one blade.
slabby	Splits uniformly along bedding planes into thick plates. Thinner than flaggy and thicker than platty.
slickenside	A polished and striated rock surface that results from grinding along a fault plane.
slip	The relative displacement of formerly adjacent points on opposite sides of a fault.
species	All of the organisms that are potentially capable of interbreeding under natural conditions; the smallest major taxonomic category.
Spheroidal weathering	Chemical weathering in which concentric shells of decayed rock are successively loosened and separated from a block of rock by water (like peeling the layers of an onion).
stamen	The male reproductive structures of a flower that are attached just above the petals. They consist of a filament (a long and slender structure upon which the anther is mounted) and the anther (structure that produces pollen and is mounted on the tip of the filament).
stem	Bear leaves. Main support of plant. Contains plant's two-way transport system made up of two systems of tubes. One system carries water and minerals up from roots. After leaves produce food, the other tubes carry food to stem and back to roots for storage.
stem succulents	Store water in stems (cacti).
stigma	The pollen-capturing tip of a carpel.
stomate	Minute pore on a leaf or stem through which gases such as carbon dioxide, oxygen, and water vapor pass by diffusion.
Stratigraphic column	The sequence of rock strata described or illustrated in a vertical column.
strike	The direction taken by a structural surface as it intersects the horizontal. The compass direction of a line formed by the intersection of an inclined plane with a horizontal plane.
stromatolite	Layered structures formed by the trapping of sedimentary particles and precipitation of calcium carbonate in response to the metabolic activities and growth of mat-like colonies of cyanobacteria and some other prokaryotes.
style	A stalk connecting the stigma of a carpel with the ovary at its base.
subduction	The process of one lithospheric plate descending beneath another (e.g. heavy oceanic plate dives beneath light continental plate).
subshrub	A plant with the lower stems woody, the upper stems and twigs not woody (or less so) and dying back seasonally.
syncline	A fold, generally concave upward, in which the core contains the stratigraphically younger rocks.
synformal anticline	A fold that appears to be a syncline but was originally an anticline.
synthetic fault	Smaller-scale faults parallel to and having the same sense of shear orientation as the main fault.
tailings	Those portions of washed or milled ore that are regarded vas too poor to be treated further, as distinguished from concentrates, or material of value. (Sometimes confused with "waste rock.")
talus	Rock fragments, usually coarse and angular, lying at the base of a cliff or steep slope from which they have been derived.
talus creep	The slow downslope movement of talus, either individual rock fragments or the mass as a whole.
tap-root	Main root of some plants. Extends straight down under plant.
tectonic forces	Forces generated within the earth that result in uplift, movement, or deformation of part of the earth's crust.
tephra	A collective term for all clastic materials ejected from a volcano and transported through the air.
terminal bud	Bud located at tip of stem.
terrigenous	Derived from the land or a continent.
Tertiary	A period of time in the Cenozoic era (0-65 My) that is before the Quaternary (0-2 My) and is the period of time from 2 to 65 My.

topography	The general configuration of a land surface, including its relief and position of its features.
transform fault	A major crustal fault, usually vertical, along which rocks have moved horizontally different distances on opposite sides of the fault.
travertine	A porous deposit of calcite that often forms around hot springs.
tree	A woody plant of medium to tall maximum height, with generally one relatively massive trunk at the base.
trilobite	Paleozoic marine organism resembling today's sow bugs. It lived from the lower Cambrian through the Permian. It is characterized by a three-lobed ovoid outer skeleton, divided lengthwise into axial and side regions and transversely into cephalon (head), thorax (middle), and pygidium (tail).
tuff	General term for all consolidated pyroclastic rocks having glass shards as a major constituent.
tunnel	A horizontal excavation with two openings.
vascular	Describing tissues that contain vessels for transporting liquids.
vitric tuff	An indurated deposit of volcanic ash composed chiefly of fragments of glass blown out during an eruption.
weathering	The physical disintegration and chemical decomposition of rock, by exposure to atmospheric agents near the earth's surface, with little or no transport.
waste (rock)	In mining, rock that must be broken and disposed of in order to gain access to and excavate the ore; valueless rock that must be removed or set aside in mining. (sometimes confused with "tailings.")
welded tuff	A pyroclastic rock that has been indurated by the welding together of glass shards, and possible crystals and volcanic rock fragments, under the combined action of the heat retained by particles, the weight of overlying material, and hot gases The rock generally appears banded or streaky.
whorl	Group of three or more leaves or flower parts at one node.
winze	Secondary or tertiary vertical or near-vertical opening sunk from a point inside a mine for the purpose of connecting with a lower level or of exploring the ground for a limited depth below a level.
workings	The entire system of tunnels, adits, shafts, cuts, drifts, inclines, winzes, raises, etc. in a mine for the purpose of exploitation.

Index

A

Alluvial fans... vi, 3, 23, 31, 37, 38, 41, 46-49, 56, 61, 78, 107, 108, 116, 119, 139, 142-144, 159, 166, 170
Animals ... Appendix B & C-7,vii, 2, 4, 8, 9, 11, 25, 26, 32, 43, 55, 59, 62, 69, 74, 81, 88, 92, 109, 113, 115, 120, 124, 125, 127, 132, 144, 147, 161-163

    Agnocastor Appendix C-7, 11
    Agriochoerus Appendix C-7, 13, 162
    Aplodontidae Appendix C-7, 11
    Archaeotherium Appendix C-7, 14
    Black-collared (aka collared) lizard 25, 91, 92, 148
    Blister beetle 25, 26, 50
    Brontops Appendix C-7, 12
    Brontotherium Appendix C-7, 12
    Brush lizard 91, 92
    Chuckwalla 25, 26, 80, 81, 88, 89, 148
    Chukar 32, 81, 115, 147
    Coyote I, 25, 26, 74, 81, 109, 139, 144, 145, 147
    Creosote bagworm 40
    Desert bighorn sheep i, vi, 25-27, 32, 81, 109, 120-122, 142, 147
    Desert Iguana 25, 26
    Desert Tortoise 25, 26
    Dinictis Appendix C-7, 14
    Duchesnedus Appendix C-7, 12
    Eotitanops Appendix C-7, 12
    Gamble's quail 25, 26, 59, 60
    Hesperocyon Appendix C-7, 14
    Hoplophoneus Appendix C-7, 14
    Hyaenodon Appendix C-7, 14
    Hypertragulous Appendix C-7, 14
    Hyracodon Appendix C-7, 13
    Ischyromyida Appendix C-7, 11
    Lambrocerium Appendix C-7, 12
    Leopard lizard 43
    Leptomeryx Appendix C-7, 14
    Leptotragulus Appendix C-7, 14
    Megacerops Appendix C-7, 12
    Menodus Appendix C-7, 12
    Mesohippus Appendix C-7, 11, 67
    Miacis Appendix C-7, 14
    Mojave Desert Sidewinder 25, 62
    Northern oriole 132
    Poebrotherium Appendix C-7, 13
    Poambromylus Appendix C-7, 14
    Protapirus Appendix C-7, 12
    Protictis Appendix C-7, 14
    Protitanops Appendix C-7, 12
    Pseudocynodictis Appendix C-7, 14
    Raven 25, 26
    Side-blotched lizard 62
    Speckled rattlesnake 25, 62
    Tarantula 25, 26
    Tarantula hawk 120
    Telataceras Appendix C-7
    Trilobite 6, 9, 70 87, 124, 125, 125, 127, 131, 150, 152, , 153
    Western tanager 72
    Zebra-tailed lizard 25, 26

Anticline 75, 76, 87, 107, 110, 117, 118, 124, 128-130, 132 -135, 144, 153, 166

B

Berger, Jacob (Jake) 92
Bonanza King Formation Appendix C-4,4, 6, 10, 31, 67, 68, 70, 72, 74, 75, 77, 78, 80, 86, 87, 91, 103-105, 107, 108, 110-118, 123. 124. 128-130, 132-135, 137-141, 144. 145, 150-153, 155, 156, 158
Bullfrog (Hills, Mountain, Nevada) 2, 29, 37, 38, 39, 44, 45, 56, 57

C

Cambrian Period 4, 6-9,17, 31, 37, 38, 60, 63, 65, 67, 68, 70, 75-77, 80, 107, 108, 111, 114, 124-127, 129, 150-154, 156
Carrara Formation Appendix C-3, 4, 9, 87, 89, 104, 107, 108, 112, 114-118, 124, 128-133, 151-153
Chambers, Ben 92
Christianson, L. 92
Costello, Virginia Thomas 97
Cottonwood Mountains vi, 17

D

Dante's View 4
Death Valley Consolidated Mining Company 92
Death Valley Scotty 45, 46
Donald Curry 2, 3, 11, 28
Dunford, Curtis 92

E

Eocene epoch Appendix C-7, i, 2, 3, 4, 6, 9-14, 28, 31, 68, 69, 72, 81, 159, 161-163

F

Fremont, John Charles 41, 45, 50, 53, 71, 114

G

Geology Appendix A, iii, iv, v, 2, 3, 4, 10, 31, 34, 36, 38, 47, 57, 60-64, 66, 68, 71, 73, 74, 80, 91, 103, 108, 110, 115, 116, 118, 123, 128, 130-137, 139, 141, 142, 144, 168
Glasscock, C. B. 97
Grapevine Mountains i, 9, 15, 17, 23, 25, 28, 29, 31, 37, 38, 45-47, 55, 57, 63, 65, 76, 92, 107, 113, 126, 130, 143, 150, 151, 155
Great Basin 6, 16, 17, 21, 39, 41, 51-53, 60, 76, 11, 114, 118, 129, 136, 143, 147, 148
Grove Carl Gilbert 29

Humans 3, 26, 27
Hunt, Charles Butler 29

J

Julian, Charles Courtney 28, 92, 95-97

K

Klare Spring   iv, 23, 27, 95, 107, 108, 114, 116-124, 128, 150-152

L

Leadfield v, 10, 17, 28, 29, 85, 91-109, 112, 118, 122, 123, 135, 151, 153, 155, 158
Lengner, Ken   iv

M

Metts, Frank 92

N

Native American i. iv, 27, 38, 39, 40, 41, 43, 49-53, 58-61, 63, 74, 78
New Road   (see Titus Canyon Road)
Noble, Levi Fatzinger 29

O

Odie, Tasker L.   45

P

Panamint vi, 2, 17, 27, 47, 62, 67, 72, 147, 148, 150, 151
Pictographs   27
Plants 18-23, 25, 32, 33-35, 40, 49-55, 57-61, 63, 64, 71, 73, 74, 78, 79, 82-84
    Arrow-leaf 140, 141
    Beavertail prickly pear cactus 52,117
    Big sagebrush 52,60,61
    Bird nest eriogonum 89, 90
    Bladder sage 50, 55
    Blazing star 55
    Brittlebush 23, 61
    Bursage 40, 41
    California buckwheat 51
    Cattail 3, 119, 120
    Cheesebush 22, 23, 40, 41
    Chia 59
    Cliff-rose 23, 57, 58, 60, 62, 92
    Cooper golden bush 41, 42
    Cottontop cactus 23, 32, 51, 52, 114, 117
    Coyote melon 21, 23, 139-141
    Creosote bush 21, 23, 38, 40, 42, 50, 52, 53, 57, 60, 92, 108
    Death Valley ephedra 49, 58
    Death Valley Phacelia 114
    Death Valley sage 114, 138, 140
    Desert alyssum 50
    Desert bearpoppy 24
    Desert dandelion 23, 53, 54
    Desert fivespot 143, 144
    Desert globemallow 119
    Desert holly 109, 138, 140
    Desert hyacinth 53
    Desert milkweed 74
    Desert pricklepoppy 78, 79
    Desert prince's plume v, 63, 64, 74,
    Desert purple sage 41
    Desert rabbitbrush 23, 32, 78, 89, 92, 108, 112, 113, 119
    Desert rock goldenbush 23, 88
    Desert rocknettle 140, 142
    Desert tobacco 114
    Desert-trumpet 53
    Dodder 42
    Fiddleneck 23, 42, 43
    Fishhook cactus 51-53
    Fotis hairstreak 58
    Fremont phacelia 71
    Gall midge 40
    Golden evening primrose 23, 53, 54
    Grape soda lupine 88
    Gravel ghost   143, 144
    Green ephedra 49, 57, 58, 59
    Groundsel   121
    Hedgehog cactus   90, 114, 117
    Hop-sage 49
    Indian paintbrush   53
    Indigo bush 50
    Layne milkvetch 42
    Mojave aster 51
    Mojave desert-rue 23, 90
    Napkin ring buckwheat 23, 24
    Nevada ephedra 49
    Pagoda eriogonum's 89, 90
    Parish larkspur 54
    Pebble pincushion 23, 42
    Prickle-leaf 23
    Prince's rock cress 61
    Pygmy cedar 119
    Red Stem Filare 43
    Rocklady maurandya 23
    Royal desert lupine 23, 63, 64
    Saucer plant 23, 71
    Shredding evening primrose 54
    Silver cholla 52
    Skeleton weed 89
    Spectacle-pod 55
    Spiny monodora 49, 50
    Stansbury phlox 59
    Stream orchids 119, 120
    Tackstem 23, 43
    Thornbush 41
    Threadleaf snakeweed 23, 78
    Weakstem mariposa's 52, 53
    Western honey mesquite 21, 73
    Whitemargin euphorbia 43
    Winter fat 51
    Woody forget-me-not 130
    Wooly sunflower 54
    Yellow-eyed lupine 55

R

Red Pass vi, 9, 10, 21, 23, 43, 58, 59, 64, 67, 68, 70, 71, 74-80, 85, 88, 92, 94, 96, 97, 100, 103-105, 113, 116, 132, 135, 152-154, 158, 159,
References 164-166
Reynolds, Mitchell W. D. 29
Rhyolite (town) i, 29, 37, 39, 45, 46, 55, 56, 92, 115
Rhyolite (rock) 9, 57, 63
Riparian   14, 23, 108, 117, 119, 120, 162, 163

S

Salsberry, John (Jack) 92, 93, 96
San Andreas Fault 16
Scotty Castle Road 1, 31, 38, 47, 108, 144, 145
Seaman, W. H. 92
Spurr, Edward J. 29
Staunton, W. E. (Ed) 92
Stock, Chester 2, 3, 11, 13, 14, 28
Syncline 75, 107, 110, 129, 132-134, 137

T

Tallman, Clay 92
Titanothere (animal) 2, 3, 11, 12, 28, 31, 65, 68, 69, 75, 81
Titanothere Canyon iii, v, vi, 2, 3, 6, 11, 15, 17, 23, 29, 37, 38, 67-73, 75, 78, 79, 80
Titus Canyon i, v, vi, 1-5, 7-11, 13-17, 23, 26-34, 36-39, 41, 43, 44, 46-48, 50, 51, 62-81, 86, 87, 89, 92, 93, 103-113, 115-118, 121, 123, 124, 126-133, 135, 138, 141-145, 149-151, 153, 155, 158-162
Titus Canyon anticline 107, 118, 124, 130, 144
Titus Canyon fault 117, 118, 123, 124, 128-129, 144
Titus Canyon Formation Appendix C-5, i, 9, 10, 17, 31, 62, 64, 65, 67-78, 80 103, 105, 112, 116, 158, 159
Titus Canyon road (aka New Road) 28, 38
Titus, Edgar 2
Tonopah 2, 43
Troxel, Bennie iv

W

Western Lead Mines Company 92, 95, 100, 101, 105
White Pass vi, 17, 31, 37, 38, 50, 63-65, 67-71, 74, 76, 79
Wood Canyon Formation Appendix C-1, 6, 9, 10, 37, 62, 63, 72, 79,107, 108, 113, 117, 118, 123-130, 149-151, 159

Z

Zabriskie Quartzite Appendix C-2, 4, 6, 10, 31, 37, 62, 63,72, 76, 79, 80, 87, 104, 107, 108, 115, 117, 118, 123, 124, 128-131, 149, 151-154, 159